Micha Feldmann

On Wings of Eagles

The Secret Operation of the Ethiopian Exodus

Cover Design: Tchiya Rosenthal, Jerusalem
Typesetting: David Yehoshua

First set of photos © Doron Bachar, Photo Archive Bet Hatfutsot: The Museum of the Jewish People
Second set of photos © Moshe Edri

ISBN: 978-965-229-569-9

1 3 5 7 9 8 6 4 2

Gefen Publishing House Ltd.
6 Hatzvi Street
Jerusalem 94386, Israel
972-2-538-0247
orders@gefenpublishing.com

Gefen Books
11 Edison Place
Springfield, NJ 07081
516-593-1234
orders@gefenpublishing.com

www.gefenpublishing.com

Printed in Israel

Send for our free catalogue

To my wife Ruti
and my children Amit, Yifat, Liad, and Kfir,
and to the Beta Israel community,
who opened their hearts to me and taught me much
about loving one's fellow human being

Grateful acknowledgment is made to the following sponsors,
without whose generous assistance the publication
of the English-language edition of this book
would not have been possible:

Bernard Hasten

Jody and Ari Storch

Atalia Katz

Orna Simkhai

UJA-Federation of New York – Richard J. Spitz, Regional Director, Westchester

Hart N. and Simona Hasten Family Foundation

Maury S. Friedman

Jane Sherman

Gary Shiffman

Brian Hermelin

Mathew Lester

UJA Federation of Greater Toronto

Contents

Abbreviations and Glossary

AAEJ: American Association for Ethiopian Jewry

aliyah: Literally "ascent," the term commonly used for immigration to Israel, hence "to make aliyah" means going to settle in Israel

Almaya: A JDC subsidiary organization assisting the Jews in Ethiopia

Bariya: Slaves who were converted to Judaism in Ethiopia

berari: Fast messengers who distributed money to Jews in the Sudanese refugee camps

Beta Israel: "House of Israel" in the Ge'ez language – the term used by Ethiopian Jews for themselves

Chanukah: Mid-winter festival of freedom, celebrating the victory of the Maccabees over the Syrian Greeks in 165 BCE

chelema: "Darkness" in Amharic – clandestine night-time operations.

djellaba: Long robe

enkalwa: Fabric bag for carrying a baby on one's back

Eretz Yisrael: The Land of Israel

Falashas: Once commonly used as the term for Ethiopian Jewry, but in fact a derogatory term, as in Amharic it means "outsiders," i.e., strangers without rights

Felesmura: Ethiopians whose Jewish forefathers converted to Christianity

Ge'ez: Holy tongue of Ethiopian Jews

Gematria: A Hebrew system of numerology, using letters as numbers

havaja: "Master" in Arabic

HIAS : Hebrew Immigrant Aid Society

IAF: Israel Air Force

ICEM: Intergovernmental Committee for Migration (a UN subsidiary)

IDF: Israel Defense Forces – official title of the Israeli army

JDC: American Jewish Joint Distribution Committee – the overseas arm of US Jewry for rescue and relief of Jews worldwide – colloquially known as "the Joint"

Kaddish: Mourner's prayer

Kayla: Similar to "Falasha"

kebele: Neighborhood management committee in Ethiopia

Keren Hayesod: Israeli fund working with United Israel Appeal to raise funds in countries other than USA for Jewish Agency programs

kes (pl. *kessoch*): Spiritual leader, equivalent to rabbi, among Ethiopian Jews

Kiddush: Prayer over wine, recited on Sabbath and festival eves

Kupat Holim: HMO (literally, "sick fund")

lika kahanat: Head of priests

Magen David: The six-pointed Star of David

Magen David Adom: (Red Star of David) Israel's ambulance and paramedical services, equivalent to the Red Cross

Ma'on Hayeled: Children's institution

matzah: Unleavened bread eaten on Passover

mergam gojo: Separate house used by women during menstruation

meshenya: Travel permit within Ethiopia

Muhabarat: Sudanese secret police

NACOEJ: North American Conference on Ethiopian Jewry

netela: Traditional white scarf

oleh (pl. *olim*): Immigrant to Israel (literally, "one who ascends")

Operation Magic Carpet: Mass airlift of Yemenite Jews in 1949–1950 (also commonly referred to as Operation On Eagles' Wings)

Orit: The Ethiopian Jews' Book of the Law

ORT: International educational network

parokhet: Curtain in front of the holy ark in a synagogue

Pesach: Passover (festival celebrating the Exodus from Egypt)

Rosh Hashanah: The two-day Jewish New Year festival

Rosh Hodesh: First day of the Hebrew month (when there is a new moon)

Seder (of Passover): Start of the Passover festival, celebrated with a meal, readings, songs, and prayers

Shabbat: The Sabbath day, when no work is performed

shiva: The seven-day mourning period when the bereaved receive condolence calls at home

shmagelie (pl. *shmageloch*): Elder(s) of the Ethiopian community

succa: A booth (tabernacle), traditionally built on Succot, the festival of the fall harvest (the festival of Tabernacles)

tallit: Prayer shawl

tisrih: Travel permit within Sudan

UJA: United Jewish Appeal

wadi: Valley or gully

yekana abat: An older man who serves as a patron to a younger man in the Ethiopian community

Youth Aliyah: Jewish Agency's organization to facilitate the immigration and absorption of young people

zemed (pl. *zemedoch*): Extended family

Some of the People Involved with the Ethiopian Exodus

JEWISH AGENCY STAFF

Zimna Berhanie
Simcha Dinitz
Yehuda Dominitz
Matti Elias
Esther Eyob
Uri Gordon
Haim Halachmi
Arnon Mantver
Avi Mizrahi
Moges Meheretu
Asnakew Sendeke
David Zevadia
Mamuye (Mamush) Zerie
Shoshana Zinger
Aleph – in charge of clandestine operations
Etan – on Aleph's staff
Yehoshua – "The black man sent to Sudan" for Operation Moses

USA OFFICIALS

Princeton Lymon
Dick Krieger
Jerry Weaver – "The Crazy American"

ISRAELI OFFICIALS IN ADDIS ABABA

Ambassador Chaim Divon – Ministry of Foreign Affairs
Uri Lubrani – special government envoy
Ambassador Asher Naim – Ministry of Foreign Affairs
Michael Shiloh – Ministry of Foreign Affairs

JDC STAFF

Ami Bergman
Eli Eliezri
Yehiel Eran
Kobi Friedman
Michael Schneider
Doron Tashtit

ETHIOPIAN OFFICIALS

Kassa Kebede – senior adviser to the president
Col. Mersha Ketsela – deputy minister of the interior
Kifle – the man in room number four
President Mengistu Haile Mariam
Col. Salomon – head of the Emigration Bureau

Introduction

Beta Israel, House of Israel – this is the name that Ethiopian Jews call themselves, observing an ancient tradition passed down through hundreds, perhaps even thousands of years. *Our fathers arrived from the west and the day will come when we will set out westward.*

This tradition has been substantiated by a large group of historians who believe that the Jews of Ethiopia are descendants of Jews who went to live in Egypt before the destruction of the First Temple. There they established a large Jewish community on Elephantine Island in the center of the River Nile at present-day Aswan in southern Egypt. The general opinion is that a group of these Jews continued their wanderings along the upper part of the Nile until they reached Lake Tana, the source of the Blue Nile in northern Ethiopia. And indeed, the approach to Lake Tana along the upper Nile is from the west and the Lake Tana region is one of the areas inhabited by Beta Israel.

Despite various suppositions, researchers possess no documentary evidence relating to the origins of the Jews of Ethiopia, but other theories are to be found, beginning with the theory that they are descendants of the companions of Menelik the First, the son of King Solomon and the Queen of Sheba. These companions possibly accompanied him to Ethiopia after he had spent several years in Jerusalem learning the art of government from his father. Another theory holds that Ethiopian Jews are descended from soldiers in the army of Dhu-Nawas, ruler of the Jewish kingdom in Himyar (today part of Yemen), who remained on Ethiopian soil after the war against the Ethiopian kingdom in the seventh century CE. Lastly, there are those who believe they are descendants of tribes who at some point in history converted to Judaism. It should be noted that the last approach is totally rejected by the Beta Israel.

It seems that the origin of the Ethiopian Jews will remain concealed in the mists of time. On the other hand, it is clear that the Jews played a most important role in Ethiopian history, even maintaining an independent kingdom in the highlands of Ethiopia for hundreds of years. This kingdom successfully fought not only local princes but also the Ethiopian kings themselves. When the Jewish kingdom fell at the start of the seventeenth century, the situation of Ethiopian Jews deteriorated to the lowest condition possible. From that time on, they became known as "Falashas," a term meaning strangers without the right to own land. Since they could not own land, the Jews were forced to rent ground from their Christian neighbors, paying them as much as half of their crops. The Jews therefore became craftsmen. The men were the weavers and blacksmiths of northern Ethiopia and the women were potters. In the course of time, some of them left the villages and went to live in the towns – usually the younger generation that wanted to acquire an education, and some of them found jobs as civil servants. Even though the community elders approved of education for its own sake, they did not favor the youngsters' leaving for the cities, as they feared that education would bring assimilation in its wake – a fear that proved correct in many instances.

In any case, throughout their history the Beta Israel never considered themselves as belonging to Ethiopia but as outsiders in exile from their own land – Jerusalem – to which one day they would return. The Jewish Ethiopian prayers are infused with longing for Jerusalem and entreaties to the Creator of the world to assist them to return there. It is no wonder that at the core of Ethiopian Jewry's unique festival – the Segd – are prayers and pleas to the God of Israel to bring the exiles back to Jerusalem.

But the Ethiopian Jews did not make do with prayer alone. In 1862, Aba Mahari, one of the Jewish monks, declared himself to be the messiah, who would lead the people to Jerusalem. Thousands abandoned their homes and fields and flocked after him. After walking for several months, with hundreds dying on the way, Aba Mahari and his followers reached the banks of the River Tekeze. It was during the rainy season and the river had overflowed its banks. Aba Mahari believed that he was on the shore of the Red Sea and just as Moses had done during the Exodus from Egypt, Aba Mahari raised his staff and waved it over the water. But it did not part. Many of the believers jumped into the water and drowned. Many others died from hunger on the way back to their villages and at the head of the group of several hundred people was Aba Mahari, returning beaten and in despair, to his own village.

Six years afterwards, Professor Yosef Halevi, from the Sorbonne in Paris, reached the villages of the Jews. He was sent by the Alliance Israélite organization (Kol Israel Haverim) in response to a report from white missionaries claiming to have found Jews in the mountains of north Ethiopia. Since these Jews believed that they were the last Jews on earth, they were amazed that Professor Halevi looked so different from themselves. It took him a long time to convince them that he, too, was a Jew. At long last, however, after being cut off for hundreds of years, the Beta Israel were in contact with the rest of the Jewish world.

But almost forty years went by before that contact was reinforced thanks to another man, Dr. Jacques Faitlovitch, a student of Professor Halevi. From his first visit to the Beta Israel in 1904 and until the day of his death, Dr. Faitlovitch worked to link them to other Jews. During his visits to the Ethiopian villages, he witnessed the destructive activity of the Christian missionaries, and realized that only through Jewish education would it be possible to rescue Ethiopian Jewry from total obliteration. Faitlovitch, who was called "Our teacher Jacob" by the Ethiopian Jews, was a religiously observant Jew. He brought mainstream halakhic[1] Judaism to Ethiopia and tried to impart it to the whole community, including the elders and the *kessoch*, the community's spiritual leaders.

Dr. Faitlovitch took young Jews from Ethiopia to Europe and to Eretz Yisrael, the Land of Israel (at that time called Palestine) to educate them in Jewish schools. In the course of time, he set up a Jewish school in Addis Ababa and made Jews throughout the world aware of the distress of the Jews in Ethiopia. However,

1. Halakha is the body of Jewish law supplementing the scriptural law and forming especially the legal part of the Talmud.

in spite of these positive steps, the Ethiopian Jews remained isolated. It is true that there were fewer villages in which a Passover sacrifice was offered, as was the custom before the introduction to Halakha, and there were some villages where the men started wrapping themselves in a *tallit* (prayer shawl) during Sabbath and festival prayer services, but, in general, they continued to observe most of their old religious customs, such as the rules of separation requiring that menstruating women occupy a separate hut – the menstruation house.

There was tremendous excitement when the news of the establishment of the State of Israel reached the villages of the Jews in Ethiopia, but disappointment soon followed. The Jews of Ethiopia were not brought on aliyah like their brothers from Europe, Asia, and other countries in Africa. While the Ethiopian Jews continued to observe the Torah commandments and to struggle against the missionary activity in their midst, the political and religious leadership in Israel wrestled with the question of their Jewishness. These discussions continued until Adar 7, 5733 (1973), when the Sephardi chief rabbi, Ovadia Yosef, issued a responsum to an application by Hezi Ovadia. Known popularly as "First Sergeant Major Hezi," Ovadia was in charge of discipline in the military camp where every soldier in Israel spends the first days of service. The rabbi's ruling stated: "Therefore I have reached the conclusion that the Falashas are the descendants of tribes of Israel that went south to Cush...and I have decided that in my humble opinion the Falashas are Jews and they must be rescued from assimilation and intermarriage, and their aliyah to Israel should be speedily carried out, to educate them in the spirit of our holy Torah and to involve them in the building of our holy land, and our sons will return within their borders."

In 1975, the Law of Return was applied to the Beta Israel and the way was opened for their aliyah to Israel. But meanwhile, in Ethiopia, a revolution had taken place: Emperor Haile Selassie was toppled and Mengistu Haile Mariam assumed the reins of power. The Jews of Ethiopia were forbidden to leave the country, though this policy did not apply only to them: none of the country's inhabitants was permitted to leave.

By that time, about 150 Beta Israel were living in Israel. They asked the government and the prime minister at the time, Menachem Begin, to bring their brothers to Israel. In secret negotiations, Israel agreed to give weapons to the Ethiopian government, to be flown to Ethiopia in Israel Air Force planes, and the Ethiopian government agreed in turn that these same planes would bring back Jews on their return flights. The first such operation took place in August 1977, bringing sixty Jews to Israel. Another similar operation followed in December of the same year. But this deal – Jews in exchange for arms – came to an untimely halt in February 1978 when Moshe Dayan, the foreign minister in Begin's government, admitted to reporters in Switzerland that it was taking place, causing the Ethiopian government to abruptly withdraw from the operation.

At the end of the 1970s, tens of thousands of Ethiopians, mostly opponents of the Ethiopian regime, began streaming into neighboring Sudan. Among them were a small number of Jews. All the refugees – Christians, Muslims, and Jews – were housed in camps in the Gedaref region in the south of Sudan, where they were cared for by the Red Cross and other humanitarian organizations.

The Ethiopian community in Israel appealed to the Israeli government to bring the Jews in these refugee camps to Israel. The stumbling block was that Sudan was, as it still is, an enemy country; nevertheless, Israeli officials agreed to send emissaries to Sudan with the intention of getting the Jews to Israel in spite of the inherent dangers. Initially, the Jews were brought out with the assistance of international organizations, first to Europe and then to Israel. The news that a Jew going to Sudan would eventually reach Jerusalem quickly spread through the villages in northern Ethiopia. Hope was rekindled. Family after family, especially those in villages near the Sudanese frontier, started the difficult trek over the border.

Whole families, including the women, children, and the aged, struggled through the desert and over the mountains. Because their departure was illegal, they could walk only at night, hiding themselves during the day in caves and forests. En route, they were not only in danger of encountering government soldiers but also highwaymen. Some did not have the strength to endure the rigors of the journey and died on the way. They were buried by their relatives by the wayside.

In spite of all the hardships, the number of Jews in the camps constantly grew. It was decided, therefore, to organize operations by sea. First, small groups were brought out of the camps to the shore of the Red Sea. There, commandos of the Israeli navy would be waiting to transfer them in rubber dinghies to an Israeli ship anchored on the high seas, and this ship would bring the immigrants to Sharm el-Sheikh, which was still in Israeli hands at that time. The first naval operation took place on November 18, 1981, bringing 164 Ethiopian immigrants to Israel. The first initiatives were so successful that word spread and the number of Jews fleeing to Sudan grew. Additional operations had to be organized, some by sea and some by air.

Jewish organizations also operated at that time in Sudan, mainly the American Association for Ethiopian Jews (AAEJ). On more than one occasion, these organizations attacked the Israeli government on the grounds that it was not doing enough to rescue the Jews, and there were even some who accused the State of Israel of not wanting Ethiopian Jews as citizens at all.

Although the contribution made by these organizations to the aliyah of several hundred Ethiopian Jews cannot be ignored, the fact is that most of the work was accomplished by the State of Israel itself, through its emissaries and its secret operations. Indeed, by the middle of 1982, it had succeeded in bringing some three thousand of the Beta Israel to Israel and many more continued streaming into Sudan. This stream continued through Operation Moses, which took place from November 21, 1984, through January 5, 1985. The Exodus from Ethiopia culminated in May 1991 with Operation Solomon, a dramatic direct airlift from Addis Ababa. The story of these operations – and what happened in between them – is the main theme of this diary.

Part One

By Secret Ways

Behold, look, I am coming to you, my land,
Sing as I laugh and let us rejoice.
Embrace me with others who once were alone,
Embrace me, kiss me, feed me fine fruits of choice.
Stretch out your hands to shelter those ground in the dust,
Stretch out your arms, ignoring distance and bounds.

This poem, in Hebrew, was composed by Galit Halili, a girl of twelve, who was actually born and raised in Israel, the daughter of Iraqi immigrants. Her poem's words were echoing in my head as I descended from the plane that brought me back from Addis Ababa at the end of Operation Solomon.

I remember very little of those moments that created such a stir in Israel. Clearer in my mind is the memory of the sun, dazzlingly bright just before setting. I was tired, dirty, and exhilarated, because within the space of a day and a half we had managed to bring some fifteen thousand immigrants to Israel. Below, in the reception area on the tarmac, stood all the VIPs ready to greet us with hugs and kisses, as though we had returned from a battle. In truth, I had not yet fully absorbed the meaning of the tumult around us and only became really excited when Boaz Shviger, a senior adviser to Uri Gordon, head of the Immigration and Absorption Department of the Jewish Agency, handed me a telephone and I heard the voice of my wife, Ruthie. I had left for Ethiopia on Wednesday and now it was Saturday. I only managed to say, "I'm here," when the amazement at the other end of the line exploded in my ear, "Here?"

"We've done it. This is the end," I said. The beginning of the story – the story of my connection with the Jews of Ethiopia – started eight and a half years before that, at a nearby airfield.

NOVEMBER 27, 1982, 4:30 A.M. – AN AIRFIELD SOMEWHERE IN ISRAEL

At the end of the runway stands a group of people, some dressed in army uniform and some in civilian clothes. I am absorbed in my own thoughts. About four months ago, I was appointed by the Jewish Agency to coordinate the aliyah of immigrants from Ethiopia. My first days on the job were difficult, as I really didn't have a clue concerning all that had been explained to me – my head had been a jumble of words in the Ethiopian languages of Amharic and Tigrinya, reports on refugee camps and Sudanese marriages. Would I ever sort it all out?

The runway is wet, reflecting lights from the surrounding area. Up to now, 2,203 immigrants have arrived here from Ethiopia via Sudan. In the second half of 1981, the government decided to try a different route, by sea, and since November 18, there have been five naval initiatives bringing in about nine hundred Jews from the refugee camps in Sudan to the Israeli port of Eilat. These operations were based on the ship *Bat Galim*, that very same ship that had been stopped by the Egyptians in the 1950s when it tried to pass through the Suez Canal. This morning, the sixth group is about to arrive, ferried by air from Eilat.

Suddenly, there is a general stir and all heads turn southwards. From afar, we see two small lights piercing the cloudy skies. Two minutes later, the Dakota lands, the door opens and one of the crew peeps out. I climb aboard and am immediately hit by a disturbing smell. On the seats arranged on each side along the whole length of the plane, quietly sunk in their own thoughts, as though those thoughts make them invisible, sit twenty-five new immigrants. The black eyes, contrasting so strongly with their white clothing, express mistrust, or perhaps it is just fear that they have not really arrived in the Promised Land. A light wind is blowing outside and morning is near. The first person to venture out into the dawn is a young man dressed in Western clothing. He seems more self-assured than the other immigrants. The others follow him, the older ones dressed in traditional, rather dirty garments that had started out white but had been soiled during the time in the refugee camps. Their expressions are frozen. Perhaps they don't realize that their exodus has reached its end. Or is it that Ethiopian culture forbids open demonstrations of emotion? There is much I need to learn about these brothers.

Tsehaye Elias, a man in his forties, tall and bearded, is one of the welcoming party. He has entered the plane and comes out carrying Lilay Solomon, a paralyzed old man. I wonder how Tsehaye can bear the strong smells and the dirt in the plane and I envy him this ability. In time, I will learn to bear these things myself. Tsehaye is used to hardship. He was one of the first to arrive in Israel from Ethiopia back in the sixties when the Law of Return and the immigrant rights it confers did not apply to those from Ethiopia. Tsehaye somehow managed alone for three months in Ashkelon, eating only potatoes. Since he was in Israel illegally, he was afraid to leave the place where he was staying. Only after three months did he dare leave the apartment.

We count the new arrivals. Twenty-five. A small group. Without further delay, they accompany us to the bus waiting on the tarmac to take them to the absorption center. Morning has broken and the red roofs and green fields of their new-old homeland are in view. I especially watch the children as they drink in the unfamiliar landscape. Suspicion is still obvious in the parents' eyes but has completely disappeared among the children. They are relaxed although they have not yet uttered one word.

Ulpan students from nearly every country in the world are already gathered in the dining room of the absorption center in Kfar Sava. Their astonishment on seeing this peculiar new group is patent. Where on earth do these black people come from? The newest immigrants are served breakfast, but they prefer just to drink the coffee and break off bits of bread. Only the children are prepared to try cheese and tomatoes – indeed, they even try to use a knife and fork, as they see others doing, but abandon them after the first attempt.

Lilay Solomon is also in the dining room, brought in by Tsehaye Elias. After being seated close to the window, he turns to Tsehaye and asks, "Are we really in Jerusalem?"

"Yes, your journey is ended." Tears well up in Lilay's eyes. His hand, long clenched by the paralysis, slowly opens and – wonder of wonders – he stretches out his arm to the bread that is in the basket on the center of the table and says, his voice trembling: "The Lord has opened my hand and my feet are also moving. I have been privileged to reach the land of my fathers, Jerusalem and Zion."

We acquaint ourselves with the immigrants. I join a couple of the interviewers, a social worker and Tsehaye Elias, who together are interviewing a young man called Adisalem Fiseha. Right from the start of the conversation, his name arouses debate. The social worker reflects aloud, "What do we do with the name Adisalem? What Hebrew name is suitable for him?" And then our director enters the discussion: "What's the problem? Adisalem sounds like Eddie." I jump as though bitten by a snake. I'm still a newcomer to this department, still learning; I can't say anything. But Eddie? What kind of Hebrew name is that? And why does he have to change his name at all? And why don't they consult Adisalem about any change to his name? I ask Tsehaye to explain what the name Adisalem actually means. He answers: *Adis* means "new," and *alem* derives from *olam* ("world" in Hebrew), so Adisalem means "new world." I think that's terrific. A boy is born and his parents give him the name "New World." How much thought his parents devoted to finding just that name. How is it possible to turn it into Eddie? But it turns out that there's nothing to be done about it now. Adisalem himself wants to be called Eddie. What a pity.

Adisalem also receives a new family name. He won't be called Fiseha anymore, the name of his father, but rather Tesema, the name of his great-grandfather. And after helping him to work out his age – in a way that I really don't understand – we send him on his way to his new home. Adisalem-Eddie travels to Arad with the other young people while Lilay Solomon, again carried by Tsehaye Elias, is put on the bus that will take him and his family to Ashkelon. I envy Tsehaye's closeness to the people and his ability to speak with them in their own language.

While driving to Ashkelon, my thoughts turn to all that happened in the last few hours. I am stunned by this encounter with the immigrants, by their restraint. I wonder whether their first hours in Israel will not leave them scarred – after all, we've damaged their sense of their own identity from the moment they landed. Enters one Adisalem Fiseha; exits one Eddie Tesema. If I stay on in this job, I'm going to make sure that the *olim* retain their own original names, names of such meaning and beauty.

During that day with the immigrants, I learned further details about our marine enterprise. Our people in Sudan bought a vacation village called Asor from an Italian company. Originally a fishing village, it is situated on the shore of the Red Sea, not far from Port Sudan. At its center there is a one-story building containing the dining room and offices. In order to validate the cover story, our people publicized Asor among European travel agencies as a diving site. And indeed, for several months the village was a tourism success, attracting diving enthusiasts from Germany, Switzerland, and Austria. Ironically, the constant stream of tourists was so great that it sometimes interfered with the real mission: aliyah.

The person behind these efforts in Sudan is "Aleph," who naturally is working under this assumed name. He has light-colored eyes and a mass of curls down his neck that are the delight of the refugees. In his undercover life, he changes into the kind of daring Israeli who is undaunted by the most dangerous challenges.

ADISALEM'S STORY

For some reason, not all those summoned to the assembly point arrived, but Aleph instructed us all to climb onto the small truck that was waiting and we set out. His car drove in front of us with Aleph himself at the wheel – he drove like a madman. On the way we were stopped several times at checkpoints manned by Sudanese army soldiers and each time we saw the same sight: Aleph would stop his car and engage the soldiers' attention, offering them all cigarettes and sticking money into the hands of the officer in charge.

Morning dawned. In front of us, we saw Aleph's car turn off the road onto a dirt track and into a *wadi* whose walls became higher and higher until we arrived at its very end, where we were enclosed on three sides by walls some eighty meters (260 ft.) high. Aleph gathered us together and explained: "We call this place Nakeb al-Yahud, the Valley of the Jews, since this is where we rest during the day on our way to Eretz Yisrael. So, rest here until the evening and tonight we'll continue to Port Sudan and from there to Jerusalem."

The whole journey took a day and a half and we arrived in the evening in a place that to us looked like it belonged in another world. There were straw huts, like we were used to in Ethiopia. In the center was a large building, very well lit. We entered the straw huts, family by family. Toward morning, we were summoned to leave the huts and get ready to move. In the background, we heard a sound that we couldn't identify. It sounded like swarms of gigantic bees coming near, then withdrawing, first near and then far, in turn. Later, I understood it was the sound of the motors of the rubber dinghies, but it was only after we were seated in these boats that we understood that we actually had left the land behind. Not one of us dared to open his mouth to ask any questions. We only knew that we were on our way to Jerusalem and that was the main thing, never mind how frightened we were. Within half an hour, we reached a large wall that looked like it was rocking on the water. I could see at its end the words *Bat Galim* written in English. One of the people said, "It's an Israeli ship and it will take you to Eretz Yisrael."

Once on the deck, we were received by people from the Israeli navy and also by an Ethiopian-born counselor called Zimna. The journey from Sudan to the port of Eilat lasted about two and a half days. Most of us immigrants suffered from sea sickness, but who cared? We were on our way and would soon reach Jerusalem, the city we had heard so much about on Sabbaths and festivals when we sat and listened to the elders' stories about the land flowing with milk and honey, a land of surpassing beauty that every Jew dreams of reaching.

JANUARY 24, 1983

In less than two weeks, 121 immigrants have arrived in two naval operations. The first, on January 12, brought fifty-seven newcomers, and today another sixty-four arrived. However, in the interval between these operations, Aleph has had little chance to rest. He just now got back after obtaining the release of "Effi," one of the Ethiopian-born Israelis working in Sudan. Effi had been on the staff of the Prisons Service in Ashkelon when he was recruited to work in Sudan. He served there as Aleph's driver, under the cover name of Yideg Biadgo. He was actually scheduled to return to Israel when he was caught without proper papers in one of the raids on Ethiopian refugees and was transferred to an unknown prison.

Aleph ran from office to office until he remembered a friend of his, a colonel in charge of police investigations in that area. He met with him and said that an Ethiopian worker called Yideg had disappeared and he had to find him. The officer's initial response was simple: "An Ethiopian? We're holding thousands of them in prison. Take another one."

Aleph leaned close to his friend and whispered, "There's no one else like Yideg. He's really something special." The colonel nodded, "If that's the case, okay, let's get on with it." The two of them entered the headquarters of the secret police. Its door had once been a smart gray, but its paint was now badly scarred and peeling. In the center of the room stood an old table illuminated by a bare lightbulb. The table was covered by a heap of hundreds of slips of paper. The colonel said, "We've got to look for your Yideg in this pile of paper."

"Don't worry. I'll find him," Aleph said.

And indeed, three hours later, the right slip of paper was discovered. The spelling of the name was incorrect, but it clearly referred to Yideg and stated that he was being held in the prison in Gedaref. That was on Thursday afternoon. With a letter to the prison commander in his pocket, Aleph rushed off to Gedaref, which is about four hundred kilometers southeast of Khartoum, about two hundred kilometers from the Ethiopian border and about seven hundred kilometers from the shore of the Red Sea. Toward the time when all business shuts down on Fridays, which is always a short working day, Aleph arrived at the home of the prison commander. A servant opened the door and Aleph handed him the letter. The commander received the unexpected guest, summoning coffee with a clap of his hands. Aleph gulped down the coffee, impatient to get the prison commander moving without delay. Two youths were summoned to carry the commander and his guest on their backs across the road – the prison was on the other side of the road and heaven forbid that such important people should dirty themselves in the mud. At the very entrance to the prison, Aleph came upon a shocking sight: people who looked like shadows were tied to iron posts. Some of them had already passed beyond this life and others were close to doing so. "Don't worry," the prison commander said. "Your man didn't get this kind of treatment."

Eventually Effi was brought. He fell into Aleph's arms and whispered in Hebrew the opening words of the *Shema* prayer, "Hear, O Israel, the Lord our God, the Lord is one," immediately adding, "I knew you'd come." He then vowed that when he arrived back in Israel he would slaughter a lamb in thanksgiving. Aleph wanted to take Effi away then and there, but the prison commander did not have the authority to release prisoners. So Effi had to wait another two days for his freedom.

After his release, only three days remained until the next naval operation. The briefing for it was carried out under a tree near the market in Gedaref. Present were Aleph and his deputy, as well as Effi and two young members of the Committee of the Ethiopian Jewish community. About five minutes after the briefing commenced, Aleph spotted a Sudanese police jeep approaching, apparently attracted by Aleph's white face, a rare sight in that area. Here was trouble, but Aleph had a flash of inspiration. The jeep stopped near them and an obviously irate police officer dismounted and asked them in English, "What are you doing here?"

"Can't you see?" Aleph answered the question with another question, while pointing toward his deputy, who was crouched low, looking most embarrassed, with his pants pulled down and his face screwed up as though answering a call of nature. The officer and his driver burst out laughing and drove off, leaving behind them four men who also burst out with pent-up laughter. But the fifth was not laughing. Effi was pale with fear. He had been so scarred by his experiences in the prison that Aleph decided to give him false papers and send him back to Israel immediately via Greece. The day after his departure, a truck laden with Jews set out for the fishing village on the seashore.

Toward midnight on January 20, the truck reached the coast, after stopping during the day in Nakeb-al-Yahud. Everything went as planned. The *Bat Galim* was already anchored outside the territorial waters of Sudan, and three rubber dinghies, manned by elite commandos of the Israeli navy, were already moored on the shore. The unit's doctor was positioned at an observation point and equipped with night binoculars. He spotted four figures approaching and passed on the information by walkie-talkie. Two dinghies were already on their way to the ship and the one still remaining on the beach was so heavily laden it was proving hard to move. With a smile on his face, Aleph went out to greet the approaching Sudanese. Suddenly, there was a burst of gunfire and the dinghy was severed from its mooring. The *olim* got such a shock they jumped out of the boat, which floated away.

Meanwhile, it became clear that these were not four ordinary Sudanese but a troop of soldiers, and some of them started to shoot toward the boats. Aleph ran to the officer in charge, shouting, "Have you gone mad? These are tourists and they're fishing for lobsters that we're planning to present tomorrow to your commanding officer!"

The Sudanese officer realized that he could not hold back the boats, but he still wanted to detain the people on the beach. Aleph quickly shifted the responsibility onto himself, saying: "If you must arrest someone, arrest me."

"You're under arrest," the officer responded. "Come with me."

"I'm not going anywhere now," Aleph replied. "I'll present myself tomorrow," and he made sure to slip in the name of the regional commander a few times during the course of the ensuing conversation. The officer agreed to wait till the next day. And so, our people were saved. The next day Aleph reported at military headquarters, bearing lobsters, and from that time on, he visited the commander every Sunday and presented him with part of the catch.

APRIL 16, 1983, YOM HAZIKARON – AN AIRFIELD SOMEWHERE IN ISRAEL

Four weeks ago, sixty-three immigrants arrived in another naval operation, and today another seventy-seven came. This has been the final maritime initiative. Among those who arrived was one extended family of seventeen people – the elderly parents, their children and grandchildren. For them, it is the end of an exodus that has lasted over four years, starting in a small village called Gamo in the north of Ethiopia and ending today in Israel, at last.

I paid particular attention to a young woman called Agerie Akale. She gave birth in Sudan only a week ago and looks very sick, but her eyes captivated me: such wisdom with such impishness, as though proclaiming, "Don't worry, I'll live. And how!"

AGERIE'S STORY

When my father decided to make aliyah to Eretz Yisrael, I was thirteen years old. One day, he gathered the whole family together and announced that we were setting out for Jerusalem. We could not all leave together, which might make our neighbors suspicious. There were those who might have reported us to the authorities. So Father moved his children one at a time, walking for three days with each one, always in the direction of a village he knew of on the Sudanese border. It took him a whole year to transfer the whole family.

At last we were all together, and the uncles and aunts also joined us. We organized provisions for a journey that would take at least seven days. The women baked *dabo kolo*, a sort of dried bread, while the men prepared furs to rest on at night, as well as several waterskins. Being a poor family, we couldn't buy donkeys or mules. We all had to walk the whole way on foot carrying all our goods. The luckier children were the ones wearing sandals made of old tires. I didn't have any shoes and, believe me, I felt every stone and every thorn all along the way.

Armed guides escorted us. They charged per head. Most of the guides were highwaymen, brigands who were not afraid of passing through dangerous areas. But the way went on and on and on. After one week, our food ran out and the waterskins were empty. And of all times, it was just then that we had to pass through a region that was burning hot. My little brothers wanted to go back home, but father encouraged us, saying, "You have to get to Eretz Yisrael. That's where you'll study and make something of yourselves." Because they were so terribly thirsty, the children started digging into the ground with their hands until they reached a soft sandy layer. They started to eat the moist dirt and to smear it on their faces.

The guides left us totally destitute in a small town on the Sudanese border. We were lucky that we ran into kind people who gave us food and drink. The next day father went out to search for Jews who would assist us. This proved difficult and it took half a year before we managed to make contact with Jews employed by the Israeli emissaries to give Jews financial support while awaiting their turn to make aliyah. In the course of time, it became clear to us that those employees usually gave preference to their own relatives, both in giving out the money and in deciding who had priority to make aliyah. We even heard of cases where those same employees separated wives from their husbands, forcing them to divorce because they desired the women for themselves. It was hard for us to believe that Jews could behave like that to other Jews.

A short time after we arrived in Sudan, when I was fourteen years old, I set out to look for work. Quite by chance, I met a rich Sudanese who was looking for a young woman for housework. I presented myself as being a Muslim and from that day on I became the ironing maid. That house became like home to me. The Sudanese man also taught me to pray. When I came to my own home every few days, my brothers would poke around in the plastic bag that I had brought back, looking for the leftovers that I'd had taken from my master's table.

When I reached the age of sixteen, my father decided that I must be married, as he was worried that otherwise I might catch the fancy of a Sudanese man. He chose a young Jewish man as my bridegroom. I accepted my father's ruling and soon after the wedding I became pregnant. My Sudanese master ordered me to immediately stop working but continued to pay me my wages.

We celebrated our last Passover in Sudan with the feeling that our own redemption was close. After all, we had been in the camp over three years and whatever way you worked it out, we were next in line to make aliyah. The day after the festival, when they were all busy baking the first bread after having only eaten *matzah* throughout Passover, I gave birth to my son. As is our custom, my own mother was my midwife and instructed me how to care for the baby. But on the very next day, they told us we would be departing on the following Monday. My child would then be only five days old and I didn't know how I would carry him. My mother calmed my anxiety, making a special fabric bag – an *enkalwa* – for the baby.

One of the activists, Zewudu Mengistu, arrived disguised as an Arab. He told us to set out immediately for the assembly point, which was an hour's walk away from our house. We packed up our few possessions and my father warned the little ones not to be noisy, reminding them that the Children of Israel had also left Egypt in great haste. It was toward the end of the Hebrew month of Nissan, when moonlight is very faint and the nights are very dark. I could see other families arriving at the meeting point. Altogether, when everyone had gathered, we were seventy-seven people.

Even before we'd managed to put down the children and our belongings, three vehicles approached with headlights unlit. They were pickup trucks with canvas coverings over the cargo compartments. An Israeli emissary sat behind the wheel of each one. The people were then quickly lifted into the back of the trucks. When the trucks reached the main road, their headlights were switched on. The drivers drove at a crazy speed, but underneath the canvas the conditions were ghastly. Twenty-five people were jammed into each compartment and the heat mounted. Then the first one threw up and the stench was awful. I felt I was about to lose consciousness. I barely managed to stretch out my hand toward the burning canvas overhead. I wanted to rip it open with my fingernails, but my hand lacked the strength and fell back. The heat was overpowering. I didn't know who should be my first concern. My baby? My parents? Myself? I felt I should be suckling the baby, but it was impossible to unstrap him from my mother's back. Every few minutes, I stretched my hand out to his mouth to check that he was breathing. At midday, my hand suddenly felt wet when I touched him. There was saliva on his face, but he wasn't breathing. I tried to shout, but my voice couldn't be heard. My mouth was open wide, but no sound came out of it. Only my eyes were crying. My mother saw my torment and she felt that the body on her back had ceased to move. She tried to calm me down and, stretching out her hand with difficulty, she stroked my head, saying, "Agerie, my daughter, don't be sad, with God's help we will reach Jerusalem."

All kinds of thoughts were chasing around in my head. Where would we bury the baby? In Sudan? Perhaps it would be better to wait and bury him in Jerusalem? I blamed myself – if I hadn't given birth to him before our departure, I'd have given birth in Jerusalem. What wrong had the child done that God had decided to take him back before he'd been circumcised?

On one of the bends, when all the passengers were thrown to one side, a baby's whimpering was suddenly heard. I heard my mother say, "The child is alive!" Then, when the truck stopped because a flat tire had to be repaired, I put him to my breast and could feel him feeding. A wave of joy swept through my whole body.

At the overnight rest stop, for the very first time in our lives, we ate food from cans – weird things like carrots and peas that were already cooked. But to us they were delicious because they came from Jerusalem. The next day, we left the main highway and traveled for ten battering hours on pitted dirt roads, in order to bypass the Sudanese army's checkpoints. Again we feared that we would not reach Jerusalem. What terrible death was awaiting us in this trap? But after night had fallen, we reached an open area and were told to get down from the truck. We saw dozens of soldiers and in the darkness they looked to us like Sudanese, but we quickly realized that they were Israelis. They put lifebelts on us and placed us in the boats that were waiting on the beach. We could see lights in the distance. I remembered the stories that the elders used to tell about how Jerusalem is filled with dazzling light and I truly thought that this must be Jerusalem. But when we got close to the lights, we saw it was a ship and realized that Jerusalem was still a long way away. The whole boat, with us in it, was lifted by a crane onto the deck. The children were in a state of shock as we hung between the sea and the sky, but from the deck Zimna reassured us, saying, "You've reached an Israeli ship. You're safe here."

We'll never forget the reception we had on board. In spite of the fact that we were covered with vomit and smelled foul, the Israelis hugged us. They gave us soap and towels and helped us to shower. Zimna took the baby from me and rushed him off to the clinic so that the doctor could check him right away. After we had showered, they showed us to small cabins that had beds in three tiers. But even before we finished gaping at them, we were invited to go to the dining room. The tables there were covered with white cloths and laden with strange foods. It all looked glorious and so attractive, but when we drew nearer to the tables many of us felt they had to refuse the meal. I heard my mother say, "Don't touch the food. That's not Jewish

> food. They want to test us to see if we're Jews who keep kosher." In the end, not one of us touched the food, all just making do with the fresh apples that were on the tables.
>
> When we got back to the cabin, I was attacked by anxiety about my baby – perhaps after all he was no longer among the living – many hours had gone by since he'd been taken from me and I hadn't seen him since. My breasts were sore from retaining so much milk. Again I fell into my mother's arms and sobbed, "My child is dead, he's dead." Once again she tried to soothe me but in vain. It was only around noon that Zimna came and took me to a room that was completely white. It was the ship's sick bay. My baby was lying motionless in a glass container with a sort of rubber stopper in his mouth. I burst out crying and shouted, "I knew he'd die, I knew he'd die!" The Israeli doctor explained to me that the baby was a little weak and so had been placed in an incubator, but that I could soon nurse him. He also explained that the stopper in his mouth was a pacifier, a temporary substitute for the mother's breast. He understood what was going through my mind and gave orders that I should be brought to the clinic every half hour to see that my son was alive.
>
> Throughout the two days that we sailed, they took us out in couples onto the deck, but all we could see was water. Then, on Saturday night they took us all out onto the deck – lights could be seen from afar, the lights of the city of Eilat. "It's Jerusalem," they said to us, "It's Eretz Yisrael." And we all knelt down on the deck and kissed it. In the plane that flew us from Eilat, my mother rolled up the window blind. The sunlight burst into the plane and my mother said, "You see, it's all just like we told you. Eretz Yisrael is alight with glory. This is our land, the land of Abraham, Isaac, and Jacob." I could swear that I saw my week-old baby smiling.

That evening, after we finished our work for the day with the new immigrants, Zimna told me, over a cup of coffee, about a similar incident that had happened over a year before on the deck of the *Bat Galim*. On January 27, 1982, the second naval operation had taken place, the biggest ever, bringing in 350 immigrants. Among them was a family with a daughter about six years old who was very sick. As soon as they got on board, Zimna directed them to the sick bay, but within an hour he found them crying and the child was still with them. They told him that they couldn't get into the clinic because so many people were waiting there to see the doctor. Zimna picked up the child in his own arms and within one minute she was in the hands of one of the doctors. When the doctor found out how low the girl's blood pressure was, he rebuked Zimna for not having brought her earlier. The older doctor who was there then joined his younger colleague and, after some discussion between them, they agreed that the child had meningitis. She was given medication but did not respond to it. The younger doctor rushed to the bridge to speak to the captain: "We must have a helicopter to evacuate a child. Her life is in danger."

"It's out of the question. We're sailing between Sudan and Saudi Arabia."

"I couldn't care less. We've got to have a helicopter."

"We're in hostile territory and I will not request a helicopter."

"The life of a six-year-old girl will be on your conscience. I demand that you send a cable to naval headquarters or else give me a letter in which you take full responsibility for what happens to the child."

The cable was sent.

Zimna had been in Sudan several months prior to this incident. He had seen the dying in the camps and knew how little a person's life was worth in that same place where this child had lived until the day before. The doctor's persistence amazed him. But sure enough, within a short time a reply was received in the wireless room: "Wait. The matter is now under discussion among the chief of staff, the minister of defense, and the prime minister." In the end the prime minister, Menachem Begin, authorized the departure of a helicopter escorted by two Phantom airplanes and a refueling plane. And Zimna thought, not for the first time: "What a crazy country that's about to put itself into danger and spend thousands of dollars just in order to save one little Falasha girl. What a nation!"

In the end, the little girl responded to the doctors' treatment and it was possible to cancel the helicopter.

Zimna was one of the twelve youngsters who were brought to Israel back in January 1955 by Dr. Faitlovitch, to study in Youth

Aliyah's religious boarding school in Kfar Batya. Upon completion of his studies, Zimna returned to Ethiopia in order to teach in one of the schools set up by Dr. Faitlovitch, but within a short time, he moved to Addis Ababa, where he worked for Solel Boneh, the Israeli construction firm, which was building roads and buildings in Ethiopia. After the Six-Day War, he made aliyah, served in the Israeli army, married, and started a family. But his concern for the Ethiopian Jewish community was a fire in his heart that could not be extinguished. In 1977, he began assisting the first Ethiopian immigrants and even became involved in public activities aimed at bringing the entire Beta Israel community to Israel. Since 1979, he has worked full-time for the Jewish Agency, who even sent him to Sudan where he lived for several months in the refugee camps with the Jewish community, thereby putting his own life in danger. That's how Zimna came to be the person who mentored me at the start of my own work at the Jewish Agency – and I hope that he'll always be there, right beside me.

In Israel, the government decided last month – that was March – that this would be the last naval operation. Several days before that decision, Aleph reported on an accidental encounter between one of his staff and a Sudanese fisherman. It happened one evening on the beach. The Sudanese said, "I know what you're doing here at night. I've seen how you load people onto boats and take them far out to sea. Don't worry. I won't hand you over to the authorities. What's more, I'm ready to make a deal with you. I'll pay you $2,000 for each person that you supply to me. I'm in the same line of business, but I have to put chains on the people in order to get them into a boat, so I usually only manage to get older ones. But you get young people and pretty girls into your boats and they don't even put up any resistance – in fact they're happy about it. How do you manage it?"

That was when our man in Sudan realized that the guy was trading in slaves, transporting them to Saudi Arabia. In Jerusalem, this chance meeting switched on a red "stop" light; it was clear the sea route had to be abandoned. The next few months were spent industriously developing an alternative route, by air.

MAY 4, 1983 – BEN-GURION INTERNATIONAL AIRPORT

Today twenty-three immigrants arrived in two groups via Europe. The first group included a *kes* (the equivalent of a rabbi in the Ethiopian Jewish community) called Abraham, together with his wife and four children. We spent some time with him and tried to locate his son, who arrived here some time before, but without success. The *kes*, a comparatively young man in his forties, speaks a little Hebrew and is most impressive. We sent him to Ofakim, where I was to meet him again a very short time later, but only after the dramatic conclusion of another event: with the second group, a fantastic experience was in store for us. The group included a woman with a very lined face but still very beautiful, together with her three daughters. She told us that her name was Maeysho, that Elias is her father's name and that Mekonen is her grandfather's name. Zimna, who was sitting beside me interviewing another family, jumped up out of his chair, and said to me, "Do you know who this is? This is Tsehaye's sister!"

I've had many conversations with Tsehaye, who has been waiting for his sister to come and was prepared to make any effort to bring her here. And here she is, sitting in the airport. She told me her story, a tale of the heroism of a simple woman who did not desert her mother until her dying day.

MAEYSHO'S STORY

When the Jews of our township – it's called Shire – decided to leave for Israel via Sudan, I remained behind with my three daughters and my mother, who was paralyzed from the waist down. My mother was old and she said to me, "Go with your three daughters and the other people and leave me to die here. I'm already old and it won't be long before I die. I'd rather die here and not somewhere else."

Like all the other Jews in Ethiopia, I wanted so much to reach Jerusalem. I wanted it for my daughters as well as for myself, but I wasn't willing to leave my mother behind. So I tied her onto my back, just like we tie a baby, and I set out on the way. I knew that it would be difficult carrying her on my back, but I had no other choice. The other Jews had already left and we had no man with us to defend us. It was only belief in God that kept us going. Every so often we stopped for a break to take down the beloved, heavy burden from my back. And at each rest stop, my mother again entreated us to leave her behind in that place and continue on our own. By the second day the straps on my back were already soaked in blood, but I went on. It took us three weeks to reach Humera, a town on the border of Ethiopia and Sudan. We took a room in a hotel in the town, a little room with one large bed and one chair. The toilets were a hole in the courtyard. The room cost us three birrs a night – that's the same as one and a half dollars. In Humera I met other Jews from our area, including some relatives, who put me in contact with one of the known border smugglers. In the folds of my clothing I'd sewn the little money I'd saved, and the time had arrived to put it to use.

I went to the Humera market. It was very crowded and noisy with a mishmash of languages – Amharic and Tigrinya and Arabic. That was the first time I saw Sudanese, black and tall with frightening eyes. The address I was looking for was a two-story stone house in one of the alleys. There were low tables at its entrance, with men playing backgammon, drinking arak and smoking water pipes. A woman stood behind the bar and she sent me up to the floor above. I knocked on the door and went into a room that was furnished like a room in a cheap hotel. A man was sitting on the bed; he didn't even get up and invite me to sit down. I told him that I wanted to cross the border with my mother and three daughters. The smuggler stated his price and promised to come to my hotel that same evening.

In the evening, he came, but then he suddenly saw that my mother didn't move from her seat. "What's the matter with the old woman?" he asked.

"She's paralyzed," I answered. "But I can carry her on my back, like a baby. I've done it for three weeks already when we came from Shire."

The smuggler rose up out of his seat, said he was sorry, but he couldn't take us, and went away. All my efforts to find another smuggler came to naught. Not one of them was willing to take the risk. So we stayed on in Humera. Every few days we met relations who were on their way to Sudan and we asked them to tell our other relatives – who had already gone on – not to worry, and that we, too, would soon reach the Holy Land. Every evening my mother repeated her request that we leave her behind and depart on our way, but every evening I repeated the same words to her: "Mother, I love you."

After three months in Humera, my mother died. I knew there was no Jewish cemetery in the town so I bought a hoe in the market. For the last time, I tied my mother onto my back and I carried her outside

> the city. My daughters went with me and helped me to dig the hole. In silence, we buried my mother. My daughters gathered stones and we placed them on the grave, without a prayer, without a blessing. We stood quietly around the tomb and wept.
>
> The next day we met relatives and told them of my mother's death. We didn't sit the ritual seven days of mourning (the *shiva*) but joined them since they had a smuggler to help them go to Sudan. There, in the refugee camps, we met thousands of other Jews, and every day more Jews joined us. All of us waiting.

Maeysho was in the refugee camp in Gedaref for almost two years. Then she journeyed to Khartoum, where she and her daughters stayed several days, and now, here she is in Israel after traveling here by plane via Greece.

One of the ways to get Ethiopian Jews from Sudan to Israel was through an organization called IOM – International Organization for Migration. The Mossad produced papers for our people indicating that they would get refugee status in a European country – Greece, in this case. Before they left Sudan, the *shaliach* of the Jewish Agency – in whichever country was involved – would be notified and he or she would put the *olim* on a flight from that country to Israel.

From what Zimna said, I knew how very attached Tsehaye has been to his sister, perhaps because it was she who took care of their mother until her very last day, and I wanted very much to call and tell him the news, but in the Ethiopian culture you are not supposed to talk about important subjects, like death or other emotional issues, on the phone. Then the question of whether to register Maeysho as divorced came up. It was just the excuse I needed, so I immediately telephoned and asked to speak to Tsehaye. When he came on the line, I asked him if the name Maeysho meant anything to him. He hesitated for a moment, then said, "What name?"

"Maeysho," I answered.

"It can't be," he responded, his voice trembling. I told him that his sister had arrived. He asked to speak with her. Zimna held the receiver by her ear. When they finished speaking, her body was still shaking from excitement as she prostrated herself on the airport's floor and kissed it. At one o'clock in the morning I set out for Ashkelon with Maeysho and her three daughters in my car.

Tsehaye was waiting for us in Ashkelon and when he saw his sister, all his usual calm deserted him. Indeed, we all burst into tears when Tsehaye embraced his sister and her three daughters. When we sat down in the living room of the family's apartment, Maeysho removed the white scarf covering her shoulders. I saw the deep encrusted grooves – outward signs, which will never be erased, that testify to her fidelity to her paralyzed mother. I bowed my head, humble in the presence of this heroic woman.

That same night, I drove on to Ofakim. In the east, the first indications of morning could be discerned. Near the clubhouse, the silhouettes of two people could be seen. After a few minutes, the *kes* Abraham, whom I had met earlier at the airport, entered the clubhouse. On the *kes*'s forehead, I saw traces of dust and sand where he had clearly touched his forehead to the earth. "What's this?" I asked in Amharic. In answer, the *kes* took my hands and led me to the spot where I'd seen the silhouettes before. He turned his face in the direction of Jerusalem and again bowed low while reciting a prayer of thanksgiving that he and his family had arrived in the Holy Land. I was infected by his excitement. It had been another unforgettable day.

MAY 25, 1983 – BEN-GURION INTERNATIONAL AIRPORT

This month we've had immigrants arriving nearly every week – small groups that altogether total sixty-six. Since I started working with the Ethiopian Jews on August 1 last year, 404 have arrived. Today we received another twenty, including Dinke Desalegn and her daughter, Yengus. We knew that her husband, Genetu Eshete, was expecting them at the absorption center in Atlit and we told her that they would all be together this very night. To our surprise, the woman burst into tears and said, "I'd rather die than go to my husband. He left me and his daughter and ran away to Israel while I was lying sick in bed."

Dinke asked that we send her to her father, in Afula. I asked the Ethiopian-born counselors what to do. Tsehaye was uncertain, but Zimna said without any hesitation, "Send her to her father in Afula. I met her husband last week and he told me that he had been to see her father in Afula. Her father has promised him that he would iron out their differences."

The story of what had happened to the woman's husband, Genetu, is shocking. Zimna was there in Sudan at the time and witnessed the incident. Among the Jews who arrived there prior to making aliyah to Israel was a youth whose two hands had both been severely damaged in prison by the Ethiopian authorities. The boy couldn't move his hands nor look after himself. The Israelis tried to find out which of the boy's relatives was taking care of him and the Jews who were gathered at the assembly point prior to departure for Israel pointed to Genetu. Then events happened so fast that before Genetu managed to say anything, he had already been lifted into the truck. He tried to get back to its entrance, but meanwhile more and more people were shoving in and even though he shouted out, he could not make himself heard. And so, he was put on the ship and reached Israel a year and a half ago. He had never wanted to go and leave his wife and daughter behind. His wife had not been told what had happened to him. For a whole year and a half, she was left in Sudan without anyone to support or defend her and with their daughter to raise and care for. Day after day her anger grew until death seemed preferable to ever seeing her husband again.

Taking Zimna's advice, we sent Dinke to her father in Afula. Dinke's father told her the story of exactly what had happened to her husband. That evening I called the social worker in Afula and she told me that Dinke and her husband had met. As soon as he heard that his wife was there, he hadn't wasted a moment in getting there from Atlit. When Genetu arrived, the two fell into each other's arms. Zimna's scenario proved correct.

JUNE 11, 1983, SHABBAT – THE OLD AGE HOME OF THE JEWISH AGENCY, ASHKELON

I arose at three o'clock this morning. A group of over 150 people is due to arrive today from Sudan. As planned, I made telephone calls to Tsehaye Elias and Matti Elias. Matti had arrived in Israel as part of the second group of youngsters who were sent to Kfar Batya at the end of 1956. He has become a member of Kibbutz Netzer Sereni and is married to one of the young women of the kibbutz. He was already waiting for me at the kibbutz gate when I got there. Tsehaye didn't turn up at the meeting point and later it transpired that, for some reason or other, he had thought that the meeting was set for 4:30 in the afternoon and not 4:30 in the morning.

We reached the Jewish Agency's old age home in Ashkelon. Within an hour it was abuzz with activity. The staff was all excited and Geula Levy, the director, was running about between those preparing coffee and those cooking eggs. On medical advice, we prepared a light meal for the immigrants – each one was to receive a potato, a boiled egg, pita bread, fruit, and a drink. By 7:30 a.m., the meal was prepared, but there was still no sign of the immigrants.

Three weeks ago, extra staffers were sent to reinforce Aleph and his team in Sudan. Their task was to locate and prepare a landing strip for Hercules aircraft. A suitable site was found in a thinly populated desert area called Hashem-a-Jerba, about 160 kilometers northeast of Gedaref, the regional hub. Hundreds of thousands of Ethiopian refugees are to be found there, including thousands of Jews. Our people risked making two expeditions to the planned landing strip, where they buried the equipment needed to mark out a makeshift air field. After everything was ready, Aleph radioed Israel to inform them that it was now possible to execute an air rescue operation to bring two hundred Jews on a direct flight to Israel. The date selected for the operation was Friday, June 10, Rosh Hodesh Sivan (the first of the month of Sivan in the Hebrew calendar). The choice of the date was made for operational reasons: at the beginning of the Hebrew month the nights are always dark (the Hebrew calendar is lunar, so the beginning of the month is always a new moon), while Friday, being the day of Muslim prayers when no work is done, makes it easier to find people at home.

And so, toward midnight between Friday and Saturday, three Hercules aircraft took off from an airbase in the center of Israel. Each plane carried soldiers from the elite rescue unit of the Israel Air Force, equipped with the best night combat gear. In addition, there were Ethiopian-born counselors, also dressed in military uniform. There was great excitement, as this was the first time that we were going to carry out a rescue operation by air from Sudan. According to the plan, two planes were supposed to land in Hashem-a-Jerba while the third's task was to circle overhead above the landing strip in case of some malfunction.

About the same time as the planes took off from Israel, a convoy of trucks laden with Jews set out from Gedaref. The people were only summoned to the assembly point that same evening, which gave them very little time to get ready and pack up, but their possessions were few in any case. Two hundred people were supposed to arrive at the meeting point, but only 166 turned up. Because they were all dressed in festive white clothes, they could be spotted easily even in the dark night. The convoy departed after midnight, with all its trucks and vans jam-packed. Their axles squeaked on the dilapidated road and had real difficulty in driving uphill.

In the meantime, Aleph's people lit up the landing strip with improvised torches. The two planes landed at about 2 a.m. and the third continually circled overhead – but of the immigrants there was neither sight nor sound. Our people started to worry that something had gone wrong. The pilots had been ordered not to switch off their engines while waiting on the ground, so clouds of sand were being blown up that covered the whole area. There was no communication between the trucks and those waiting by the planes. However, after an hour of fear and anxiety, the trucks were seen approaching. It was an immense relief – they felt as though a heavy weight had been lifted from their hearts.

The soldiers rushed to help the new immigrants get down from the trucks and board the planes. The immigrants, in long robes, with infants in their arms and bags on their shoulders, tried to shield their eyes from the dust. It was a new version of the Exodus from Egypt and those standing watching, hardy battle veterans though they are, could not help wiping tears from their eyes at the sight of their brothers leaving for Eretz Israel.

Because of the delay, the planes arrived two hours late in Israel, only landing at eight o'clock this morning. Every so often I went out to the road to see if the buses were in sight. At exactly ten o'clock, we saw them approaching. It was my biggest group of immigrants since I started this job. We assembled the new arrivals on the lawn in the inner courtyard of the old age home. The immigrants sat in a circle, so close to each other that it was difficult to believe that there were over 150 of them. I looked at these beautiful black Jews, who were excited but seemed embarrassed by the warmth being showered on them.

A veteran immigrant is assisting me in handling the arrangements for this group. He grouped the people according to each extended family – *zemed.* I am becoming acquainted with the important role played by the extended family in Ethiopian culture – general as well as Jewish. There, they often feel a greater attachment to a second or even a third cousin than is common even between brothers in our society. This attachment is expressed in concern for the relative's fate, as well as in an almost compulsive sharing of joys and sorrows.

The rumor that immigrants have arrived has spread to all parts of the country and, within a few hours, Beta Israel relatives start arriving at the assembly point in Ashkelon. For some reason they are not allowed to enter the facility, so I chat with them beside the gate. Just then, Tsehaye comes up to me, closely followed by an elderly man who is short and very thin but conveys a sense of great dignity. He is one of the newly arrived *olim*. I can't help but notice that his originally white robe has turned gray-brown because of the long time he spent in a refugee camp. Oddly, I notice also that this is the first Ethiopian Jew I've ever seen with a pair of glasses. Tsehaye introduces him: "This is Aba Alene. He requests permission to fulfill a vow that he swore when he left Ethiopia two and a half years ago for Sudan."

"And what is that vow?"

"He swore when he left his village in Ethiopia that when he arrived safely in Jerusalem he would taste its earth."

Out of courtesy to the elderly man and so that he would not need to bend down, I scoop up a handful of Ashkelon earth in my hand and hold it out before him. I innocently expect him to kiss the earth and thus consider his vow fulfilled, but the man takes the sand from my hand and starts to swallow it. I stop him when he starts to choke. We bring him a glass of water and he stops coughing. Then, I tie up the sand in a corner of his robe and I say to him, "This is holy earth. Guard it." I ask Tsehaye to translate a question to Aba Alene: "What did it taste like, the earth that you tasted?"

"*Genet*," the man says, and Tsehaye quickly translates it for me, "The Garden of Eden. Paradise."

I learn later that Aba Alene has immigrated alone, leaving his wife and children behind in the village. Strange. How will he cope here without them? It's going to be difficult for him to manage on a practical level, even though his Zionism is so profound.

The old age home where we deal with the new immigrants during their first day in Israel is inhabited by elderly immigrants from all over the world. I was really impressed by the volunteer spirit that they displayed. It wasn't only that they helped us in giving out food, but they brought clothing for the newcomers, some of it worn and shabby, but clothes off their own backs. This is the Jewish people at its best: these speak Yiddish and those answer in Amharic, but in spite of that – they understand one another; they are one.

JULY 17, 1983 – BEN-GURION INTERNATIONAL AIRPORT

This morning twenty immigrants arrived via Kenya. Among them was a girl whom I'll call Zena. She sat down some distance away from the others in the group. It was only when she was interviewed that we found that she was actually married to one of them. Zena has an aristocratic air with her slightly slanted eyes, somewhat reminiscent of people from the Far East, prominent cheekbones, full lips, and brown skin. Her curly black hair is neatly gathered up at the back of her head and, in spite of her youth, she radiates a strong personality. When I heard her story it was difficult for me to understand the source of her strength.

THE STORY OF ZENA

In the village where I was born, my family has lived for many generations, son following son, one after the other, including famous *kessoch*. When I was six years old, ORT opened a school in our village, but it only went up to third grade, so when I was nine I went to live in a larger village, called Ambober, at the home of a *yekana abat* of my father's. What is a *yekana abat*? He is an older man who is tied to another younger man in a relationship that is similar to that between a man and his son, even though they are not blood relations. A *yekana abat* is a patron and protector. Ambober had a larger Jewish school where I was able to continue my studies. When I finished studying at that school, I went to live in the home of my grandfather's brother in a small city not too far away where I studied at a public school. He was a man known throughout the whole Ethiopian Jewish community. By then I was thirteen years old and I loved to learn. I was ready to give up everything provided I could carry on studying; but even so, the separation from my parents was hard. I went home every two weeks, walking four hours each way. Even though the route was difficult, I never missed the opportunity of seeing my mother and my father, hugging my brothers and sisters, enjoying the Sabbath atmosphere in the village, and savoring the aroma of my mother's cooking and tasting the dishes she'd prepared.

On Sundays, when I said good-bye to my mother, I had tears in my eyes. She always gave me bread to keep for the rest of that week. I would conserve its upper part for two weeks because my mother's fingerprints were on it and each day, when I got back from school, I would kiss that bread as though I were kissing my mother. When I arrived back at the home of my grandfather's brother on Sunday afternoons, I would smile at all my relatives, but at night, in my bed, my pillow would be wet with my tears. But I loved the school, the white uniform, the stream of kids every morning looking like a river of white as they entered. My school friends were always Jewish.

When I returned to school at the end of the long summer vacation, I discovered that some of the Jewish kids hadn't come back. The word *Sudan* was heard more and more frequently in secret discussions among the Jewish students. Then, during one of my visits home, my father told me that I would soon leave with my uncle for Sudan and from there we would proceed to Jerusalem. I was only fourteen years old and none of us knew when we would see each other again. I clung to my mother, not wanting to leave her, but my uncle said we had to hurry and eventually they pulled me from my mother's arms by force. We walked all that night and for half the next day. About noon, we reached Tikula, where my uncle's brother was waiting for us. He slaughtered a lamb and made sure that we lacked for nothing.

That night, as I was lying down to sleep, I heard our host urging his brother not to proceed to Sudan. "Do you know what's lying in store for the girl? See what a beauty she is. She already looks more like a woman than a child. Brigands are sure to attack you on the road."

"I can protect her," my uncle answered.

"You don't live here so you don't know how cruel these robbers are. There is no respect here for human lives. And even if you manage to cross the brigands' territory safely, the Sudanese are next and they too lust after Ethiopian girls. Everyone knows that Ethiopian women are the most beautiful women in Africa."

My uncle relented and decided to return to the village. In my heart of hearts, I was overjoyed. I so much wanted to go back home and now my prayers had been answered. So we walked again for a day and a half, until we reached home. Everyone was pleased, except for my uncle who was angry that he'd been delayed. But if I could have seen into the future, I wouldn't have been so happy. It would have been preferable to risk meeting with brigands and with tall, black Sudanese. Perhaps I'd have been saved from what actually lay in store for me.

After returning me to my parents, my uncle retraced his footsteps, departing once again by night for Sudan. I went back to my lessons at school. Three years elapsed and more and more young people had left for Sudan. I was already in eleventh grade before the next opportunity to leave arose. Two young Jewish men, who had already spent two months in Sudan, returned to our area shortly after the festival of Passover, probably to assist some relatives to go to Sudan. The rainy season would soon start and here was an opportunity to leave with two experienced guides. This time, being older, I jumped at the chance. It was Friday and the whole village was making preparations for the Sabbath. Unexpectedly, a young man showed up with my cousin. He told us that my uncle had arrived safely in Sudan and it would not be long before his turn came to make aliyah to Israel.

My parents knew how eager I was to reach Jerusalem and gave me their blessing, but they made my departure conditional on a relative accompanying me. Eventually, one of my uncles agreed to do so. We set out one morning. I embraced my mother and her tears mingled with mine. My father was more restrained, but I wept on his shoulder. Next, I hugged my brothers and sisters. I kissed them all, promising them we would all meet again soon in Jerusalem. I took the small loaf of bread given to me by my mother and we set out.

The first day that we walked passed quickly as we talked about what we expected to find in Jerusalem. Both of us, my uncle and myself, came from families of *kessoch* and had heard many stories about Jerusalem, about the land flowing with milk and honey that is the aspiration of every Jew. That evening, we reached Wuzaba, where the two men we had met in our village were already awaiting us to act as our guides. They both seemed very self-assured. The taller one always spoke first, but it was the other one who seemed to look at me in a special way. We were a group of eight people and, as we walked toward Wogera, that fellow – I will call him Uzi – always tried to position himself close to me. He even gave my uncle all sorts of tasks to carry out in order to get him away from me. It was only later that I discovered that a woman who was both his aunt and my aunt had promised him that I'd be his wife. She had no actual right to do this, but since my parents were far away, she did so. She did this without consulting me, and even though she knew that he already had a wife in Sudan.

After several days' walking, we reached a place called Mereba. The guides said that we would be waiting there for several days, but as there was some sort of danger nearby we couldn't stay in any of the homes and would sleep in a nearby forest. The Jews of the village brought us food and water every evening. I was given jobs to do that I had never done before, such as grinding corn between two stones to make fine flour. After two days, my fingers were so battered that my hands, which had been lovely, were unrecognizable. We'd been camped there in the forest for a week when one day, as I was grinding the corn, I saw one of the guides take the hand of one of the young women, a girl of my age, and the two of them went up toward the village.

As we lay down on our bedding under the trees, while my eyes were still open and I was thinking of my parents and the pampered life I had led, a loud cry suddenly rent the stillness of the night. I recognized the young woman's voice and realized what had happened. In my imagination, I could see her face fill with horror as the young man assaulted her. The next morning, we saw her coming toward us. She looked so humiliated, so full of hurt and anger, obviously wishing she could escape our gaze.

Ever since I'd heard her cry out, I knew my own turn would come. Not a day passed without my begging my uncle to return home and wait for another opportunity, but he would not listen to my pleas. Ten days later, whatever danger there had been had passed and we were taken to live with the Jewish families in the village. Uzi took me, without my uncle, to the house of one of his relatives. After the evening meal, the family all retired to their own corners. I did not undress as I wanted to discourage any ideas he might have, but he came to me and tore off my clothes. I fought him and shouted out. I knew that his relatives could hear me and hoped that perhaps one of them might come to my assistance. But not one of them made a move. He'd told them that I was his wife and it is a husband's duty to break the hymen on the wedding night.

There was nothing else I could do but bury my head in the pillow and cry. I felt as though black walls were closing in on me from all directions. Above and beyond the physical pain, there was the agony of shame. I dreaded that my family would hear of it. I thought of committing suicide, but then I lost consciousness. When I came to, it was to find all the members of the host family standing over me and Uzi, looking worried, moistening my lips with water.

Three days later, we resumed our journey. Uzi felt my repulsion for him and suspected I might try to run away. He warned me, "If you try to escape, I will find you and make you suffer." We walked for eight nights before reaching Sudan. There was some comfort in the fact that he didn't touch me during the journey, but I was in his power and I had no choice but to walk beside him and to serve him as a wife must serve her husband. By the time we reached the Sudanese border, we had no money left. So my "husband" set off for Tewaba – the big refugee camp near the town of Gedaref – while the second guide guarded us. A week passed, but he did not return. Our provisions were finished and all we had left was water because it was the rainy season. In the end, some local people helped us. They gave us flour and, later, also enough money to hire a truck to get to Tewaba.

It was only when we reached the refugee camp that we again saw Uzi. He'd collected money for us from our relatives. For me, he had taken money from my cousin, without even thinking that if he considered himself to be my husband, it was his responsibility to look after me and my cousin. This same cousin also told me about my "husband's" wife in Sudan. I did everything he commanded me – I was like a zombie – a person without a soul. I had no future. Meanwhile, he divorced his previous wife and made me his legal wife, by having two elders as witnesses when he signed a piece of paper, as is the custom. But actually, I was his slave, carrying out his mother's orders in everything concerning housework and his orders in everything concerning bed.

Throughout the two years I spent in Sudan, it was my job to carry the water from the central water outlet, gather wood, grind flour, cook the meals, and clean the house. Everything had to be executed to his mother's satisfaction. At night, when my husband returned drunk from Tewaba's bars, I had to obey him in bed. It made me happy when I heard that he had a girlfriend in Tewaba. I hoped that meant he wouldn't bother me anymore.

One day I went with him to the market and we bought twenty kilos of corn. I knew that he had plenty of money in his pockets and I was sure that he'd lay out the tiny sum needed to hire a vehicle. But he made me carry the whole load on my back. I felt so degraded. I'd been transformed from a bright, eleventh-grade student into a slave with no rights. As on so many occasions, before and after, I thought of committing suicide, but the picture of my mother rose up in my mind and stopped me. She'd lost enough children in her life already.

I found some consolation with a group of Ethiopian Christians who lived in the same courtyard. When I was in their company, I could again become a person worth respecting, a young woman whose opinion is valuable, and a woman of importance. But there were arguments between me and my husband which grew more frequent and with them came violence. Everyone was afraid of him, so nobody dared defend or comfort me. Only his twelve-year-old sister would approach me when I was left alone with my tears.

Relatives of mine who were in the area heard about my situation and tried to get me released from him, but their efforts only made things worse. He behaved even more cruelly. In order to prevent escalation of his abuse, I asked my relatives not to interfere further and to let me be. I wanted to simply disappear and even considered going to a Sudanese family and offering myself as a servant.

In the end, I became pregnant with my first child. At first, he treated me gently, but within a short time, the situation reverted to what it had been before. I was afraid of losing the baby as a result of his beatings. Luckily, the American organization, AAEJ, recruited

> him for work and that's how we've now made aliyah, even though others have been waiting in Sudan longer than we. We traveled to Khartoum by night, flew the next day to Juba, and from there we went by jeep to Kenya. It wasn't an easy journey and twice we were almost arrested. Fortunately, because I was pregnant the policemen were persuaded to let us go. At long last, we reached Nairobi. The Americans bought us new clothes so that we would arrive in Israel dressed festively. Now I'm happy that I've arrived in Jerusalem, but I don't understand how I've gone through all that I have and still remained alive. I don't look strong at all, but obviously I'm stronger than I look.

As I now prepare this diary for publication, I can report that Zena gave birth to a son a short time after she arrived in Israel. Within two years, she divorced her husband, who had continued to abuse her in Israel.

JULY 27, 1983 – BEN-GURION INTERNATIONAL AIRPORT

Today, a small group of thirty-one new immigrants arrived. The figure who stood out most was a young man who is so black that it almost gives one a shock to see him. When I asked him his name, he said it was Melaku Tefesahaku. If I hadn't known that he was lying, I wouldn't have doubted him, because he lied with such brazen confidence. Unfortunately for him, I know the real Melaku Tefesahaku; he works for us as a translator and counselor in Upper Afula. I decided to pay the newcomer back in his own coin and telephoned Upper Afula, got the real Melaku Tefesahaku on the line, and said to the impostor that he could now speak with Melaku Tefesahaku. After that conversation, the game was up. This man's real name is Osman Hussein Ahmed. He is a Muslim who worked in the home of a *kes*, Tefesahaku Melaku's father. Since he had no other family than his master's, he followed them to Sudan and then immigrated with them. There's no doubt we'll have to keep him here, since it's impossible to return him either to Sudan or to Ethiopia. Maybe he'll agree to convert to Judaism, but meanwhile he has to be registered as a Muslim for religion and as an Ethiopian for nationality.

AUGUST 1, 1983

Today marks a year since I started working in the Jewish Agency as the national absorption coordinator for Ethiopian immigrants. Now is the time for me to take stock of the job, as well as of my own feelings about it. I love my work and it seems to me that the community members in Israel return the affection I feel for them. Indeed, Zimna told me as much a few days ago.

I visited the absorption center in Atlit today and naturally one of my first stops there was to see Aba Alene, the elderly gentleman who had wanted to eat holy soil when I met him the previous June. I asked him in Amharic how he was. "Thank God, I'm in Jerusalem," he answered. But when I probed further, it became clear that he's having a very hard time managing without his wife and children. It's more than just the important fact that he misses them; it is also his inability – being a man – to organize his home. The room he's living in is dirty and his clothes still carry stains from Sudan. He has certainly not eaten one hot meal since then. Ethiopian culture forbids a man to engage in work that is considered women's work, so no Ethiopian man has a clue how to manage in the kitchen nor do any domestic tasks. Aba Alene can't even make a cup of coffee, let alone deal with laundry. When I asked one of the translator/counselors why it's like that, he couldn't even understand my question, which from his point of view was completely illogical. But, after some reflection on the matter, he said, "If a man does woman's work, for him it's like wearing a dress."

DECEMBER 3, 1983 – THE RUNWAY OF AN AIRBASE SOMEWHERE IN ISRAEL

My car is laden with pita breads, jams, chocolate spread, tea, coffee, sugar, and candy. I arrived at the office at four o'clock this morning and after the briefing, we set off for the air force base at six o'clock. Now there, we assemble in the officers' club, where I have a cup of coffee.

Shortly after, we leave for the runway. On the horizon, a single Hercules plane can be seen, shining in the first rays of the morning light. Soon it will land. I'm excited, but the more experienced staff calm me down, explaining that it's an empty plane whose job has been to circle overhead during the operation in case of anything going wrong – it did not actually land to pick up immigrants and since it's not carrying passengers, it has returned about ten minutes before the others. And indeed, after it lands, two more Hercules planes appear. A one-legged pilot is standing on the runway – his other leg was lost during his military service. He is very stable on the one leg, and uses his crutches to direct the planes to their stopping points. The under part of the first plane opens and the *olim* emerge, many youngsters, as well as old people. Their faces are expressionless, displaying no joy. There's only one old woman who realizes that she's apparently arrived in Jerusalem and falls on her knees and kisses the ground. They quietly file into the six buses that are drawn up in a U shape at the rear of each plane. Here and there, some turmoil occurs as a father searches for his son or a mother for her daughter. The chief of staff, Moshe Levi, accompanied by his entourage, is observing the event.

From the second plane, they lift down a woman who gave birth on the sands of Sudan a short time before the plane took off. I send my secretary, Sarah Yaron, with the mother and the newborn baby to the hospital. After they are all in the buses, we pull down the curtains so that the new immigrants cannot be seen from outside, since this has been a clandestine operation during which we have transported immigrants from Sudan, an enemy country. That is also why we leave the airbase by a side entrance. Within an hour and a half, we reach the Jewish Agency's old age home in Ashkelon. We explain to the newcomers that we are going to interview them in order to issue them their identity cards, but it's doubtful if they understand what we're talking about.

The interviewing process is especially difficult since there are many cases of multiple marriages. I am reminded of how Aba Alene is incapable of looking after himself without a wife to take care of him. We know that many men who arrive in Sudan without their wives – often because the wife has made aliyah before them – take another wife. This presents us with the dilemma of how to register their married status: to the wife that they've arrived with, or the wife that they left behind in Ethiopia, or the one waiting for them here in Israel?

Today, with the experience gained in over a year in this job, I am convinced that we damage the new immigrant's identity as soon as he arrives here because aside from the place of birth, religion, and nationality, the other details that we register are often different from what the immigrant knows. As I sit opposite the newcomers, I can feel that we're doing them wrong, but no matter how deeply I probe, I am no nearer a solution.

Take, for example, the basic issue of a person's name. Here in Israel we have a first name and a family name. In Ethiopia, there are no family names and a person is identified by his name and his father's name. Here it has been decided, for some reason or other, to change the first name to a Hebrew name, and usually the original name is not even translated, but the immigrant is given a Hebrew name with a similar sound to the Ethiopian one. Thus, elderly women have ended up with ludicrously inappropriate Hebrew names such as Lilach or Osnat. I instituted two changes in the matter of the first name in order to lessen the damage caused to a person's sense of self. First, I directed the staffers not to change the first name, but to add a Hebrew name as a middle name and on no account to erase the original. Second, the Hebrew name must be as close a translation as possible of the original and not just sound like it. The affair of Adisalem-Eddie is permanent engraved in my memory.

When I started working with the immigrants, it was explained to me that since in Ethiopia there is no such thing as a family name, upon their arrival in Israel, the first name of the grandfather of the family head is given to the whole family as its surname.

But I checked into this and discovered that the issue has been dealt with arbitrarily, without delving into a name's significance, as is done in Ethiopia. After studying the matter, I instructed that the father's name should be kept as the family name for all adults whose parents are no longer living, in order to lessen the damage to identity, at least among the men.

I could thus perhaps mitigate the damage to the men's sense of self, but for married women – of all ages – the damage caused to their identity by giving them a new family name is one of the hardest things to cope with. But there is nothing I can do to save the situation. According to the State of Israel's laws, a woman's family name is changed upon marriage (she may retain her maiden name only by special request); this is not the case in Ethiopia, where a woman retains her own father's name after she marries. And so, on more than one occasion, we have experienced a disturbing thing: a woman who made aliyah without her husband, and thus was registered as the family head, did not respond when she was called by her new Hebrew first name, which she didn't recognize, or her new family name – the name of her husband's father or grandfather. However, unfortunately, these are the new realities they have to cope with and nothing can be done to alter them since every person in Israel must have a family name and that family name – by definition – is the name that unites the family.

The question of age is also not easy to deal with. The immigrants arrive from Sudan without a birth certificate or any other identification documents. In addition, most Ethiopian immigrants do not know their exact date of birth. Knowledge of one's exact age does not play a particularly important role in Ethiopian society, where there is no law of compulsory education determining that every child must start kindergarten at the age of five; neither is it customary there to celebrate a bar mitzvah at the age of thirteen; nor is there compulsory military conscription at a certain age. Indeed, there have been cases of children aged fourteen or fifteen who were drafted for military service in Ethiopia because their bodies looked developed enough. There is also no official old-age pension, at least in the rural areas. In Ethiopian villages, the adults know who is older than whom and the younger person treats an older person with respect without any need to officially register the birth date. So what's to be done, since Israel's Ministry of the Interior mandates registration of the date of birth on the ID? That's why we always sit with the new immigrants upon arrival and try to help them work out their age, using, for the purpose, important historical events such as the start of the Italian invasion, its end, and so on. It's obvious to me that here, too, we sometimes do wrong by the immigrants and I've already come across claims from immigrants in absorption centers that their ages have been registered very incorrectly.

But the greatest harm done is, without doubt, in the registration of marital status. In Ethiopian Jewish culture, girls are often married at a very young age. Sometimes parents promise their children in marriage soon after they are born. Usually, the girls are married when they reach puberty. But there are many cases of marriage at an even younger age, even as young as six or seven years of age. However, the couple does not live together intimately as husband and wife in such cases. The marriage ceremony is legally carried out and three elderly women examine the girl to make sure she is a virgin. But after the ceremony and the festivities in the bride's village and the groom's village, the girl usually spends the next years preparing for married life, some with the husband's family and some with her own family. The couple's parents also appoint a guardian from the groom's family whose role is to make certain that no harm comes to the girl, and especially to ensure that her husband does not have sexual relations with her before she begins to menstruate, officially becoming a woman.

There was such a girl in the group that we interviewed. She was about twelve years old and arrived with her parents. Her husband arrived earlier. I wish it were possible to register a person as betrothed or engaged on our ID cards, but unfortunately there is no such option. So I had to decide how to register this girl. For a moment, I thought of my own daughter, Yifat, who will be twelve in six months, and I simply could not list this child as "married." I could not write the word. In the end, she was registered as "single." We explained this to the parents, but without a doubt they still don't have a clue why. When we asked them if it was acceptable to them, they responded, as was to be expected, "You're the best judges of what is right. You're from Jerusalem."

That night, when I lay down to sleep, I was troubled, convinced that we were not doing the right thing, that our bureaucratic procedures are utterly wrong for the Ethiopians, being based on our culture, which is in no way in tune with theirs. I dreamed I saw an immigrant entering by one door – smiling, proud, and impressive – then exiting by another door a short time after, still smiling but sad-eyed and submissive. I would interpret this dream as emanating from my distress at the identity changes imposed on the Beta Israel: within one hour, the immigrant acquires a different first name, a different family name, and an arbitrary date of birth. Even the immigrant's marital status is decided for him or her.

The situation is made even worse because many workers in the system view themselves as the immigrants' superiors and consider themselves entitled to run their lives and decide what is best for them. I have no doubt that something needs to be done about this, but what? The same patronizing attitude had ill effects on the absorption of immigrants in the fifties and sixties, leading to the concept of "the Second Israel." We must not allow the Ethiopian immigrants to become "the Third Israel."

DECEMBER 8, 1983 – BEN-GURION INTERNATIONAL AIRPORT

Today, sixty-five immigrants arrived via Europe, in two groups. Building on our past experience, we now interview a couple separately. In the course of the conversation with one young couple, it was revealed that the man had left one wife behind in Ethiopia and taken this wife while in the camp in Sudan. When we revealed to the young woman that her "husband" already had a wife in Ethiopia, she was furious and, in spite of her young age – she was only seventeen – upbraided him angrily. We registered him as being married to the wife in Ethiopia, while the young woman was registered as being divorced from a husband who is also now remarried in Ethiopia. We decided to send him to Pardess Chana and her to Upper Afula. They sat together in the bus. When it arrived in Pardess Chana and we called his name to get off, she got off, too, and refused to reboard the bus, in spite of our entreaties. It seems to me that her attachment to him stems from the fact that she has no relatives in Israel.

DECEMBER 13, 1983

Zimna told me this morning that he had looked into the matter and the reason the young woman had followed her "husband" to Pardess Chana was because she was raped in Sudan and is apparently looking for a "cover story" for the baby she is carrying.

DECEMBER 18, 1983 – SAFED

Today, Zimna and I went to Safed to speak at a public information evening. The mayor told us that there is opposition to receiving Ethiopian immigrants in the city. I really do think that we succeeded – or, to be more exact, Zimna succeeded – in turning around the Safed residents and infecting them with our own enthusiasm. Zimna told them about his own childhood in Ethiopia, describing how, at the age of five, he was given the job of shepherding the calves and then, as he grew older, was given increased responsibilities. But it was when Zimna spoke of his own yearning and the longings of all the Ethiopian community for Zion that the ice was truly broken and the atmosphere in the hall swung in favor of the immigrants.

His words were so poignant that I can quote them exactly: he said that he apologized if his words inadvertently hurt anyone, but "When you want to know what Zionism is, you go to the bookshelves, take out a book on Zionism and read what Herzl, Weizmann, Jabotinsky, and others said on Zionism, and then you know about it. We in Ethiopia didn't have books like that. You can also take a book of Chaim Nahman Bialik's poetry in your hands and read his poem 'To the Bird,' and then you understand what Zionism is. We in Ethiopia don't have such books of poetry, but we, too, have a bird. Our bird is the stork, and every Jewish child in Ethiopia knows that on its way from Europe in the fall, the stork stops off to rest in Jerusalem. So in Ethiopia, the first one in the village who sees a stork landing in one of the fields calls out at the top of his voice, '*Shimela*,' which is 'stork' in Amharic, and then all the people of the village lay down their tools, however busy they are in the field or the house, and everyone goes out to the stork and sings a song to it. It's a very simple song: '*Shimela, shimela, agerachin Yerusalem dehena?*' which means, 'Stork, stork, is our land of Jerusalem steeped in good?' That's our Zionism!"

And then Zimna went on: "In Ethiopia, when a parent wants his child to do something, he doesn't threaten that he won't let him watch television, since there's no television there, or that he won't let him go the cinema, since there's no cinema in the villages. He threatens that if he doesn't behave properly, he won't have the good fortune to reach Jerusalem." When Zimna spoke about this threat, I thought about my own kids and what their reaction would probably be: they'd be bound to retort, "We'll wait and see about that." But for a child in Ethiopia, a threat from an adult is real and there's no appeal against it. And since there is no punishment greater than not reaching Jerusalem, the child will quickly obey. My love for Ethiopian Jews – a love that was kindled at the very start of our road together – has been greatly enhanced by Zimna's personality and, in particular, by the way he spoke that evening.

While we were driving back from Safed, Zimna gave me a full picture of the situation in Sudan. He started on a personal note, saying, "It's good that you're not stationed in Sudan. Two hours there would break you. You just can't imagine what suffering the people endure there. You wouldn't be able to stand it. You'd either run away or go crazy."

The first Jews left for Sudan back in 1978, when thousands of Ethiopian refugees started streaming into that country. At the start of the eighties, large groups of Jews arrived at the refugee camps near Gedaref. Our organizational setup in Sudan has constantly improved over the years. At the start, when there were only a few hundred Jews – most of them in one camp – it was like a family-type framework. But as the numbers grew, the system had to be improved, while at the same time secrecy about it had to be preserved.

Zimna spoke about the early days in Sudan. When he was sent out there at the end of 1981, his operators gave him so many warnings to beware of everything and everyone that he was jumping at every shadow. In the end, he decided to leave the hotel and go to live with the refugees and, for that purpose, he grew a beard and starting dressing like the other Ethiopians. Since he was driving the car while he was telling me all this, I was able to study his face and my eyes were drawn to his beard as he was telling me about it – how it changed his face so much his own mother wouldn't have recognized him. Suddenly his expression clouded over and every muscle in his face went taut as he started describing the conditions he found in the refugee camps for Jews waiting to make aliyah. Most of them fell sick with dysentery because of the polluted water that they drank – water in which the worms could be seen wriggling about. Many children had died because, in addition to the dysentery, they suffered severe malnutrition.

Zimna told about how he had tried to encourage the Jews, visiting them in their homes whenever he had the opportunity. On one of these occasions, he identified a Jewish house because beside it there was a *mergam gojo* – a separation house used during menstruation – which was occupied at the time. One woman was delousing another. Inside the house, he saw a woman sifting flour that was full of worms. It made him so bitter and angry. The woman was shocked to see him there and when he asked where she was from, she answered, from Ethiopia. When he persisted with his questions, asking from what place in Ethiopia, she again answered, from Ethiopia. In order to calm her fears, Zimna said that he was also from Ethiopia, but the fear could still be seen in her eyes. It was only when he told her that his own mother, like her, also made pottery vessels with her own hands, that she burst into relieved laughter because then she understood that he was a Jew like herself. When people started to gather in the women's house, Zimna was afraid that his identity would be revealed so he grasped the hand of the oldest of her sons, a youth of about seventeen, pulled him outside and gave him a note of fifty Sudanese pounds. To this day, that woman reminds Zimna every chance she gets of how he saved her children on that evening.

But it was not possible to save everyone. On one of his journeys, Zimna encountered a woman who had not yet buried her son, who had died four days earlier, because she had neither the tools to dig a grave nor anyone to assist her.

During the course of time, Zimna grasped the local problems and then he gave instructions that the Jews must conceal their identity as Jews. He said that they should cook on the Sabbath, eat meat that had not been slaughtered by the *kessoch* and do away with the *mergam gojo* (separation house). The young people accepted this, but the elders would not agree to carry out these orders.

Aliyah was not yet organized at that time; however, by the end of 1983, a system was in place and was working well, even though the aliyah activists had to be replaced each time some of them made aliyah themselves. The people called these activists the "Committee" – and even in Amharic that was the term used. The Committee dealt with two main issues: organization of aliyah and distribution of money. At the beginning, the Jews who arrived in Sudan were not systematically listed; everything that happened was based on chance meetings, newcomers meeting people they knew and being referred by word of mouth, one friend telling another, until the name reached one of the Committee. Aliyah was also handled haphazardly, without orderly lists of those waiting to emigrate.

In the course of time, the elders of the community, known in Amharic as *shmageloch,* were brought into the picture. They were given the task of determining who, out of the hundreds of thousands of Ethiopian refugees who had crossed into Sudan, was, indeed, Jewish and therefore entitled to receive assistance and eventually immigrate to Israel. But even when this system was up and running, it was not organized at a proper registration office. The registration was still carried out behind closed doors, in complete secrecy. This could result in a considerable time gap until a Jew who had already endured the trek from Ethiopia to the refugee camp came to the attention of one of the Committee members or community elders.

The Committee members were entrusted with arranging aliyah according to the length of stay in Sudan, but there were always exceptions to this rule. These exceptions included the sick, the elderly, wives unaccompanied by a husband and with children to care for, as well as those with fear of blood revenge from Christian neighbors because they had killed a family member. The Committee members were also subjected to pressure from their own family members who wanted to "jump the line" and make aliyah sooner than their proper turn and, in quite a few instances, the Committee members gave in to this pressure. In terms of Ethiopian culture, in which your first duty is always to look after the members of your own family, this is understandable. However, since the various rescue operations continually reduced the number of Jews waiting in Sudan, not many complaints were heard on this subject.

While the Israelis in the group had contact with the Sudanese men of power in Gedaref, the main town of the region, as well as in Khartoum, the capital, the Committee members nurtured special relationships with the clerks who issued the permits that allowed travel from the camp area to Khartoum. It was usually possible to obtain such a permit within two to three days. These permits were issued only to those setting out for Israel via Khartoum, where they boarded regular flights to Europe. Obviously, no permits were needed for those making aliyah in an operation referred to as *chelema* ("darkness" in Amharic) – in other words, the secret nighttime operations.

The immigrants usually traveled from Gedaref to Khartoum in crammed buses whose roofs were piled with goats, barrels of kerosene, boxes of produce, etc., so that they looked almost like trucks. Upon their departure, a Committee representative would hand the people their requisite documents and tell them that upon arriving in Khartoum they must wait at the central bus station until they were met. There were always two to three members of the Committee at any time in Khartoum. They went to the central bus station twice a day, once around one o'clock in the afternoon and once toward evening, to collect the new arrivals. Since there was no regular communication between Gedaref and Khartoum, they would arrive at the station at these regular times and search for Jews whom they might or might not know already. Sometimes, if they had the feeling that they were being followed or they saw too many policemen in the vicinity, they would abort their visit to the station and instead would go at night to Khartoum's Ethiopian neighborhood, Khartoum Talatta. Sure enough, in the cheap hotels there, they found the Jews who had arrived that day or the previous day and would then take them to the safe houses that had been rented for the purpose in Khartoum. The immigrants were given strict instructions not to go out, and, indeed, the only time they went out was when it was necessary to take their photographs. Then, it was a quick trip to the photographer and back to the house. Within a few days, Israelis who were stationed undercover in Khartoum obtained refugee passports for them stamped for a European destination. These papers and the plane tickets were put in the hands of Committee members.

Waiting around in closed, strange houses in Khartoum was hard on the people, but the most difficult time of all for them was the last night. It always seemed endless – the hours of darkness between receiving the announcement that the next day they would set out for Jerusalem and the actual departure early in the morning for the airport. That night, not one of the adults ever managed to sleep and they would even wake up the children in the middle of the night to get ready. Then, dressed in their best clothes, they awaited the coming of the white man and the Committee member who would take them to the airport.

Before setting out, each of the immigrants received a plastic bag marked ICM, the international emigration organization, to facilitate their identification until they arrived in Israel. A Committee member accompanied them from the house to the airport in one of the closed Toyota pickup trucks that are used as taxis in Khartoum. The Israeli was always in the vicinity, observing events from a distance and leaving only after seeing the last of the immigrants enter the airport, where they came under the authority of the ICM representative.

The Committee was also responsible for distributing money. One of the Israelis would leave every few months for Europe, returning with a suitcase full of dollars. In this way, every year several million dollars made their way from Israel via Europe to Sudan. This money was to be given out once a month to the Jews in the refugee camps. Every three weeks, one of the Israelis took some money out of the suitcase, the dollars were exchanged for Sudanese money, and the Israeli then traveled with two Committee members to Gedaref. It never once happened that they were stopped on the way, though there were many checkpoints. It was simply taken for granted that the Sudanese considered a white man as a *havaja* ("master" in Arabic).

Upon arrival in Gedaref, the Committee members donned sunglasses in order not to be recognized by the Sudanese Secret Service and police and that same evening they met with the *berari*, the fast messengers whose job it was to distribute the money to Jews in the various refugee camps. The *berari* were supposed to disburse the cash the next night in accordance with the Committee's lists, with the exact sum corresponding to the size of the family. That same evening, the Israeli would disappear from the area, unless a night aliyah operation was scheduled. The Committee members who had come with him from Khartoum would remain in Gedaref for at least a week, in order to supervise the money distribution and to update the list of those receiving benefits.

Throughout all the years that the system operated, complaints were constantly heard from immigrants arriving in Israel that the Committee members and the *berari* did not hand over all the money they were supposed to, but that a portion of it always found its way to their own pockets, so they enjoyed an extravagant mode of living while the other Jews were on the verge of starvation. Similar complaints were also raised about the *shmageloch*, and these were investigated, but it was only on rare occasions that we were able to right a wrong.

DECEMBER 19, 1983 – BEN-GURION INTERNATIONAL AIRPORT

Never a dull moment!

At three o'clock this morning, eight immigrants arrived from Sudan. They were all young and single – six young men and two young women. Two of them, a boy and a girl, are the siblings of a young man who has been in Israel for a while, and they looked very happy to have made their aliyah and were very eager to see their brother again. They asked Zimna about him and to my surprise Zimna answered with a smile that they would soon see him – in spite of the fact that he knew the brother died over a month ago.

I asked Zimna to accompany me to one of the corners of the hall. There I began shouting at him, the blood rising to my head in anger: "How can you delude these poor people in such a way?" With the calm that is so typical of him, he gave me a lesson in Ethiopian culture, which helped me to understand one of the important differences between it and our own culture. Among us, when someone dies, a doctor, army officer, social worker, or simply a friend announces the sad tidings to the spouse or family. In Ethiopia, when a person passes away – and especially when it's an adult or an old man – people assemble who knew the deceased and the relatives are brought to the home of one of the relatives who already knows of the death. The family members usually burst into bitter tears because the very fact of the gathering and the composition of its participants make clear that their loved one is no longer among the living. Because of this, Zimna did not tell this brother and sister about their brother's death. After the new immigrants dispersed, we took the siblings to their brother's home so that their sister-in-law, and not we, could tell them the sad news.

JANUARY 1, 1984 – OFFICE OF THE JEWISH AGENCY, TEL AVIV

Today, David Zevadia returned from a four-week mission in Ethiopia. David is the son of Aba Getie, one of the most respected *kessoch* of the community in Ethiopia. He gave David his Jewish education: as a child David studied a chapter of the Torah in Ge'ez every evening with his father. At the end of each lesson, he would kiss his father's hands and feet, and only then was he allowed to go to bed. David made aliyah at the end of 1974 and started working in a factory, but when the aliyah from Ethiopia grew, he was recruited by the Jewish Agency and has been working with us ever since.

On November 19, 1983, David was called to our office and told to get ready to leave for Addis Ababa. His mission would be to encourage the Jews of Gondar to join their brothers who had already made aliyah from Sudan over the last four years. Only a few hundred Jews still remain in the refugee camps as, in the second half of 1983, we brought out 760 in three naval operations and another 1,056 in twenty-nine small groups through Europe. After David arrived in Addis Ababa, he invited leaders from the Gondar region to meet with him in order to tell them how to get the Jews to Sudan.

At first, he based himself in the Finfine Hotel in the town center, but the next day he felt that he was being watched and he feared that those visiting him would arouse the authorities' suspicions. He decided to move to the home of Hailu Desta, one of Dr. Faitlovitch's students. Some of the invitees were already in Addis Ababa and others arrived from Gondar. Among those who came were his brother and brother-in-law. As a surprise for David, they brought his mother with them, although his father, Aba Getie, being no longer mobile, remained behind in the village. It had been nine years since David left his village and now he had returned in order to organize a Jewish exodus, but when he saw his mother again, he was once more like a small child and wept in her arms.

On December 18, all the invitees arrived at Hailu Desta's home, where the finest refreshments were offered by his wife. David started the proceedings by saying, "Our message is clear. The State of Israel wants all Ethiopian Jews to make their way to Sudan. You have to send messengers to all the villages in the Gondar region and they have to tell the Jews to leave everything behind and set out for Sudan. Those from Wogera will go via Inkash and the people from the town of Gondar will leave via Gayna."

One of the elders asked to take the floor, but not in order to discuss the difficulties involved in walking hundreds of kilometers through a mountainous region; the Ethiopian Jews had already demonstrated their ability to overcome the hardships of the route. He raised a different question: "We're talking here of thousands of people who have to reach Sudan within four months. How will it be possible to cross the Gondar-Asmara highway without arousing the authorities' suspicion? That's a busy road with military and police everywhere."

In fact, our people have already addressed this issue. Contact was made with the famous brigand Berihun Gebreyesus, the uncrowned king of the Armachiho district of the Amhara region. The area under discussion is not ruled by the government or by the anti-government rebels. It is an area of refuge for robbers, brigands, people with blood on their hands because they avenged the death of relatives, and your ordinary, run-of-the-mill murderers. It was an easy matter to persuade Gebreyesus to assist our people since, in addition to receiving money from us, there is a Jewish angle: his wife – the mother of his children – is Jewish and her parents are among the candidates for departure. Our emissaries were asked to tell the departing Jews that they must at all times be especially careful in front of other community members since there are informers among them. Our emissaries were also told that when the Jews set out for Sudan, our contacts in the area would be very helpful and especially the brigand Gebreyesus.

David summed up, "The ultimate goal is to bring thousands of Jews within four months to Gedaref, which is the main city of the region and also the largest center for refugees in Sudan. Once there, they must seek out the people of our Committee who will deal with their maintenance and make sure that they eventually get to Israel."

David waited in Addis Ababa another two weeks until he received word from his contacts in Gondar. The message ran, "We are gathering the grain and soon the rains will start." He knew then that it was all right for him to return to Israel.

Today David reported to his superiors that the community is on its way. We now have to get organized to receive thousands of people in the near future.

JANUARY 15, 1984 – THE ABSORPTION CENTER, ATLIT

Three weeks ago, this year's first group arrived – sixteen immigrants, including three community activists, one of whom is Zegeye Mamo. He is tall, with shining eyes, and he behaves in a patronizing manner, even to the Israeli staff dealing with his absorption. Here began a perfect example of the complications we deal with continually. The day before yesterday, even before I left my house in the morning for the office, the absorption center in Atlit called me to ask in which house Zegeye should be placed. We had sent him to the woman whom he declared to be his wife, Alem Beyene, the granddaughter of the chief *kes* of the Jews of Tigre. However, in Atlit there is another woman, Natshatey Alemu, who gave birth only two weeks ago to Zegeye's son and she, like Alem Beyene, is registered with the family name Mamo. Obviously they were both married to him in Sudan.

In my mind's eye, I pictured a potentate and his harem. That's how some of the activists have behaved in Sudan. In the refugee camps, they are the kings who rule the community. They have the money and they have the power to rescue or to imprison. Quite a few girls have given themselves to this sort of king to rescue their families, and more than one father has sacrificed one daughter in order to save his other children. Zegeye belongs in the same category as the two young men who cruelly raped Zena and her friend. There must be an investigation here in Israel into the deeds these people committed in Sudan and if the stories are proved to be true, the guilty activists must be punished. As to the question the Atlit staff posed about Zegeye, I asked them to leave the situation as it is until I get there.

This morning, we traveled to Atlit and ensconced ourselves there in an office at the absorption center. Sitting with me were the director of the absorption center, Tamar Carmeli, the social worker, Nehama Sarabernik, and her counselor, Na'ama Malihi, as well as the on-site translator/counselor. The first person to enter was Zegeye Mamo. With a penetrating look he surveyed all those present in the room and only after making sure that he had instilled in everyone the feeling that he was the person in control, he sat down on the vacant chair. He claimed to have divorced Natshatey. How? Before Natshatey boarded the aircraft, he told her that he divorced her. This disdainful way of treating the person who had been his wife – though perhaps "slave" would be a more correct term – made me furious. I quickly asked him what he thought about the fact that just two weeks previously Natshatey had given birth to his son. His condescending answer made me want to hit him: he said that only a medical test could prove his paternity.

The next one to enter was Natshatey, a tall young woman, about twenty years old, very beautiful, with delicate features. When she came into the room, I wanted to hug her and defend her with my own strength. To my surprise, she did not request to be reunited with Zegeye. Her only concern was that he admit to being the father of her child. Natshatey arrived in Israel with the group that came on June 13 last year. We sent her then to her first husband, who was living in the absorption center in Afula, where he was one of the old-timers and already had a job. When she reached the absorption center, she was directed to her husband's apartment, but then her brother intercepted her and warned that if her husband saw her, he was likely to kill her, since he'd heard of her marriage in Sudan to another man. That was when we hurriedly transferred her to Atlit.

Zegeye came back into the room and announced that even if it meant he would be hanged until dead, he would not agree to live with Natshatey. All he wanted was to live with Alem Beyene, who is registered as the widow of Avraham Mahari. In the meantime, we have heard that Avraham Mahari is not dead at all but is living in Sudan with another wife.

Complicated?

There is no doubt that the problem of marital status among the Ethiopian Jews is more complicated than we've ever encountered with any other immigrant group in Israel. Apparently, over half of the adults have been divorced at least once in their lives. This is perhaps because, on the one hand, most of the first marriages were arranged by the parents when the couple was still at a very tender age, and, on the other hand, divorce among Ethiopian Jews has been much simpler than in Israel or other Jewish communities. But there is another factor aggravating the situation: their stay in the refugee camps in Sudan often involves family separations with some family members going to Sudan while others do not. As a result, families do not always make aliyah together as a unit. Many families have split up with some staying behind in Ethiopia, some remaining in Sudan, and others making aliyah. It must be assumed that this situation will have a negative influence on the immigrants and on their children. All of us – they and we – will have to cope with the effects.

FEBRUARY 4, 1984 – THE RUNWAY OF AN AIRBASE SOMEWHERE IN ISRAEL

Early this morning we assembled, eighteen of us, in the Jewish Agency office in Tel Aviv. There should actually have been twenty people present, but I didn't manage to find either David Zevadia or Matti Elias. For the last two days, I've been hearing rumors that we've got to prepare for a major initiative; then yesterday morning at 10:30 a.m., I was given an authorization for the arrival of over 350 immigrants. I immediately went out to do the shopping for them that has become my standard pattern: hundreds of pita breads, chocolate spread, jam, sugar, coffee, tea, and other items. It would be interesting to find out what my grocer thinks of these strange shopping sprees.

At 6:30 a.m., it is still a little dark as we drive to the airbase, but by the time we make our way to the officers' clubhouse the sun is already warming us. It's really a bit rude to make an all-out assault on the delicious cookies that the army cook – who really deserves the title "chef" – prepares each time that we deploy to meet a group of immigrants at this airbase. After just a few minutes, we go out to the runway. This time, the two planes have already landed and the six buses are stationed behind them. At the planes' doors, I see well-known faces: Zimna, Matti Elias, and David Zevadia. Now I understand why I couldn't find them yesterday. There is great excitement. Their three faces reflect all their strenuous efforts but also their tremendous exhilaration at having had the chance to take part in such an important and dangerous operation. Once again, I am jealous of those privileged few who go into the abyss, rescue Jews from it, and then return home. This time the minister of defense, Moshe Arens, is among those welcoming the new immigrants.

I've accepted Zimna's recommendation and recruited Yosef David and Avraham Kehati to work in absorption. Both are Kfar Batya graduates who returned to Ethiopia at the start of the sixties and worked as teachers in Jewish schools there. A few years ago, they both made aliyah. They understand the complicated facts regarding matrimony, and at the same time have a status in the community that endows them with the ability to use their authority to resolve intricate problems. As usual, Zimna knew more than he actually said, and he knows that this time really difficult problems are awaiting us regarding marriages in Sudan and underage marriages. Also as usual, Zimna was right in the choice of people. In Avraham Kehati, we've found a person who is capable of tackling these difficult issues. Less complicated was the happy moment when we witnessed his emotional reunion with his firstborn son and oldest daughter, who are among the latest arrivals. I was watching Avraham's face when they met and I confess that when his eyes filled with tears, so did mine.

In order to show just how tangled the whole matter is, we monitored the first cursory interview with the immigrants that took place at the old age home in Ashkelon, which, as usual, was their first stop. Even Zimna, who warned us ahead of time, was shocked by the complexities. Although these people were only in the camps in Sudan for a relatively short time, there are many cases of second marriages – without a prior divorce – among the men, as well as among the women. There are even instances in which one man has two or indeed three wives. Because it is so terribly complex, it was decided to carry out the in-depth interviews in Safed, where we are going to send most of the immigrants. All the buses left directly for Safed except one, in which I myself traveled. That one set down immigrants at different stops en route – in Pardess Chana, Afula, and Nazareth.

At the first stop, in Nazareth, the most moving experience of all was awaiting me. The arrivals included a boy of about ten called Ajalew. He was barefoot, very scrawny, his head shaven except for locks of hair in front, and with sad but very wise eyes. His clothing was torn and his only possession was one little khaki bag. His father is Zemene Mandefro, whose name I found in the file where details of previous arrivals are compiled. I know that he is now living in the Hermon Absorption Center in Nazareth. It was evening when we arrived. I took Ajalew from the bus into the absorption center. We made our way to apartment number 1, Zemene Mandefro's home. I placed my hand on the boy's shoulder and tried to imagine what thoughts must be going through his head. Zemene opened the door and behind him I saw Workitu, his wife. Her eyes rested on the boy. For a moment, it seemed to me that she didn't recognize him. Then suddenly, she ran toward us and hugged him as tightly as she possibly could.

WORKITU'S STORY

Seven months ago, after three years of waiting in the refugee camp in Sudan, we heard that there were aliyah permits for seven elderly couples. I put in a request that my parents should be accepted, and my request was granted. On my way to tell my parents the news, a new idea popped into my head – that my son Ajalew should join them. In Amharic, his name means "Considered." In our miserable straw hut in Tewaba, we had another three children living with us and I was in the fourth month of pregnancy. At that time, the price of flour had just gone up and the money from the activists didn't always arrive. I've got clear memories of one night when I was alone with the children in the hut. Outside it was pouring cats and dogs. I tied the baby onto my back, held the second child in my arms and placed the third on my knees. I covered them all with the blanket we'd bought in the market for the winter.

Suddenly I heard a sound. It was as though the wind was rising up out of the earth, shaking the whole structure. Its central pole, which supported the hut, was on the point of falling and crushing us all underneath it. I kept my wits about me. I jumped with the children off from the bed and pushed the bed to the pole that was about to fall – and all this with only one hand free. That's how I saved myself and also saved my children. The next day we rented another house. That's when I vowed to use any chance to save the lives of my children and here I had just such an opportunity. I decided that my son would go with my parents, but first of all I had to persuade Zemene, my husband. He was not happy at a separation between father and son and asked Ajalew, "Do you want to go with grandfather and grandmother to Jerusalem?"

The child was embarrassed. He replied, "Well, I'll go, but how will you get there?"

"We'll arrive after you do."

The boy agreed, with tears in his eyes. The next day we all went to escort Grandfather and Grandmother from Tewaba to Gedaref. It was decided that my parents would wait with the boy for their papers in a relative's home and we would return to Tewaba. It was hard to part. Everyone was crying. I suggested that we go back to our own home and that the next day I'd come back to Gedaref. My mother forbade me to do so as it would only make the parting more difficult than it was already. However, that same night I regretted the decision we'd made and wanted to bring my son back. I also wanted to have my mother beside me when I gave birth, as she has always been at such

> times, ever since my firstborn. But Zemene had a serious talk with me and persuaded me not to make the journey.
>
> And meanwhile, people who returned from Gedaref told us that the group hadn't left yet. I'm strong, the sort who always thinks of what is best for her family, but I couldn't hold out any longer. My husband and I came to an agreement that the next day I'd go with my sisters to Gedaref and bring my son back. My young sister – she's the clever one – knew that on the same day as we planned to go there, the group would be leaving Gedaref for Khartoum and that's why she cooked up different excuses to delay our departure. At long last we left, but my parents and son were no longer there. The group was on its way to Khartoum.
>
> When it became clear to me that my sister had fooled me, I lost my temper and attacked her with clenched fists. "You tricked me! You knew that they're leaving today and so you made us late. I'll never forget what you've done!"
>
> But my sister only laughed and confidently exclaimed, "In another two days they'll be in Jerusalem. They'll live in a tall building with many floors and will eat from the finest produce of the land."

But things did not turn out that way at all. About an hour after the plane took off to fly the group to Europe and from there to Israel, it was forced to make an emergency landing at an airport in Libya. The authorities discovered that the passengers were Jewish and immediately returned the immigrants to Khartoum, where they were all imprisoned in a Sudanese jail for three months. In the meantime, the rest of the family's turn came to make aliyah. Zemene and Workitu and their children, together with Workitu's sister and her husband, made aliyah in one of the air operations. Before they landed, our Zimna sat with them and gently prepared them for the fact that they would not yet see their son in Israel. He told them what had happened, but soothed them, saying that the group was about to finish its term in prison and would be brought to Israel soon. Workitu didn't believe it. She was sure that they had all died and she would never again see her son and her parents. They all wept, in particular Workitu's sister, who blamed herself for the deaths of her parents and nephew.

The day after they arrived in Israel, Workitu gave birth to a son. The family decided to name him Abraham because at long last they had arrived in the land of the patriarch Abraham after a journey that was no less difficult than Abraham's from Ur of the Chaldees.

A month later, the prisoners were released from the jail in Sudan, but they had to wait another three months until it was their turn to make aliyah. Today they landed in Israel. The elderly parents were sent to Afula, to the home of their younger daughter, while Ajalew went with me to be reunited with his parents.

FEBRUARY 5, 1984 – THE ABSORPTION CENTER, SAFED

This morning we started the in-depth interviews. I was faced with some of the most difficult cases possible – and there are no routine solutions.

Throughout the day, from all corners of Israel there has been a stream of people who arrived previously, and among them is Samay. Yesterday, Zimna had advised him that his wife, Tegist, had arrived with this latest group. Sarah Alperovitch, a longtime staff member who dealt with Samay in his first year in Israel, knows how worried he has been about his wife and greeted him with a wide smile. After we found his wife's apartment number on the list, I saw Sarah and Samay heading that way, smiling with delight. I followed them so that I could witness the exciting reunion between husband and wife, but when Tegist opened the door, there were no hugs or kisses. They both stood frozen-faced when she said she didn't want him because she now had another husband. Samay instantly became haggard and drawn, obviously feeling like he'd just fallen off a cliff. His body, previously upright, crumpled, and a broken man stood before us.

I summoned them both to my makeshift office and that was when their appalling story was revealed. Samay left Tegist behind four years ago to come to Israel. It was understood between them that after he got to Israel, he would deal with her and their baby's aliyah. There had been no contact between them since. After some time had gone by, Samay's parents asked Tegist to vacate the house that they had built beside their own, perhaps because they could not support her anymore. This was a terrible blow. She returned to her own parents' home, awaiting some sign of life from her husband. But after two years of hoping in vain, she decided to make her own way to Sudan. There she formed a relationship with a young man and it was with him that she made aliyah. They are not married, but when she saw Samay at the apartment door, she told him she was married to the young man because she wanted to hurt him for abandoning her and for not making the effort to get her out of Ethiopia. Although we attempted to mitigate the anger that has grown in her over the years, the rift between the couple is too wide.

After a whole day of especially trying interviews, all I wanted was to collapse into bed and forget everything, but something pulled me back to apartment number 1 in the Nazareth absorption center, the home of Zemene Mandefro and his family. Once again I was given a royal reception, as though it was I who had rescued their child from the inferno. Workitu told me that they had not been able to sleep at all the previous night and her pillow was wet with tears. She was afraid all the time that the child might disappear, that perhaps it was all only a dream. That morning when the children woke up, their parents gave them the news that their brother was alive. They kissed him and were so overcome with happiness that they then licked him all over his face and his ears.

MAY 4, 1984 – THE RUNWAY OF AN AIRBASE SOMEWHERE IN ISRAEL

Six days ago one of the largest-ever immigrant groups arrived – 379 in number – and yesterday we were informed of another such group due today. The experts among us explained that the reason for the arrival of such large groups so close together is that the rainy season will start soon, which will make it difficult to carry out operations, thus slowing down departures from Sudan.

After the usual excitement, we quickly led the immigrants to the buses and counted them during the journey to Ashkelon. This time "only" 314 immigrants arrived. The new arrivals look exhausted. It was only after many of them came up to us with requests to help locate their relatives that we understood what had happened.

There had been problems in Gedaref. In contrast to previous times, when the organization beforehand was methodical and the number of immigrants was strictly kept to around three hundred, this time our people lost control. After night fell, the two trucks arrived, each of which holds between 120 and 180 immigrants, but over five hundred Jews were at the assembly point, waiting to be taken under cover of darkness by plane to Jerusalem. They stormed onto the trucks and, in the end, the Israeli in charge instructed the drivers to start moving, in spite of the fact that some people were still clinging to the sides of the trucks. The man had only two alternatives: either to cancel the whole operation or to slice through the pandemonium. However, when the trucks did start to move, one of them broke into two. The people on it tumbled out, one after the other, as though thrown through a gigantic funnel. The remaining truck was packed with over three hundred people and it, too, was on the verge of collapse, but it finally crawled onto the improvised airfield that our people had set up that day.

The unfortunate ones who were left behind in Gedaref quickly scattered to their own homes or to the homes of relatives. Meanwhile, in the open space where the broken, deserted truck stood, there remained only the bodies of two dead children with the parents wailing into the hot Sudanese night.

In Ashkelon, our labors did not end until it was almost morning. A considerable part of that time was devoted to soothing the newcomers, who again and again came up to us with requests to help them find family members who might or might not have managed to be on the flight. Among these were a brother and sister, who seemed to me to be about thirteen or fourteen years old. When they discovered that I speak Amharic, they approached me with great hesitation, standing near me like two lost souls, with the brother's hand on his sister's shoulder. For a moment I saw in my mind's eye my own son and daughter – how would they feel if they'd suddenly arrived in an unknown country? I went up to them to give them a hug and then asked their names. "We are the children of Genetu Dessie and of Debora Admasu," they said. My hug, intended to cheer them, had the opposite effect and instead caused them both to burst into tears. And then I heard the brother, the older of the two, whispering to his sister, "Tell him. Tell him what happened."

ZEWDITU'S STORY

We left our home in Azezo, near the city of Gondar, six weeks ago. It was the time of year when we were busy with preparations for Passover and we were already happy that all the family would be getting together for the festival. But one day our father suddenly announced that we were leaving for Sudan, to make our way to Jerusalem.

We left at night, so that the neighbors wouldn't spot us. Three guides led us who had been paid to show us the way. Father said that we could trust them, but all sorts of unpleasant things happened on the way, so that in the end Father said that maybe they tricked us.

We always walked at night and hid during the day because the government had forbidden anyone to flee from Ethiopia to Sudan. But that wasn't the terrible thing. What was shocking was when brigands assaulted us. They were terrifying; their eyes shone in the moonlight and the shots they fired shattered the night. We were attacked twice and we were forced to give them nearly all the money that my parents had sewn into our clothing. But the worst disaster of all happened one dark night when the guides brought us to a dark forest and told us to get ready for a steep descent, where there was danger of our falling and getting hurt. My father carried my two young brothers on his back and placed my five-year-old sister, Manale, in the charge of the Jewish guide who was leading us. It was indeed a very difficult route, but when we fell down, we actually found it funny. The disaster waited for us down below.

At this point in her tale, Zewditu burst out crying. Her brother tried to give her courage, but he also had tears in his eyes.

When we reached the bottom, we realized that our sister had disappeared. The guide said that he didn't know where she was. We looked for her all that night and the guide and his people carried on the search during the day. The next night we again looked for her, calling out her name, but she'd disappeared as though the earth had swallowed her up. My father wanted to stay there in order to find out what had happened to her. Both my grandmother and great-grandmother said there was no way back.

In the end, we carried on walking without my sister. Two weeks later we reached Sudan. On the way, the guides deserted us and we were left without food or water, but eventually we got there. I was amazed at the size of the refugee camp where we were to live in Sudan. It contained tens of thousands of people, jam-packed, living on top of each other. Many died, especially the children. No other tragedy struck our family, but the loss of my sister continued to cast a dark cloud over us and the misery it caused never left our temporary home.

Unlike other people that we met who had already been in Sudan months and even years, it seemed that we were going to be lucky. The night before last, a relative who is a member of the Committee told us that the next night a group would leave by what is called the *chelema* (darkness) method. The group would leave in trucks for the desert and from there by plane directly to Israel. Our relative said we should be in the area of the assembly point at eight o'clock in the evening after darkness fell.

We set out together, the whole family. My uncle carried my great-grandmother on his shoulders and all the others went on foot. My grandmother – my mother's mother – took one baby on her back and my mother took the other. My father led us all. We were so happy. We children were already describing to each other what Jerusalem looks like, how it's a city of gold with two rivers running at its foot, one of honey and the other of milk. Only Father interrupted our joy, reminding us of our sister who had been left behind on the way.

We were new to the area and got lost and found ourselves in an unfamiliar neighborhood where people only speak Tigrinya. Fortunately, we ran into a relative who told us how to get to the assembly point. When we arrived there, the trucks were full and people were hanging onto them on all sides. Father lifted me up from the side and then placed my brother, Eyayu, between the driver's cabin and the rear body of the truck. When my brother saw that there was more room beside him, father passed up the younger ones to him but had to take them down when mother announced that she would not mount onto the truck.

The pressure from all sides was terrible. I would have liked to get off, but against my will, I tumbled into the truck where I could hardly breathe. I tried to shout that I wanted to leave, but it was useless, and I remained trapped in the mass. I couldn't even see the sky, I was stuck so deep down inside. I almost choked and begged to leave. I cried that I wanted my mother. Suddenly the truck got going and moved slowly forward. There was the sound of an explosion from beside it. Afterwards I heard that the second truck had broken up. After a little progress, our truck almost stopped. From the back there was the sound of children wailing and somebody said that children had been crushed. However, we did leave and after several hours we reached the place in the desert and people started to descend. I cried because there was nobody to lift me down. Eventually, I managed to get down by myself and I started looking for my parents. I think my voice couldn't be heard when I called out the names of my father and mother. But suddenly I heard my brother's voice. He was also looking for them. I fell into his arms and cried. Meanwhile, the two planes landed, raising clouds of dust around them. The whole area was lit up and it was like being in a fog. In the dust, we searched and searched for my parents, but they were nowhere to be found. Young men with weapons got off the planes and pushed us through the dust and onto one of the planes. My brother tried to hold onto my hand the whole time, but once again we got separated. I was frightened I was going to lose him too and shouted out, but one of the Israeli soldiers carried me in his arms, with me struggling against him every inch of the way, and put me on the plane. I calmed down once I was inside the plane and eventually I found my brother.

I fell asleep on his shoulder and slept until we landed. Through the loudspeaker someone announced in Amharic, "*Enquan dehena metachu*" (welcome). We were exhausted, but when one of the people started to clap, we all joined in. The person sitting next to me kissed me and I got caught up in the general rejoicing, but my thoughts soon turned back to Sudan, to my mother and my little brothers. I wasn't aware of crying, but somehow my eyes were wet. We've arrived in Israel, in Jerusalem but without joy. We feel so strange here without our parents.

I promised the two children that I would check into what had happened to their parents, even though at the time I didn't know how I would manage it. However, they looked more relaxed. I saw them again as they got onto the bus that would take them to a Youth Aliyah religious boarding school, Ma'on Hayeled, in Tel Aviv.

In the course of our interviews with the adults in the group, we got an optimistic picture of the situation in Sudan. Apparently, only several hundred Jews remain there, and so David Zevadia's journey was made at the right time. However, there are some among us who think that there was no need to send David so early and that he should only have gone to Ethiopia now, since his journey there in December will lead to Jews arriving in Sudan in the coming weeks, at the height of the rainy season. During that time, it's impossible to carry out large rescue missions and many of those in the camps are likely to die from the diseases that are so prevalent during the rainy season.

This evening, a telegram was received from the Israeli embassy in Washington, confirming our information that the number of Jews in the refugee camps has decreased to a few hundred.

SEPTEMBER 11, 1984, AFTER MIDNIGHT – AT THE DINING ROOM TABLE AT HOME

During the last four months, about ten thousand Jews have arrived in Sudan from every corner of the Gondar region. The news from there is dreadful. Here, every day we encounter children who just cannot learn because they are so worried about their parents back in the refugee camps. Community activists state that at least twenty Jews are dying every day, many of them women and children. Indeed, recently many widowers have arrived here, some with children and some without. One of them, called Yitzhak, arrived alone. His wife and four children all died in Sudan and he was forced to bury them with his own hands. The thing that troubled him above all else was the lack of a proper Jewish cemetery in the refugee camps. Anyone wanting to provide a proper burial for his loved ones is in danger of being revealed as a Jew and so the burial is usually carried out at night.

The most difficult incident occurred when Yitzhak had to bury his eldest son. His wife, two daughters, and younger son had already died from malaria. The sickness did not spare his eldest son. He died quietly, as though he didn't want to disturb his mourning father. One morning, his father found his son lying dead in bed. He went through the same agony with his older son as with his wife and other children, unable to mourn them properly, according to the dictates of law. In the refugee camps, it is impossible to observe *shiva*, the seven days of mourning, and relatives cannot come to console the bereaved. But worst of all, it is impossible to hold a memorial service seven days after the death. In the villages of Ethiopia, all the relatives would come from near and far, as well as all the others who wanted to pay their respects. The family would slaughter lambs and cows and prepare a meal in honor of the deceased. Only after the *kessoch* had recited the prayer for the dead would the dead person's soul be released from its earthly fetters. Yitzhak had not released his dear ones from the material world. Their souls are still hovering between worlds and so his pain is double: he has lost his family in this world and has not released them to the next world.

Then, faced with the dead body of his son, he had to do something that was even more painful. The activists had spread warnings about terrorist organizations' attempts to identify Jews and hand over their names to the authorities, so Yitzhak decided that it was better not to bury his son outside the refugee camp in the improvised cemetery, and he buried him in the same tent where he lived. Yitzhak had in his possession a small hoe and a spade that he used in his employment as a digger of holes for the camps' public toilets, work carried out by a Sudanese contractor with financing from the Red Cross. Using his work tools, he dug his son's grave in the center of the tent. On reaching a depth of eighty centimeters he came to a layer of rock. He had no water to wash the corpse, but he cupped in his hands the little water that was in the corner of the tent and used it to clean the face of his beloved son. Yitzhak kissed his son and carefully placed him on the rock within the grave. For some time he gazed at his son's peaceful face, before eventually covering him with earth. Afterwards he sat sunk in his own thoughts beside the fresh grave, refusing to believe that he did not have one person left alive to live for. He wished only to die.

When I heard this story my hair stood on end. I couldn't grasp how Yitzhak had retained his sanity. If such a tragedy had happened to me, I would surely have put an end to my own life.

SEPTEMBER 30, 1984 – THE OLD AGE HOME OF THE JEWISH AGENCY, ASHKELON

Since May 4 of this year, thirty-seven new immigrants have arrived directly from Ethiopia and another fifty-seven have come via Kenya. But the largest number came through Europe: the total of those arriving by the European route, together with today's group, comes to 433 *olim* in fifteen groups.

When we sit down and question the newcomers, the situation in the camps in Sudan becomes more and more clear. Half a year ago, a few hundred Jews remained there, who have all been brought here in the last few months. But meanwhile, over ten thousand Jews have flocked into Sudan, many motivated by David Zevadia, and many others by a lifelong desire to make aliyah. They have filled entire areas of Um Rakoba, Wadihilu, and Tewaba and, as feared, the immigrants report many deaths.

When I interviewed the first family and registered the name of the head of the family, Genetu Dessie, his name sounded familiar. After writing down the usual identifying particulars, the realization struck me that Genetu and Debora, sitting opposite me on the veranda of the old age home, were the parents of Eyayu and Zewditu – the brother and sister who arrived in Israel six months ago. Their shocking story was still clear in my mind, about the hard trek to Sudan, about the sister, Manale, who was lost on the way, about their sudden separation from their parents, brothers, and sisters. I visualized again the youngsters' distraught faces – and here were their parents, now sitting with me.

Genetu and Debora were surprised by the kisses that I showered on them. It was only when I told them that I know their children, and that they are well and studying in a boarding school and being properly taken care of, that they understood why I felt such a special closeness to them. Their joy was indescribable.

GENETU'S STORY

We spent a whole year making preparations for our departure to Israel, but it was only toward Passover that the opportunity arose to sell all our assets for 6,000 birrs. We didn't get the guides that we really wanted and made do with a Jew, a Christian convert, and a Christian. They led us overnight to Duwadu – a village of Jews. There the price was fixed – 100 birrs per person. There were over seventy of us, nearly all relatives. They included my wife's mother and even her aged grandmother, whom we loaded onto the back of a mule since she couldn't walk. I was asked for a payment of 800 birrs – a married couple with six children. No sooner had we left Duwadu after the evening meal than we were already surrounded by local Christian converts, shooting at us from all sides. One of the mules, on which three of my younger children were sitting, broke free of his straps at the sound of the shots, threw off the kids, and escaped. I ran after it, but the converts said, "Leave the mule, because if you don't, we'll kill you." "Kill me, but I won't leave the mule," I answered. Our great-grandmother had also fallen off the back of her mule. So we had no choice but to return to the home of the Jew. We stayed there for two days and were asked to pay another 900 birrs. Because we had no option, we paid but I decided that from then on I would carefully watch what the guide did, because I thought that he was in collusion with his convert neighbors. One evening the converts came to us and said, "You're Falasha, you're Kayla, why are you running away from our country?"

The converts are the descendants of Jews who converted to Christianity long ago and there is animosity between Jews and them. The word *Kayla*, which is similar to the term *Falasha*, is considered a derogatory expression for the Ethiopian Jews. Some people think that its origin is the Hebrew word *kehilla*, meaning "community." Genetu continued his story.

We didn't respond to the converts' remarks. On the second evening, the head of the region came and said, "Don't go by the main route. Go through the forests and when I come back tomorrow, I don't want to see you here." That was how he was in effect taking care of his territory while at the same time also hinting to us not to go by the main route where soldiers ambush people fleeing to Sudan. We walked all that night, and toward morning we reached the village of Korkombel. We knew from what our relatives had told us that it is a village inhabited by converts who live by robbery. It was frightening and the guide suggested that we put him in charge of the money that was sewn into the children's clothes. I refused, saying, "I'm not handing over the money. This money is for me to rescue my children."

We hid in the forest and the guide went with the other guides to meet the people of Korkombel. They returned in the evening, bringing with them containers of water for which they demanded a price of five birrs for each container. Then the guide said, "You really ought to be put on trial in the regional capital, Ayekl, for fleeing to Sudan, but the people of Korkombel have intervened on your behalf and that's how you've been saved." Once again we had to pay 800 birrs for eight people. It was as though he wanted to pacify us when he added, "Soon you'll reach Sudan and won't need money." In my heart of hearts, I felt that he was in league with the robbers and I vowed to myself to be even more wary of him than before.

During the last remaining hours before sunset, we hid ourselves in the forest and in the evening we carried on with our journey to Sudan. After two hours we reached a steep slope that stretches from the Chilga region toward Armachiho. The guide took my daughter Manale from me, since I was already carrying two other little ones. As we made the descent, everything was dark. There were no stars that night and we couldn't see each other, only hear their breathing. Many of us slipped and got hurt before we reached the valley at the foot of the mountain. We gathered together beside a pool of water. We all rushed to drink because we were very thirsty and it was only after drinking that I realized that Manale wasn't with us. I ran to the guide and asked him where my daughter was. I nearly lost my mind when he said, "I don't know where she is. Maybe some cruel animal has eaten her, maybe a tiger, or a wolf, or maybe a snake."

I felt helpless facing this scoundrel. I put down the child who was fastened onto my back and tied up the donkeys and went off to search for my daughter. Everything around was dark and depressing. After two hours of searching I returned, beaten, to the place where they were gathered. When I got back, I found that the guide had disappeared, leaving us on our own. We went on looking for the child all that night, but without results. The suspicion that the guide had sold my daughter started to creep up on me. For sure, I thought, at this very moment he was handing her over to serve as a slave to one of the rich people in the area. Once again I felt so powerless – I, who was considered a big shot only one week before, a man of prominence in his region, and now I wasn't even capable of defending my children.

The guide returned toward morning and made a pretense of helping us with our search. All that day we looked for my daughter. We cried. He made a show of trying to soothe us, but we didn't believe him. He definitely must have taken the girl in order to steal the money that we'd hidden in her dress and maybe he did indeed sell her to someone. I suggested to Debora, my wife, that she continue on with the rest of the family to Sudan and I would stay behind to search for our daughter. I even offered the guide money to bring back my daughter to us, but he warned me off, saying, "If you come near me, I'll kill you." After those words, he went away, but he returned that evening to announce that he would not lead us to Sudan and that we should leave the vicinity if our own lives and our children's lives were precious to us. We had no other alternative. We carried on to Sudan using our own resources.

When we were one day's walk from the Sudanese border, our supply of water finished. Fortunately for us, we met a man who was searching for his donkeys and he led us to Sudan. We stayed there for about nine months and now the Lord has helped us and we have reached Jerusalem. Now we'll meet our children who came here before us. But what is going to be the fate of our lost five-year-old daughter? Why did we leave her? Why didn't we carry on looking for her?

I have promised Genetu that from this moment on I consider his daughter as being my own daughter and I will not rest until I find her. I have made the promise, but will I be able to keep it?

Part Two

The Crazy American

OCTOBER 6, 1984 – THE JEWISH AGENCY OFFICE, TEL AVIV

It is becoming more and more difficult to endure, ignore, or discount the news arriving from Sudan. During the first months, I thought the immigrants' stories must be vastly exaggerated – there could not be so many deaths. I have tried to put all the troubling things I have been told out of my mind, but now the extent of the situation has become known to all. The reality is that there is not one single person among the last groups of immigrants who has not lost some relative in the refugee camps. The numbers are particularly high among children and women who were too weak to fight off the ravages of disease, hunger, and thirst. There are now more widowers like Yitzhak: men whose physical toughness kept them alive, but who were forced, before coming here, to bury their wives and children with their own hands. The camp where the greatest number has perished is Um Rakoba. Thousands of our people there have succumbed to hunger and disease, and I feel the responsibility for these deaths is ours.

In one of the last groups, there was an old woman with a deeply wrinkled face. There is no light in her eyes, and she has a weary, dragging walk. When she sat with us, she told us that the night before she left to come here, she buried twenty-eight people with her own hands. By the time she reached the last burial, she believed that her own would be the next. She sat in the improvised cemetery at Um Rakoba waiting for death to come and take her, but then one of her grandchildren came and told her to hurry back home because the next day they were to make aliyah to Israel.

In another group, a woman arrived who looks truly aged, though she is only thirty-five. When it was announced that at long last they had reached a safe haven, this woman stepped out from among the crowd with an *enkalwa* (a bag for carrying a baby) on her back. She danced a very repetitive dance in which her feet hardly moved and the upper part of her body bent backwards and forwards, while the fingers of both hands were stretched all the time toward heaven. It was the death dance through which Ethiopian Jews express mourning.

Then suddenly the woman stopped dancing and began to weep. Her sobs racked her whole body. From her throat there emerged a sort of squawk that could hardly be heard: "Now I'm in Jerusalem, I've reached the land of which I've dreamed since the day I was born. But what is left for me? Who is left to me? I carry an *enkalwa* on my back, but I do not have one child left to carry in it."

Nearly all the recent arrivals are relatives of the activists in Sudan. This may be further proof that the situation there has indeed deteriorated to a grave extent and the reports of so many deaths are not exaggerated. The activists wish to save their own relatives since every additional day in Sudan endangers the lives of the people there. Zimna and Matti Elias are very angry about this and I understand them, but I also try to understand what the activists must be going through.

Zimna told me today that about two weeks ago, in early September, he was supposed to prepare for a large Air Force rescue operation, but it was canceled because the activists, who were meant to assemble the people under cover of darkness, started to transport their own relatives to the assembly point during daylight. In consequence, the Jews, and perhaps also the non-Jews in the camp, saw clearly that something big was about to take place, and hundreds of people flocked to the assembly point. Aleph and his people had no choice but to inform Israel that it was impossible to implement the operation.

I've tried to understand the activists, but now, in light of this, I think that they have the blood of thousands on their hands. They are immoral and greedy.

OCTOBER 10, 1984 – BEN-GURION INTERNATIONAL AIRPORT

Today a group of fifty-one immigrants arrived via Europe, and in another four or five days another group should arrive by the same route, comprising over seventy people. After I received the newcomers with the traditional blessing, a young man came up to me. He was short, looked to be somewhere in his twenties, and was dressed in a suit, not the traditional loose robes. He presented me with a blue and white plastic bag bearing the symbol of the international emigration organization the ICM, inside which were the group's flight tickets and passports. The immigrants look weak and thin, and their faces have the yellowish hue of sickness. They all wear traditional clothing and all their garments are dirty. Indeed, the only one in a suit is the one who gave me the bag of documents, and I could see that he wanted to tell me something. I took him aside and he told me his story, speaking in English.

MEKONEN'S STORY

My name is Mekonen Tesfay Ayehon, and I'm one of the members of the Committee in Sudan. I asked our superiors to release me and let me make aliyah, since I couldn't bear to go on seeing the suffering of my brothers. You must know that dozens of people are dying every day – people with only skin on their bones and with faces that are just large, sad eyes. Most of the dead are children. What have they done to God that He lets them die? Two of my own brothers have also died there. I just couldn't bear to stay longer and suffer – and so here I am.

You must hear complaints against us, the activists, but please realize that our work was not at all pleasant. Oh, yes, on the one hand, we got some of life's pleasures. Our "fathers" – that's what we call the Israelis who work with us – gave us a lot of money, but, on the other hand, we lived in fear the whole time. We've had encounters with policemen and Sudanese soldiers more than once, and you're never sure how such conversations are going to turn out. It might be with a slap on the head, or a blow to the stomach, or you might end up in jail. But the fear of the Sudanese is nothing compared with what I saw when I visited Um Rakoba two months ago. I wandered among the thickets in the Jewish area of the refugee camps until I couldn't suffer the sights any longer, and I decided to leave it all and make aliyah.

Each corner had a man carrying a dead child or his dead wife. There were several familiar faces among them, and some of them even greeted me, but I couldn't identify them, either because they had become so thin or because I was frightened to remember what they had been. In each of the open spaces among the thickets, there were gatherings of family members, all sunk in their own thoughts, holding their heads in their thin hands and crying for those who had died. And the improvised cemeteries are constantly growing and filling up, and the people just don't have enough strength to dig to the required depth for a proper grave for their loved ones.

Every home was bursting with pain. Every thicket was completely filled with sick people – so sick that they are just waiting for death to take them. There's not even enough water. In one of the alleys, a young man came up to me and announced that he is organizing a group to return to Ethiopia. I remember his words exactly: "At least we'll have a grave there." I gave him money to shut him up. But I suddenly felt myself running without a destination, just in order to get away from the awful sights. In the end, when I stopped, I knew I couldn't stay in Sudan any longer. I returned to Gedaref immediately and announced to Gedam, one of the Committee heads, "I'm going back to Khartoum. I'm not prepared to carry on. I'm going to Israel." Then I asked Gedam, "Have you visited Um Rakoba?"

"Yes, two weeks ago. True, it's disgusting, but there's nothing we can do about it," he answered.

So I said, "Don't hand out money, and don't hire apartments in Gedaref or Tewaba. Let's transfer them to Khartoum."

Then Gedam shouted at me, "And what will I give them to eat? My own body? Until we have rescue operations and move some of the people out so that there is more space in Gedaref, I won't transfer anybody anywhere."

I wanted to be on my own, I wanted to get away, but Gedam trapped my arms and said quietly, "If you want to, go to Khartoum and convince the white men."

Within two days, late at night, Worku Abuhay and I went to see our Israeli liaison, and I said to him, "You Israelis are sleeping while our people are dying." Then I added, "I only wish you should be buried in

Um Rakoba." Not one muscle in his face moved and at first he didn't answer at all. Then he quietly asked, "What's happening there?"

I tried to keep my answer quiet too. I said, "Nearly all the people are ill. Dozens are dying every day and here we're playing."

His voice was again very quiet as he asked, "How many people do we have there?"

"I don't know."

"I'm asking you how many people there are there, and I know that you know."

I asked that a rescue operation be organized, but he said that since it was still the rainy season, there was no chance of it. Perhaps in order to soften my anger, or perhaps since it was really so important, the Israeli repeated his question about the number and persisted until I told him that in my estimate there were about seven thousand Jews. He then asked me if there are medicines in the camps and which medicines could be sent, and in the end he said, "Next week I'll go with you and take a supply of medicines to Gedaref."

Worku and I left his apartment with the feeling that we had not succeeded. And although many small groups left in the following weeks via Europe, at the same time there was a large influx of Jews to Khartoum, so that their numbers there increased. Some arrived in the city on their own initiative, paying the expenses of the travel permit themselves; others were sent by the Committee, either because they were ill or old or had a relative in the Committee. Gisme and I were the last of the Committee left in Khartoum, and every day we had to listen to the newcomers complaining, "You, you lack nothing, you have food and drink, while in Um Rakoba people are dying every day."

The number of newcomers flocking into Khartoum increased constantly, just when most of the Committee members were in Gedaref. All the worries fell on Gisme and me. We had to meet them when they arrived in the Khartoum central bus station, put them up in rented houses, purchase food for them, buy them clothing and shoes, have their photographs taken, obtain the documents they needed, and assist them to the airport.

And then it happened. One day I went to the Umdurman market to buy clothing and was already on my way back with my assistant, who was carrying a bag full of garments on his shoulders, when suddenly a police car stopped beside us. One of the cops grabbed my arms and said, "Get in the car."

They took me to the detectives' headquarters and immediately ushered me into the office of the regional commander, a police officer with the rank of colonel. He was tough, but somehow there was something very human about him. First of all, my pockets were emptied and they found the money that I had in them. I thanked the Lord that they didn't also search in my socks, because that's where most of the money was. The colonel spoke to me in English: "You killed one of my people."

"No, I didn't," I answered.

"So why did you come here? Tewaba is your place of residence."

"I'm on my way to Canada."

"And what's the source of your money?"

"My parents. They own property. They live in Gojam, they're opponents of the government." I noticed a slight change in his face and went on, "I've only been a day and a half in Khartoum."

"Okay, you're going to be transferred to the prison," he ruled.

I decided to work on his feelings, so I said with tears in my eyes, "Only you can help me. My parents are not here. Help me."

"I can't help you," he answered. "You belong in Tewaba."

"I'll work for you, I'll do everything you tell me to do," I continued pleading.

After making a telephone call, he agreed to release me, telling me to report the next day. But then he suddenly changed his mind and instructed that I remain locked up. I was given a bucket for my bodily needs and was taken to a sort of dark cage. The next morning the colonel appeared and said, "You will be my fourth servant."

He took me to his house in his red car. There he gave me an iron, showed me where I would sleep, and told one of the maids to give me food. I ironed several *djellabas* (long robes) and then suddenly one of the servants came, put a bucket of water in my hand, and ordered me to fill a container that was in the courtyard. When I went outside into the courtyard, I suddenly realized that the colonel's house was only three houses away from one of the houses where I'd placed the immigrants, and I also saw that the red car was no longer there. Within one second I came to a decision. I threw down the bucket and ran.

The residents of the rented house were very surprised at my sudden appearance because rumors of my arrest were already circulating. That same evening I met the Israeli. He understood that my decision was final and authorized my aliyah. He also gave me some money. The day before yesterday I left Sudan, and now here I am.

Mekonen's account gripped me. I didn't doubt his words for one moment and through his story I could feel the suffering of the Jews in the Um Rakoba camp. On the way to the bus that was to take us to Safed, Mekonen wanted to tell me something else: "Now you'll have people coming to you and accusing me of raping girls. They'll ask you to arrest me. Please, don't believe them. And even more important, please do something. We have to rescue the people in Sudan; we have to stop the deaths."

OCTOBER 15, 1984

A week ago a high-level meeting took place in the Intercontinental Hotel in Geneva. The initiative for it actually came from the man still working behind the scenes who is in charge of the various operations that have transported – either directly from Sudan or via Europe – 80 percent of the 6,649 Ethiopian Jews now in Israel. His identity still cannot be revealed.

Among those who took part in the meeting were Princeton Lymon of the US State Department; Dick Krieger, a Republican in charge of refugee affairs at the State Department; Yehuda Dominitz, director-general of the Aliyah Department of the Jewish Agency; and Neale Katz, director-general of the United Jewish Appeal in Israel. But without a doubt, the one who stood out most was Jerry Weaver, who is in charge of refugee affairs at the US embassy in Khartoum.

Jerry is known in Khartoum's diplomatic community as the "crazy American" because, unlike other diplomats, he does not devote his time to cocktail parties or sporting activities but rather spends most of it in the company of the Sudanese, whom he admires.

Jerry is tall and broad and looks more like a football player than a diplomat. He has been monitoring Israel's actions in Sudan for almost two years and has even reported to the State Department that the Sudanese are aware of what is occurring. We also received a copy of this report, through our embassy in Washington, though at a later date. Weaver supports our evacuating the Ethiopian refugees from Sudan. He is so much in favor of the Israeli initiatives that he has even pushed his superiors to provide some sort of covering action. At the end of the day, Operation Moses was supported by the Americans, but Weaver had to fight for it.

Weaver has visited the Gedaref area many times during the last two months, even visiting Um Rakoba. At the Geneva meeting, he painted a very black picture, describing the grimmest conditions imaginable, and said that of the ten thousand Jews who arrived in Sudan over the last five months, dozens are dying every day. All the people there are suffering from malnutrition, and their chances of survival are slim. He compared the Jews in Um Rakoba to those who were found by the American liberators when they entered Bergen-Belsen, Dachau, and Sachsenhausen.

Following this description, the Israelis at the meeting suggested dispatching immediate financial and medical assistance to the Jews languishing in the camps, but Weaver turned this down. He feared that Israel would consider such steps as sufficient instead of effecting a speedy rescue. When he succeeded in convincing the Israelis that the Sudanese would agree to an evacuation operation, it was decided that on that same day a working group would meet, consisting of Weaver, Krieger, Dominitz, and the anonymous Israeli. The four of them assembled toward evening and Weaver then presented his plan: with the knowledge of the Sudanese, and with agreement from Khartoum's international airport, the Jews would be flown out, apparently to the USA and Europe, even though everyone would be aware that Israel would be their true destination. Weaver accepted the responsibility for coordinating this plan with the Sudanese. Indeed, that same evening, he met with his Sudanese friend and liaison, who authorized the plan on condition that no Israelis actually appear on the scene.

The next day, Weaver said that all the Jewish refugees could be evacuated within five to six weeks – assembling them in the Gedaref area, transporting them to Khartoum in special buses, flying them out of Khartoum International Airport to Europe, and then on to Israel. He told the Israelis that the only condition set by the Sudanese was that no Israelis play an open part in the operation. Eventually, in a further meeting, it was agreed between Weaver and his Sudanese liaison that "in order to identify the

Falashas, one black man would be present." The Sudanese liaison didn't see any problem with this, even though it obviously meant flying in one of the Ethiopian Jewish community from Israel to Sudan for the purpose.

By the end of the discussions, it was clear that Israel would bear responsibility for the financial aspects, including the purchase of buses and small cars, several tons of fuel, and communications equipment. It was understood that all these items would remain in the hands of the Sudanese afterwards. Israel would also be in charge of organizing the flights. Neale Katz immediately contacted the UJA in New York and arranged for the necessary funds to be available, while an anonymous Mossad agent's assistants started searching for an airline that would be acceptable in Sudan and would agree to fly ten thousand Jews – that is the estimated number – from Khartoum to Europe and from there to Israel.

In their last working meeting, Weaver and the Israelis agreed that further communication between them would not be direct but would be made by cable from Weaver in Khartoum to Washington and transferred from there to Jerusalem. In his concluding telephone report from Geneva to Washington, Weaver stated, "Having no other choice in the matter, the Jews have decided to place the fate of the Falashas in the hands of a fat American they don't know and a Sudanese they don't trust."

Weaver returned to Khartoum with a quarter of a million dollars of Jewish Agency money in his suitcases. He immediately started making the practical arrangements for the operation. He hired cars, built straw huts in Tewaba, bought five thousand liters of fuel, rented houses in Khartoum, and sent money to Gedaref. Within a few days, he had only about $30,000 left. He sent a telegram to Washington, asking that the Israelis be informed that he needed more money, for purchase of the buses and medical equipment.

According to foreign press reports, in their search for a suitable airline, the Israelis came across a Belgian Jew, Georges Gutelman, the owner of Trans European Airlines. TEA operated many flights in the area, including flights for pilgrims from Sudan and other Arab countries to the Muslim holy sites in Saudi Arabia.

At meetings held in Geneva, it was agreed that the operation to rescue Ethiopian Jews from Sudan would start within a month and would terminate within six weeks. All the Israelis, Americans, and Sudanese involved in organizing it have their hands full – and time is short.

OCTOBER 22, 1984 – BEN-GURION INTERNATIONAL AIRPORT

Even while the major rescue operation is being planned, small groups continue to arrive. Today seventy-four flew in via Europe. Most of them are families from the Gondar region and are, in light of what we know, in better physical condition than expected. Among them, I spotted a young woman, very thin, dressed in a cheap Sudanese dress in shades of yellow. She sat huddled up into herself, her head on her chest, apart from the others. It looked like she had no relatives or friends among them.

As I went near her, I could feel how her whole body was shuddering with fear. I asked her name, but she only told me her brother's name, adding, "He came here about six months ago. I want to see my brother. Please help me find him." I brought her a glass of water from the kitchen and she started to be more at ease with me. She began telling me her dreadful story. As I listened to it, I studied the lines of her face and body. She was so beautiful and delicate, she broke my heart. Her long, bent head was a sort of continuation of a still-childish body. Her legs were tightly held together, barely allowing space for the hands grasped between her knees.

GENET'S STORY

When I was about sixteen years old, we sat together – my parents, my brother, and I – in the courtyard of our village home and my father said, "Most of the young people around here have already gone to Sudan. Now it's our turn. We're only waiting for Grandmother to recover from her illness, and then we'll sell up. In another two to three months, we can buy a horse for Grandmother to ride on to Sudan. But you youngsters are going to leave now."

My mother prepared provisions for the journey. My cousin joined us, and on the way we met up with other Jews, so that within one day we'd become a group of seventy-two people – men, women, and children. Already on the second night, when we were in the Armachiho area, brigands attacked us. They demanded 700 birrs to let us pass. We had no choice in the matter, and each of us paid 10 birrs. The next night, the same robbers attacked us again and this time they demanded the donkeys. For two weeks we walked every night and hid during the day. From time to time robbers attacked us.

When we were close to the border, we had no water left. Three children had already died from hunger and thirst, my brother was sick, and I couldn't move any further. I felt it was the end, that I'd die there, but one of the young men had the courage to cross the border to Sudan. There he met Sudanese who agreed to escort him. We were all lying on the ground, waiting for death to redeem us from our agony, when the Sudanese arrived, bringing us water on the backs of donkeys. I tried to drink, but I couldn't, at first. My throat was too swollen.

After we were somewhat recovered, we managed to cross the border. The Sudanese took everything of any value from us and conveyed us to Um Rakoba. There, we were given a large tent for the fifty-seven of us who were still alive. Fifteen children hadn't survived the journey and had been buried on the way.

The number of people in the tent grew smaller and smaller as every few hours various relatives arrived and took this one or that one away. In the end, we were left by ourselves – just me, my brother, and my cousin. We heard that it was advisable to get to Gedaref and we were happy when we met one of the activists, who gave us enough money to travel there. At Gedaref, we found a relative and he shared his house with us.

After five months in Gedaref, I fell sick and my brother decided that it was absolutely out of the question for me to remain there. He went out to work and he worked day and night until he had enough money to buy me the *tisrih* – the permit for passage to Khartoum. I didn't want to leave him alone, but he was determined that I make aliyah immediately because if I didn't, something bad might happen to me. When my brother brought me my *tisrih*, I knew there was no point in arguing with him anymore. I tucked the document into my clothing and went with my brother to the assembly point.

We traveled to Khartoum in a packed bus. There were twenty-three Jews on it but I didn't know any of them. There were two families with children and a group of youngsters who were also related.

I linked up with the youngsters and they were happy to have my company. One of them even said, "From now on, we are your family. Don't worry." I thanked the Lord for meeting up with them.

After a journey of two days we arrived in the central bus station of Khartoum. Because of problems on the way, our arrival was four hours late and none of the activists who were supposed to receive us was there. We all huddled into one corner of the bustling bus station. I couldn't see anything except for the sand that I was sitting on, but I could hear the tumult of people and cars and I could smell the different smells of the capital of Sudan.

Meanwhile, night fell and the noises decreased, maybe because by then there were fewer vehicles around where we sat, or maybe because we'd just gotten used to the place. Suddenly someone stopped by us and spoke in Amharic. At first I thought that someone had arrived to take care of us, but this man was a Christian Ethiopian who wanted to warn us of the dangers that lurk in Khartoum for strangers. He said, "It's not good that you stay here. The girls, especially, are in danger. If a Sudanese man desires them, then there'll be no help for them, save from the Lord alone. You should find yourselves rooms in Khartoum Talatta – that's where all the Ethiopians live."

We took his advice and went to the Khartoum Talatta neighborhood and paid in advance for three rooms. There were two beds in our room, but we were six people, so none of us managed to sleep. There was a wind howling outside and my thoughts blew with it. I wanted so much to be back with my brother in Gedaref or with my parents in the village. In the morning, we went out to search for the two families who had stayed in the other two rooms, but we couldn't find any of them. They'd simply disappeared. One of the boys volunteered to go out and search for the activists, but in the afternoon, it was they who found us. I don't remember who they were; I only remember that I was as happy to see them as if they were my own relatives.

They brought us to one of the houses that are rented especially for hiding the Jews until they leave Sudan. The activists told us not to leave the house and to wait for them. After sunset they returned with all sorts of good things to eat. We were hungry and we women immediately started preparing a meal for everybody. After we finished eating, they started questioning us, to make sure that we really were Jews. Then, after they were convinced, they asked each of us for three photographs so that our aliyah documents could be prepared. When I left Gedaref I had hidden three photographs in my shoes. I brought them out and handed them over to one of the young men. I never learned his name.

We waited for two days to receive the papers and then something happened. Ruben, one of the main activists, came to our room. He handed the other young people their papers, and left me till the end. And all the time, while he was explaining to them what was going to happen next, he was looking at me. The truth is, I felt as though he was undressing me with his eyes. I lowered my own eyes. "Give me three photographs," he said to me.

"I've already given them."

"Don't lie," he said firmly.

"I'm not lying," I answered.

"So, who did you give the photographs to?"

"To one of the activists who was here two days ago."

"Don't dare lie to me; if you lie to me, I'll hit you."

I didn't know what to do. I was miserable. The young people that I was with tried to come to my assistance, but Ruben shut them up by threatening, "Do you want me to take your papers away from you?"

They were silent and I wasn't angry with them. I understood. Then Ruben went on the attack, saying, "You're a whore! I know you. You were a prostitute in Gedaref. You slept with soldiers, whore!"

"Who are you talking about? I've lived all my life in a village. It's not true."

"Good. So give me the photographs."

"I don't have them. I already told you..."

"Shut up. You're a liar."

I was silent. What could I do? I wanted my brother beside me.

We all passed two nerve-racking days and then Ruben came back, this time with several of his friends. He took me aside and said softly, "Come and be my wife. I have a lot of money and you'll live like a princess."

"I can't, I'm betrothed to someone in Israel," I lied, giving him the name of a cousin who went on aliyah a few months before.

"You're lying to me again, just like with the photographs. You don't have anyone. You're a whore."

I was silent. My silence enraged him. I could see the veins on his forehead swelling, but I maintained my silence.

"Okay, come with me and I'll take you to be photographed."

It was late at night and obviously no photographer works at that hour. So I refused to go with him. He let me be. But the next evening he returned with his friends and once again took me aside. This time he said, "Come with me, I'll take care of you, you won't lack anything."

"I've told you – I've got someone who is waiting for me in Israel. I can't."

I could see the rage rising to his head again. He grabbed me by my shoulder and said, "I'll kill you."

"So what? Kill me. I'm lost anyway."

One of his friends tried to calm him down but that made him even madder.

The next day the others all left for Israel and I was left alone. I was frightened of what was going to happen next and I left the house. Suddenly, I saw a distant relative, a person who was also waiting to make aliyah. I told him in a few words what was happening to me and he said, "Don't worry anymore, I'll protect you, you're not alone."

That night one of Ruben's underlings arrived and the story of the photographs came up once more. After the usual argument, he said that he'd been told that I'm not Jewish at all, so I can't make aliyah and ought to return to Gedaref. "Good, send me back there," I said, and in my heart of hearts I was already looking forward to being reunited with my brother. How much I needed him then by my side. My relative tried to intervene, but the man silenced him. In the end, the business of the photographs was brought up again but this time in order to get the papers to return me to Gedaref. For some reason, this time I believed him and left the house with him. My relative called out that he would wait until I returned.

We walked a long way on foot and then we went in a taxi. We reached a dark house. The man put me inside and closed the door from outside. The room was completely empty of furniture, except for a sort of bench along one wall. A lightbulb hanging from the ceiling lit the room. After I recovered a little, I saw that a girl, older than me, was sitting on the bench. She said hello and asked why I'd been brought there. "To be photographed," I answered. She nodded her head but didn't say anything. I understood that there was no photographer and no camera in the place. We sat and talked and it turned out that I knew her sister from school. Suddenly, Ruben appeared, accompanied by another friend. The friend took the girl to an adjoining room. Ruben stood beside the door and ordered me to come to him. I refused. I saw his eyes glittering. I hated him and cursed myself. From the other room there came the sound of the girl screaming. I knew there was no chance at all of anyone else hearing her. And even if anyone were to hear her – no one would come to help her because a man is permitted to do anything to a woman that he wants. I knew that my time had also arrived. Ruben dragged me to the corner of the room, then tore my dress off. I felt as though I was paralyzed. "Come on, whore," he shouted at me.

I tried to appeal to his better nature and said, "I'm a virgin."

"Liar. You slept with all the soldiers in Gedaref!"

"I swear to you that I'm a virgin. Have pity on me."

"We'll see if you're a virgin."

I realized that the worst thing of all was about to happen to me. I tried to make my senses numb. I thought that if I don't see and don't hear, the pain would be less. I didn't have any chance of persuading Ruben with words and the only thing left for me was to force myself not to feel what he was about to do with me. In spite of my attempts, I couldn't but feel him when he penetrated within me.

When the blood from my hymen spurted forth and covered the floor, I looked at his face and saw his amazement. Here he had the proof that I was a virgin. Was, and am no more. I remained in the corner, in pain and humiliation, torn apart.

Ruben smoothed down his clothing and left the house. His friend was already waiting for him outside. The other girl crawled from the other room into my room. We hugged each other.

In the next two weeks, Ruben came back every night and raped me; sometimes, several times in one night. I silently vowed that I would have revenge for my stolen, spilled virginal blood. Occasionally he came during the day, in order to try to persuade me to remain with him. He promised he'd take me to Canada, which is where he intends going, but I was true to myself, and said that my brother is waiting for me in Israel. I no longer spoke of a betrothed, since I'd lost my virginity anyway. When Ruben saw that he couldn't persuade me, he tried to ingratiate himself with me so that I wouldn't ever say anything at all about what he was doing to me. He wanted me to promise that when I got to Israel, I'd say that he's my husband and that I'm waiting for his arrival. It was only after I promised to do so that he released me.

In the plane on the way to Jerusalem, I cried quietly, so that no one would be aware of it. I managed the hard trek to Sudan, I survived the refugee camps where dozens of people die every day and I really was at the end of my journey, at last. And now, just now, this cruel man had to ruin everything and dishonor me. I'll never forgive him.

OCTOBER 29, 1984 – THE JEWISH AGENCY OFFICE, TEL AVIV

It is now certain that a major operation is about to take place to bring all the Ethiopian Jews who are wasting away in the refugee camps in Sudan on aliyah. The news from the US embassy in

Khartoum is encouraging: the Sudanese are being helpful with all the arrangements. Indeed, they have even found four bus chassis in Saudi Arabia that now only have to be taken to Khartoum to have the upper parts fitted. At the same time, a Red Cross team has been organized for Um Rakoba to provide the Jews with medical care until their evacuation.

Here in Israel, Yehoshua has been recruited for the operation. He is the son of a leader of Ethiopian Jewry who was one of Dr. Faitlovitch's students. Yehoshua's father studied in Jerusalem, Frankfurt, and Zurich during his youth and, when he returned to Ethiopia, Emperor Haile Selassie appointed him to a senior position in Ethiopia's Ministry of Education. He left this position at the start of the fifties when missionary activity among the Jews increased and there was concern about their future. That was when the Jewish Agency established a Jewish school in Asmara and he was appointed its principal. In the following years, he initiated and established schools in many villages and devoted most of his time to the Jewish public. Six years ago he made aliyah and has continued the battle to save Ethiopian Jewry. Indeed, from his home in Petah Tikva, he has recently been warning once again that unless Israel carries out some sort of "Operation Entebbe" to rescue the Jews of Ethiopia, there will be none left to save, since he foresees the community's demise through assimilation, intermarriage, and conversion if they remain in Ethiopia or in Sudan.

His son, Yehoshua, who was among the first Ethiopian immigrants to arrive in Israel, finished high school at the French school in Addis Ababa. He is a thoughtful and reliable man who will understand the necessity for secrecy and seems an excellent choice for the job of "the black man to be sent to Sudan to identify the Falashas," as the Americans and Sudanese have defined the role. Yehoshua has shared the suffering and pain of Israel's Ethiopian community as they hear of more and more deaths in the refugee camps. Like all our staff members, he has relationships with families who have been touched by these tragedies.

Yehoshua agreed to bear the responsibility for the operation without a moment's hesitation. His training for the job began immediately and the entire operational plan was disclosed to him. He learned of the American involvement and the expected cooperation from the Sudanese secret police. In the next few days, he'll be fully briefed on every aspect, such as the order of evacuation from the various camps, cooperation with the Committee members, liaison with the Americans, and so on.

Meanwhile, an agreement has also been signed with Georges Gutelman whereby he has undertaken to fly a group of two hundred Jews once every two days from Khartoum to Brussels or another European airport, and, after a short touchdown in Europe, the same plane will then continue to Ben-Gurion Airport in Israel. There will be a doctor on each plane to care for passengers who are in serious condition.

At the Jewish Agency, we've also started to feel the bustle. In the rooms on the third floor, cartons are piling up stuffed with every item imaginable, from ID cards prepared specially for hanging around the necks of the new *olim*, to stationery supplies in all colors and sizes. At the Jewish Agency's old age home, we've started to stock the storerooms with a supply of clothing and shoes in all sizes. According to Ora Donio, head of the Jewish Agency's Welfare Department, not even one word is uttered about the imminent events, in spite of the fact that everyone knows that a major initiative is underway and the staff are all thrilled about the rescue of the families left in Sudan.

NOVEMBER 15, 1984 – THE JEWISH AGENCY OFFICE, TEL AVIV

According to a report from Jerry Weaver in Khartoum received via Washington, the first Jews from Um Rakoba have arrived in Gedaref. They have been housed in a number of houses rented as part of the preparations for the operation. From these houses, they will set out in buses for Khartoum in another few days and from there to Israel. Weaver expects the operation to commence within a very short time; they are now waiting for Yehoshua's arrival.

In Yehoshua's home in Petah Tikva, everything has already been packed and ready for the last two days. Today, he'll receive his passport and learn what his name and nationality will be for the period of the operation. Tomorrow he leaves for Sudan via Europe and will land in Khartoum in another three days. His main role will be to identify those entitled to make aliyah and to allow only these people to board the buses. The plans took into account the possibility that there might be some tumult during the identification process, so, through the channel of Jerry Weaver, the Sudanese secret police will cooperate throughout the entire evacuation.

But meanwhile, we are facing problems in Israel. This morning I visited Ma'on Hayeled, which is in an old three-story building surrounded by an unkempt garden in Yad Eliyahu, Tel Aviv, not far from the basketball stadium. For the last few months, it has housed boys and girls from Ethiopia who arrived in the last two big rescue missions. Most of them left their parents behind, some in Sudan and some in Ethiopia. I've visited there many times in the past and the children have always been happy to see me. They always clustered around me, asking what's new in Sudan and in Ethiopia. This time my reception there was so reserved that the children actually ignored my presence entirely.

I discovered the reason for their puzzling behavior over lunch with the staff. Yesterday, Baruch Tegegne visited there. He is one of the Kfar Batya graduates of the fifties and has been living in Canada for many years. He has just returned from spending time in Sudan and Kenya. I don't know who he works for, but his goal is to organize the kids to demonstrate in public. When he gathered them together in the clubhouse, he stood before them and, crying as though his own mother had just died, he pointed at one after the other of the children and called out, "You don't know that your father has died, that your mother is already dead?"

Baruch got what he wanted. Within less than an hour he turned the clubhouse into a room full of mourners with the children all sobbing for their dead parents. They were ready to go out and demonstrate on the spot. Obviously, such a demonstration must be prevented as it could endanger the very existence of the operation. I know to the depths of my soul how very difficult it is and will be to keep the forthcoming operation a secret, but it is unbelievably harder to do so when faced with a boy of fifteen who is going out of his mind with worry about his parents wasting away in Sudan, and wants to raise public awareness by demonstrating with his friends. It would be marvelous if I could only go to him and say, "In another week, the State of Israel is going to start evacuating all the Jews who are now trapped in Sudan. Your parents will also arrive and you'll be able to embrace them." If I could say such things, no one would feel any need to demonstrate, but obviously I'm forbidden to drop even a hint. I can only pray that no demonstration will be held, or if one is held, that it won't cause any harm.

NOVEMBER 19, 1984 – THE JEWISH AGENCY OFFICE, TEL AVIV

Everything is ready and in high gear for the big initiative. Yehoshua has already managed to meet with our people in Khartoum and late yesterday evening was introduced to Jerry Weaver. Jerry was concerned that Yehoshua doesn't know how to use a gun and so he agreed with the Muhabarat – the Sudanese secret police – that one of its jobs would be to provide bodyguards for Yehoshua.

At the last working meeting with the Sudanese, we were asked that the operation commence with the evacuation of the Jews from Tewaba, where there is the largest concentration, and only then move on to Um Rakoba, Wadihilu, and Gedaref, where the situation in the camps is better in comparison.

This morning, Yehoshua arrived in Gedaref and tomorrow he will send off the first group of immigrants in a TEA plane to Europe. The day after tomorrow they will land here at Ben-Gurion Airport.

Even before his first working meeting with the Committee people, Yehoshua toured the Tewaba refugee camp, escorted by Ruben, that same young man who so viciously raped Genet.

When Yehoshua passed among the trampled thickets in the Jewish area of the camps, he didn't recognize one person there; even if he should have known them, it was impossible for him to identify them because their faces and bodies had changed beyond recognition, having become so drooping and gaunt. He saw many sick people and it was clear to him that some of them would not survive long. In the afternoon, the Committee members gathered. One of the Israelis with whom the Committee has worked for many years opened the meeting. He introduced Yehoshua and told those assembled that henceforth Yehoshua's instructions must be obeyed without question.

When it was Yehoshua's turn to speak, he first talked of his tour in the Tewaba camp and about the terrible sights he had seen there. He then announced unequivocally that the sick and the old would make aliyah first. This caused an uproar among the Committee members. It had always been the Committee's prerogative to decide who is first in line for departure and they were adamant that this should not be in the hands of a person, however distinguished, who lives in Israel and has not endured the same sufferings as the people in Sudan. It was only the Israeli's authority that managed to stifle the commotion. But their opposition to Yehoshua increased by the minute as he repeated his words, stressing, "The sick and the old will leave first and only afterwards will we send the other people, according to their length of stay here." But finally, they did agree that priority should be given to the sick and the elderly.

From Yehoshua's countenance, it was impossible for a bystander to know what was going on inside his brain. His nerves were taut, anticipating upcoming events. On the surface, everything appears organized. He has four buses in reasonable condition at his disposal and tomorrow morning 220 people will board them and be driven to Khartoum, where a plane will be waiting to fly them to Brussels. After a short stopover, they will fly on, landing in the afternoon of November 21, in two days' time, at Ben-Gurion Airport.

There was a minor incident that same evening when Yehoshua asked one of the Committee members to include his cousin, who is very old, on this flight. The Committee people refused on the grounds that the cousin's condition did not entitle him to preference. To the Israelis observing this incident, it was clear that there is going to be further tension between Yehoshua and the Committee.

In Israel, preparations are also at their height. At the Jewish Agency's old age home in Ashkelon, clothes, underwear, towels, jogging suits, dresses, baby garments, shoes, and parkas are constantly being added to the storerooms. Anyone who chanced to be in the vicinity of Ora Donio's office during these last days would think that we're about to take a long journey. The office has been in ferment with Ora herself going in and out, rushing from a top secret get-together with the chief of staff to some other confidential briefing, then afterwards meeting with us and not passing one remark about the big secret that we all share.

It is now evening and my thoughts are again with Yehoshua in Sudan. How will he cope with the tremendous responsibility he bears? How will he stand up to the pressures? How will he manage when things go wrong?

NOVEMBER 21, 1984 – BEN-GURION INTERNATIONAL AIRPORT

It is almost two o'clock in the afternoon and a plane with markings never seen here before is landing. It is a TEA Boeing 707 and in it are 283 frightened Jews, most of them sick and old, but also young children. The plane is ordered to land in a remote corner of the airport and we set out to meet them in one of the six buses that have been hired to transport the *olim* to Ashkelon.

The plane comes to a halt and the steps are trundled over to it and attached to the forward exit. Excitement grips all those waiting. Everyone who is anyone is here, from the prime minister, Shimon Peres, down to the lowliest El Al technician. They all press forward toward the steps in order to see the miracle, but only a few are allowed to ascend to the door of the plane.

The forward exit is opened and in the doorway is a tall, blond flight attendant wearing a pale blue uniform and white gloves. The first to go into the plane is Zimna. I try to join him but am pushed aside by a woman who works in the prime minister's office. The minutes pass and no one comes out. I don't understand what can be causing the delay. Afterwards, it was explained to me that Zimna asked everyone to wait until the very sick had exited.

And here, carried by Zimna, comes the first beneficiary of this operation, looking out at the rain-soaked fields of our land, so different from the yellow, dry fields in Sudan. With his right hand, Zimna is holding an infusion bag and with his left arm he is supporting the old man.

I quickly use the commotion to board the plane. As soon as I reach the door, the smell of urine and excrement hits me. I think of the elegant flight attendant standing at the opening with the regulation smile fixed on her face. I admire her for that, but I don't waste much time on these feelings as I am required to carry an old woman, weighing some thirty-five kilos (about seventy-seven pounds), who is also hooked up to an infusion. She, like many of the others, will not be taken to Ashkelon but will go directly to the hospital, so I carry her in my arms down to one of the ambulances that are parked beneath the aircraft's wings and pass her to the doctors.

Again I board the plane and help Zimna to transfer the other immigrants to the buses. Now that the initial thrill is behind us, Zimna also gives vent to his feelings and shouts out to me, "We've done it. Success at long last!"

Within less than half an hour, we're already on our way. We travel in six buses with their curtains pulled down, as in previous secret operations, but this time we know that every two days the planes will be arriving, with over two hundred Jews in each. Today, 283 reached here by TEA and another forty-three arrived by the previous system, via Europe.

I feel that I am a partner in an enterprise that penetrates to the most basic essence of the State of Israel – the rescue of Jews because they are Jews, as the most irrefutable response to the persecution of Jews because they are Jews, at any time and in any place.

***

I make use of the time spent traveling to Ashkelon to study the faces of our new citizens. I see how sad their eyes are after witnessing death day after day. It is difficult to believe that they will ever be able to recover from the tragedies that befell them while they were waiting for their aliyah.

At the entrance to the Ashkelon old age home, many of the staff are already waiting and they immediately crowd around the newcomers. The love passing directly from the workers to the *olim* is demonstrable and I am sure that the immigrants can feel it. The turmoil is enormous. For us, tomorrow will be a day of interviews, of reunification of families, and of placement in absorption centers. I start to digest the thought that we are faced with the absorption of thousands of new immigrants within a very short time. Do we have enough places? Have we made sufficient preparations for all of them? There is certainly going to be a great deal of work to heal family rifts and our staffers are going to need a wealth of understanding and much, much love!

NOVEMBER 22, 1984 – THE OLD AGE HOME OF THE JEWISH AGENCY, ASHKELON

We've just been informed that the second group, with 235 new immigrants, is on its way. However, in the cable from the Israeli embassy in Washington it says that after the immigrants descended from the buses in Khartoum and boarded the plane, Jerry Weaver's Muhabarat friends immediately went over to him and remarked that the passengers this time were very well dressed and don't look at all like sick and elderly refugees, as the agreement stipulates. A similar remark was heard by Yehoshua. That same evening he summoned Worku Abuhay and said quite unambiguously that he would not agree to people from Gedaref making aliyah before those from the camps in Tewaba and Um Rakoba. Of course, Worku's response was, "Don't worry, it'll be okay." The question is, what is Worku's assurancc worth?

NOVEMBER 23, 1984 – BEN-GURION INTERNATIONAL AIRPORT

The 235 immigrants arrived. There are far fewer sick and elderly among them.

NOVEMBER 24, 1984 – THE OLD AGE HOME OF THE JEWISH AGENCY, ASHKELON

In Sudan this morning, four buses left with 220 immigrants. According to the preliminary report, this time too there will not be many sick and elderly in the plane. Yehoshua even reports that Committee members were seen receiving money from Jews living in Gedaref, in order to allow them to get priority and make aliyah before the sick and the aged. In Jerry Weaver's report to Washington that same day, he calls the Committee members "travel agents."

Yehoshua has received stringent instructions to put an end to this business because if he doesn't, the whole operation – yes, the whole shebang – will be placed at risk.

That same evening, our people heard of a previous grave incident. At the daily meeting with the Committee, Yehoshua gave instructions that Zimna's brother, Chekole, with his family, should be put on one of the next flights because it was known in Israel that he was very ill. The angry response of the Committee members was loudly voiced by their undisputed leader, Gedam Mengistu, a man who parades around the camps with a gun in his belt. When Gedam speaks, everyone else keeps silent. Yehoshua's Israeli partner was not present at the meeting and Yehoshua felt that he was alone against the entire Committee, with all of them shooting darts of hatred at him from their eyes. Gedam started off by saying, "You were born with a silver spoon in your mouth. You lived all the time in Addis Ababa and now you've come to us straight from the fleshpots of Jerusalem and you've never suffered – not even one day – in the refugee camps here in Sudan. And you dare to decide who makes aliyah first, before the others? Who the hell do you think you are?"

Yehoshua answered with his usual calm, "I am here as the representative of the State of Israel. I am here in order to organize the rescue of the Ethiopian Jews."

Yehoshua held his own against Gedam on this particular occasion, but when he analyzed the situation afterwards with Jerry Weaver, it was clear to both of them that either Ruben or Gedam would have to go in order to stave off future problems. They agreed that Ruben would be removed, which would at the same time lessen the opposition to Yehoshua and constitute a warning to the others. Jerry even suggested that Ruben be eliminated altogether, but in order not to embarrass the Sudanese, it was agreed that he should be sent to Israel at the first opportunity.

NOVEMBER 25, 1984 – BEN-GURION INTERNATIONAL AIRPORT

Today 217 immigrants arrived by TEA and another thirty-six came via Europe, by the former method.

NOVEMBER 26, 1984 – TRANSITION AND PLACEMENT CENTER FOR OPERATION MOSES, ASHKELON

In the plane that left Khartoum this evening, there are two passengers who are special for entirely different reasons. One of them is Chekole Berhanie, Zimna's brother, who was brought with his family to Tewaba after Jerry Weaver met with the Committee and got their agreement to accept Yehoshua's authority and to cooperate with Yehoshua in implementing the operation. The second special passenger is Ruben, who was tricked into boarding one of the buses in Tewaba.

It was Jerry who suggested that we recruit Ruben to carry out the passenger count in the buses. The four buses usually halt a few kilometers outside Tewaba in order to count the passengers. Ruben was asked by Yehoshua to be responsible for this task. When the buses stopped for the inspection, Yehoshua and four Sudanese soldiers descended, one from each bus. Ruben obviously had a sudden flash of suspicion that they were about to trick him, but it was already too late. When Yehoshua asked him to get into the third bus to count the passengers, he tried to make a run for it, but two grim soldiers, tall and imposing, pushed him inside the bus. Instead of counting the people, he was forced onto the rear seat from where, over a soldier's shoulder, he saw Jerry Weaver's threatening expression. Jerry said to him, "It's better to live in Israel than to die in Sudan." Then he commanded the soldier, "You're responsible for making sure that this man reaches Khartoum today. If he tries to move from his seat, shoot him in the forehead, but don't waste more than one bullet."

To the amazement of all the passengers, this potentate, this ruler of the camps who had held life and death in his hands and had taken for his own gratification any girl who aroused his fancy, sat without moving until the bus reached Khartoum. He made no resistance to boarding the plane and tomorrow he will arrive in Israel.

NOVEMBER 27, 1984 – BEN-GURION INTERNATIONAL AIRPORT

Today 217 *olim* arrived. Among those receiving Ruben was Haim Halachmi, the representative in Israel of HIAS (the Hebrew Immigrant Aid Society). Haim has been dealing with the aliyah of Ethiopian Jews for years. The Israelis in Sudan have asked him to send Ruben to the USA or Canada because they are afraid that his life will be in danger in Israel where there are too many people with accounts to settle with him. In any case, he is not interested in living here. Haim Halachmi decided that Ruben would not join those traveling to Ashkelon.

The other special passenger, Zimna's brother, Chekole, is on the bus to Ashkelon. Toward evening, when the sun is about to set and the shadows of the people walking from the dining room to the registration area are becoming longer and longer, a shout is heard. It is a sound that will long remain engraved in my memory, a strange mixture of joy and pain. I hurry to the source of the strange cry, making my way through the huddle of people in the center of the lawn. It comes from Sagi, Zimna's younger brother, who happens to be in the crowd. His face expresses the pain of the fourteen-year separation from Chekole, his older brother. It was Chekole who reared him in the village, taught him the work in the fields, and was like a father to him until he left for Israel. They stand with the head of the one pressed into the shoulder of the other. Then slowly, very slowly, the pain turns to joy, the joy of reunion, and the joy of knowing that Chekole and his family are alive and have escaped from the horror.

I ask for Zimna to be called so that he, too, will be part of the happiness that is sweeping over everyone here. He arrives on the scene. And when he does, he is transformed into the same village child who bows his head before his older brother and is at his command. All around us the people weep, the tears flowing faster as the brothers hug tighter and tighter together.

While this was happening, a dramatic event of a totally different kind was taking place in Gedaref. Gedam spent the whole night looking for Ruben, who had not turned up at their regular meeting place. After a protracted search, he had no doubt in his mind: Yehoshua must be behind Ruben's disappearance. Gedam found Yehoshua among the people waiting to make aliyah and angrily confronted him. The Sudanese police guarding Yehoshua charged at Gedam, trying to get him away from Yehoshua, but Yehoshua signaled to them to let him deal with it. Gedam and Yehoshua stood challenging each other, the eyes of both filled with animosity. Gedam spat out through clenched teeth, "You killed him. You hated him so much that you killed him."

"No. The truth is that we haven't killed him, even though he deserved to die. We've sent him to Israel so that he won't prey on anyone here anymore," Yehoshua answered, trying to maintain his composure.

"Well, from now on you're on your own. There is no Committee anymore; we all quit," shouted Gedam and turned away.

Within a few hours, Yehoshua appointed a new Committee, composed of former teachers, some of them known to him from their meetings with his father in Addis Ababa and some of whom were recommended by friends. At his meeting with the members of the new Committee, Yehoshua explained the reason for the previous Committee's resignation and asked for their assistance to bring the operation to a successful conclusion. He then went into more detail about the problems that he had had with the previous Committee and concluded by saying, "The success of the operation depends on your being able to bring all the Jews to Tewaba. You must on no account repeat the methods of Gedam and his people. Please, first bring all the sick and elderly and don't give in to pressure from any family members who want to have priority over others. Remember that, in any case, in just another month, you'll all be in Jerusalem."

And here in Ashkelon, the immigrants have gone to sleep and the counselors and home management advisors have retired to their rooms. I meet with Avi Mizrahi, a social worker by profession who has been active in the aliyah of the Ethiopians from the very start, even going to Ethiopia in 1982. He has been appointed by the Jewish Agency to direct this transition and placement center for the *olim*. We sit down in order to sum up the first days of the operation. We are in a great mood. Our high spirits spring from the meeting between Chekole and his brothers, as well as from seeing old friends, long settled here, welcoming their relatives, and also from being active partners in this tremendous Zionist endeavor.

Our discussion is cut off when Alemu Kedebe Eshete enters the room. In the Ethiopian community, he is known as Little Alemu because he really is very short. He is one of the few professional artists to be found in the community in Israel and, at present, is studying at the State Art Teachers' College. I know Alemu as a friendly guy, usually smiling, but when he comes in, he is obviously distraught. He has learned from recent *olim* that his father died in Um Rakoba and now he is worried that his mother, whose whole life depended on her husband, is not going to cope. I see a young man suffocated by a dark cloud of misery. I offer him a seat, but even before I manage to ask him what's happening with him and why he's here, he says, "I can't sit calmly and study while this is happening, when my family – my mother and sister – are in the worst refugee camp of all, Um Rakoba, where my father died." And with lowered eyes, he goes on, "I want you to give me work here. I'm ready to volunteer since I just can't study feeling as I do."

The truth is that we are in need of additional counselors. All the staff are working very hard, with their work day starting early in the morning and finishing toward midnight, and there are always extra things to be done, such as accompanying sick people to the hospitals. I ask Alemu if the principal of his school knows of his departure. When he answers in the negative, I agree to take him on if he brings authorization from the school principal. We allocate him a place to sleep and then at last, even we go to bed.

NOVEMBER 28, 1984 – THE TRANSITION AND PLACEMENT CENTER FOR IMMIGRANTS OF OPERATION MOSES, ASHKELON

This morning, while rousing people, I found Alemu sitting on his bed, leaning against the wall with his head covered by a *netela,* the wide, white scarf that serves as both clothing and covering to Ethiopians. Alemu hadn't managed to sleep. He spent all night thinking about the anticipated reunion with his mother. Would he know her? Would she recognize him? He imagined how he would hug her, how he would console her for his father's death.

During the afternoon, he came back and said that the school director had released him from his studies until the end of the Chanukah vacation in another ten days. Let's hope his mother arrives by then so his studies don't go down the drain.

A report has come in from Sudan that tomorrow we should expect another group of immigrants, comprising some 220 people.

NOVEMBER 29, 1984 – BEN-GURION INTERNATIONAL AIRPORT

Today 220 immigrants arrived. Since the start of Operation Moses, 1,172 Ethiopian Jews have arrived on five flights.

DECEMBER 3, 1984 – BEN-GURION INTERNATIONAL AIRPORT

Today another 219 new immigrants arrived on the TEA flight.

A cable from Sudan reported that since the buses are going to be exchanged for new buses, a group will not arrive in two days' time. However, there are rumors that the delay is because the new Committee is not managing to transfer Jews to Tewaba. The fact is that all the Jews who arrived in the last week were still organized by the previous Committee and were already waiting in Tewaba to make aliyah. No new arrivals came to Tewaba.

Another mishap reported in the cable is that there has been a fire in the straw huts that house the immigrants prior to their departure for Khartoum. It is not clear who is responsible for the fire. Was it an act of retaliation by Gedam and his friends, or is one of the Ethiopian underground movements responsible? They are aggrieved because the Sudanese police confiscated their houses for the Jews to stay in before their aliyah. Jerry is inclined to believe the latter version.

In another cable that Jerry sent to Washington, he reported a serious incident with the Russians. Throughout the whole operation, an American intelligence-gathering plane has been parked on a side runway in an isolated region of the Khartoum airport. This black plane is, in fact, the most advanced monitoring and broadcasting station in the world. The plane that has been flying the immigrants landed beside it. Today at noon the Sudanese secret police discovered a group of Russian diplomats photographing the immigrants' plane from inside their car. It is suspected that the Russians' real objective was the spy plane. The Sudanese followed in two cars behind the Russians' vehicle and when it reached the airport exit, it was stopped at the control point. A Muhabarat man with the rank of colonel approached the driver, pointed at the camera and asked, "What's this?"

"A camera."

"Do you have a license for it?"

The Russian didn't answer, but his face clearly expressed anger; however, the Sudanese stood his ground. "And what's this?"

"Cigarettes."

"Did you pay customs duty on them?"

"No. I'm a diplomat."

"Okay, you all have to come to make a declaration in the customs house."

The incident did not last longer than five minutes. The official in the customs office apologized for the bother and the Russians were escorted in a dignified manner back to their car. It was only after they returned to their embassy and handed over the film for developing that they realized that while they were inside the customs house, the Muhabarat people had exposed the film to daylight. Perhaps this is also a reason for the delay of the operation.

DECEMBER 7, 1984, FRIDAY – THE TRANSITION AND PLACEMENT CENTER OF OPERATION MOSES, ASHKELON

This morning, like most mornings, when I woke people up I found Alemu in the same position, seated on the end of his bed with his body wedged into the corner of the room and his head covered by the same *netela*. When he removed it, his eyes were so sad. He said that until his mother arrives, he won't return to his studies. The day after tomorrow his school reopens after the vacation so he is likely to lose everything he has invested in his studies.

Today, there were many journalists at the airport, which is maybe why so many politicians were there, welcoming the immigrants. Perhaps as a result of all the fuss and perhaps as a result of the experience I've gained, I managed to slip through them all and reached the doorway of the plane before the first *oleh* came out. Zimna was already inside with a microphone and loudspeaker, giving them the traditional blessing on their arrival.

The plane's interior stank from excrement and urine, and I once again looked with admiration at those blond flight attendants in their pale blue suits and white gloves, smiling cheerfully as though no stench could bother them. These reflections were cut short when Zimna placed in my arms a girl of about twelve years whose weight could not have been more than twenty-five kilos (fifty-five pounds). It was only when I reached the bottom of the steps from the plane that I realized that her body was cold. I entered the ambulance with her. It's the first time in my life that I have held a dead body. And she was the same age as my daughter, Yifat. I didn't know how to shake off my anger at her fate.

And there in the ambulance was the doctor who had accompanied the flight. Presuming that, like the rest of the crew, he was not Israeli, I muttered in Hebrew, "What sort of doctors are you who can't save a young girl? Absolutely useless! You don't deserve to be called doctors." The doctor did not react, not even by raising an eyebrow. But that evening, when I related this to Zimna, he corrected my error – all the doctors on the flights are Israelis. I was ashamed of my rashness.

On the way to Ashkelon, we counted the immigrants, including the sick and the girl who had died. Altogether they were 216. In the bus that I traveled in, an elderly couple sat on the front seat. The man fascinated me. He sat so upright and even though his clothes were dirty, his whole bearing proclaimed dignity. That couple conquered my heart. Wanting to know more about them, I struck up a conversation.

ABA SAMUEL'S STORY

Like all the Jews in Ethiopia, we also dreamed of having the privilege of reaching Jerusalem. Nearly all our children are already in Israel. A lot of the youngsters, who did not want to be forced into the Ethiopian military, had already fled to Sudan, so there were not many of us left in our region. We walked for ten days until we reached the home of my daughter. She is married to the chief of the brigands in the area. We stayed with her for about a month and then we left for Sudan in the company of her sons – my grandchildren.

In this new country, where we didn't know the language or the customs, we were transferred from one camp to another. Since we had none of our children with us to take care of us, we were afraid we wouldn't succeed in ever leaving that burning inferno. We barely managed to survive on the money we'd brought with us and had already accepted that death was near. It was a pity that we wouldn't see our children and grandchildren or Jerusalem with its golden roofs and heroic people, but we already realized that people without children or relatives to assist them were fated to die and be buried in the sands of Sudan.

On one of the last evenings, when I was sitting at the door of our straw hut, I heard my neighbors talking about a rescue mission. I knew them. They were Jews who came from another region. One of them even said that tomorrow his nephew would be coming to take him to Tewaba. I was so envious, but we had no alternative but to go on waiting – perhaps, somehow, someone would come and take us, too. And to our surprise, one of our distant relatives, indeed, hadn't forgotten us and he came and took us. We journeyed in an open truck to Tewaba. We were placed there in a group of about fifty people and someone wrote us down on a paper. There were old people, young people, and families with children in the group. Some of them were known to us and we said hello to them. Someone said that we were making aliyah, but we had no idea how long it would take us to arrive. Also, I'd reached the stage where I didn't believe that we would ever reach Israel.

At sunset four buses arrived and it was only then I realized that we were sitting in four groups. We were asked to rise, and started moving toward the bus that was allocated to our group. Suddenly someone stopped me and said that we were surplus and didn't appear on the list. I didn't have the strength to argue, but happily our relative was in the vicinity and he intervened on our behalf.

Before we boarded the buses, every two people were given one blanket between them. We were told that the place where we were going is cold at night. After traveling for six hours we suddenly saw many lights on the horizon. Obviously it was Khartoum, the capital of Sudan, referred to in the refugee camps as the gateway to Jerusalem. Even before we managed to recover from all the new sights that met our eyes, the buses entered the airport. It was midnight when we mounted steps into something that looked like a large chicken or fish.

Inside this large chicken, young women were going here and there. They were strange-looking, with very light skin and eyes of such a light color that it was as though they hardly had eyes at all. Their hair reminded me of linen and didn't look like hair at all. They smiled all the time and spoke with us in a strange, unclear tongue. They seated us in high padded chairs that were arranged in a peculiar formation, and they even fastened us to the chairs. Then a minute later the lights of the city started to move more and more quickly and suddenly this thing that we were sitting inside separated itself from the ground and we could only see the city's lights when we looked down. After some time, they disappeared and that's when we also started to feel some sort of movement. Eventually, we fell asleep.

When dawn broke, we found ourselves on the ground once more, but within a few minutes, we were once more in the air. Then after several hours passed, we were on the ground again. I didn't know what they were doing with us and what was happening to us. I didn't know where they were taking us, even though it was said that we were on our way to Jerusalem.

Suddenly I heard a voice that I recognized, blessing us with the ancient Ethiopian blessing, *"Enquan dehena metachu."* Then a few moments later I realized that it was the voice of Zimna Berhanie welcoming us. I hadn't seen him in over twenty years, but his voice has hardly changed at all. With my eyes I searched for him, and suddenly he was standing by me. I wanted to rise and embrace him, but I was tied by the strap to the seat. Zimna bent down over me and let me kiss him and hug him. We both cried and then he said, "Uncle, at long last I have the privilege of seeing you arrive in Jerusalem. I thank God."

In Sudan I thought that I would die and never reach Jerusalem, and here I was, embracing Zimna. I could barely manage to get out the words to answer him, but I did manage to say, "Thank God that I have reached this day, and thank you."

With my hand, I wiped the tears from Aba Samuel's face. This meeting has helped me to a fuller understanding of the miracle that is happening right in front of my own eyes.

In Ashkelon, we parked the buses beside the side entrance of the Kupat Holim convalescent home, a particularly beautiful place of lush greenery on the shore of the Mediterranean. The immigrants didn't see any of this beauty as it was already evening. In fact, it was past time for lighting the Sabbath candles and the *olim* still hadn't a clue where they were and what was happening. They walked slowly, hesitantly.

Suddenly a shout was heard from the far end, where the fourth bus was parked. The voice sounded familiar to me, but even so, I couldn't identify it immediately. It was Little Alemu. He'd been with me in the airport and, as with previous arrivals, I'd seen him scrutinizing the faces of the *olim* but without finding his mother. It was only now, when the immigrants were on their way to the dining room in the convalescent home, that he suddenly realized that one woman seemed a bit like his mother. Alemu's arms were loaded down with cardboard boxes, but when he saw this woman, he started making his way in her direction. At the same time she started walking toward him. Suddenly, the woman started running and he threw down everything that he was carrying and ran to her. For long minutes they were locked in a tight embrace, with the tears streaming down their cheeks. While still hugging his mother, Alemu felt someone pulling at his shirt. It was his niece, his brother's daughter, who also wanted to be part of the hugging and kissing. The girl's name is Fasika, meaning "Passover." She was born during the festival of freedom and arrived in Israel during Chanukah, the festival of lights.

The day after tomorrow, the Chanukah vacation ends and Alemu will be able to return to his studies.

At the entrance to the dining room, we'd set up a table on which strips of paper were stacked, each one bearing the individual details of one immigrant. When these strips are fastened around the necks of the *olim*, they remind us of dog collars, and that's the nickname we've given them. I feel uncomfortable each time I see this and each time we use the term, but I must admit that the system is efficient. The immigrants wear these "dog collars" at all times and they really facilitate identification.

The festival of Chanukah is reaching its end and in the dining room both Sabbath candles and Chanukah candles are lit. The atmosphere is festive. The immigrants sit down at the tables and are served a simple meal of a potato, an egg, bread, and tea. We wanted to give them a much more sumptuous meal, but the doctors instructed us to serve only light foods. This is to prevent immigrants from having to be hospitalized afterwards from overeating, as happened with Holocaust survivors (some of whom even died from the rich foods given them by their liberators).

Once again I am struck by the size of this enterprise that we have undertaken. I stand up with a cup of wine in my hand and I make the Kiddush blessing, "And on the seventh day, the heaven and the earth were finished and all their host...," and I stress the words "in remembrance of the Exodus from Egypt," because what is happening to us here and now, at this very minute, is another exodus, and it is such a privilege to take part in it.

Suddenly a man sitting in a corner of the room rises. He looks about thirty-five years old and three children are sitting with him. No wife. It's safe to assume that he is a widower and from his head covering, he is obviously a *kes*. Some of the staff want to silence him, but I ask them to allow him to do as he wants.

The room grows silent and the *kes* starts with a blessing of thanksgiving to God for allowing him and his children and all this holy congregation to reach Jerusalem. Toward the end of his prayer, the congregation responds "Amen," and also after each sentence that he utters. I, too, join in, even though I don't understand Ge'ez, the holy language of the Jews of Ethiopia.

Someone beside me whispers that this is Kes Birhan, meaning "Light," and that his wife died in Sudan. From what I already understand of the status of a *kes* and of the limitations that apply to him, I know that it is going to be hard for him to manage in Israel. It will be difficult to remarry suitably, since a *kes* is permitted to marry only with a virgin from a good home. And in general, the *kessoch* have a hard time fitting into Israeli society since they are not officially recognized as rabbis. They therefore suffer from their loss of importance and prestige even more than do others who had a high social standing in Ethiopia.

However, at this moment we are all captive to the *kes*'s penetrating gaze and monotonic blessing.

DECEMBER 9, 1984 – BEN-GURION INTERNATIONAL AIRPORT

Today 213 *olim* arrived by TEA and another fifty-one by the previous method, through Europe. Also today, Little Alemu returned to his studies.

DECEMBER 11, 1984 – BEN-GURION INTERNATIONAL AIRPORT

Today another large group, with 239 *olim*, arrived by TEA. During the interviews, Zimna found out that one of them is a Christian, named Fikadu Teshome. I asked Fikadu to tell me his story and how he'd managed to arrive in Israel.

FIKADU TESHOME'S STORY

I was born in Eritrea, in a small town near Asmara. My father was a soldier and when he got divorced from my mother while I was still a small child, I went with him. That is the custom among us in Ethiopia – if a couple are divorced, the daughters go with the mother, and sons older than about five or six go with the father. I've not seen my mother since then.

Since my father was in the military, I moved with him from place to place and eventually we reached the Gondar region, where the Jews lived. Naturally, I made friends with them and even when I followed in my father's footsteps and joined the army, I always searched out Jewish company. So it was natural for me that when many Jews from the vicinity left for Sudan, I went with them. When we reached Sudan, I discovered that the Jews, and even the Committee members, thought that I was the brother of one of them who was my very close friend. I didn't deny it, but when the Committee people offered me support, I refused, on the grounds that I had a job in a Sudanese shop that provided enough for my needs.

One day Abera, my "brother," came to me and said, "Take my house. I'm moving to Port Sudan with my family." I was happy to take the key from him, and I moved in. I believed him and I even maintained that he'd moved to Port Sudan when others told me that he'd gone to Israel. But in time the truth sank in and I realized that he was actually in Israel.

Then one day one of the Committee members met me and said, "Abera is already in Israel. What are you still doing here? If you want to go to Israel, come tomorrow to Tewaba."

On the one hand, I wanted very much to go to Israel, but on the other hand, I couldn't just walk out on the grocery store owner who had been good to me. He paid me well and relied on me. He only stopped by there once every two or three months to collect his profits. Luckily, he turned up just that day. So I said to him, "My family in Port Sudan has sent me money, so now I can join them. I really appreciate everything you've done for me." I handed him the keys and he gave me the Arabic blessing for a safe journey.

Two days later, I was at the assembly point for departure to Israel. My brother and sister went there with me, saying all the time, "Don't go to Jerusalem. We've heard that the Israelis throw all the Ethiopians into the sea when they arrive in Jerusalem." But I'd decided to tie my fate to the fate of the Jews and so I decided to take the risk. We've landed here now and I've been waiting every minute to be thrown into the sea, when your assistant – I think he's called Zimna – greeted us in the plane, he said that we are welcome. Now I'm positive that nothing bad is going to happen to us. I see the reception you are giving us – the best of everything. Now when I think how worried my brother and sister looked, I pray that they will also be lucky enough to reach this good land. If you permit it, I'll write them a letter.

In spite of his optimistic words, I saw the worry in Fikadu's eyes. So, first of all I offered him a cigarette, which he lit with tremendous pleasure. I calmed him down and told him not to worry. For the present he has a bed and food and in the course of time we'll find the proper framework for him. As to the letter, I couldn't be encouraging. I know that letters to refugees never arrive in Sudan, but he sat down to write it anyhow.

Unsettling reports are arriving from Yehoshua and Jerry. Journalists are starting to sniff around the departure area and there is grave concern that the whole operation might blow up in our faces. Yesterday, when the buses traveled from Gedaref to Khartoum, the Sudanese spotted a car following them with an Ethiopian driver at the wheel and an American journalist inside. In Sudan, they deal with such incidents in a way that ensures they will not recur. They found some pretext to stop the car at one of the roadblocks and separated the journalist from his driver. The journalist returned to his hotel and, with encouragement from the Sudanese, has left Khartoum. However, the driver was less fortunate. His hands and feet were bound and he was lowered three times upside down into a deep well. He will clearly no longer be interested in driving any journalist following the tracks of the Jews.

In spite of what had happened, the journalist managed to send his article to the *New York Times*. In it he wrote that every two days hundreds of Jews are leaving Sudan for Europe and from there to Israel. The article's publication has worried our people very much, but to everyone's surprise the Sudanese are not all that disturbed by it and have continued to authorize the departure of the Jews.

In Um Rakoba the Jews are still dying. In lists drawn up by the camp management, the number of the dead has risen to over two thousand, of whom about fourteen hundred are children, aged fifteen and under. But in the other camps, too, many Jews have died and the incidents of death have not ceased during the aliyah operation.

Yehoshua decided to accompany the buses and arrived yesterday in Khartoum, where he met with his Israeli operators. The meeting took place in the bar of a hotel overlooking the Nile. Yehoshua didn't touch the cold drink he was served. His thoughts were too occupied with those suffering in the south. He stated that the number of people who have died is four thousand. Our people reacted with disbelief. We in Israel also don't credit the number. Perhaps we don't want to believe that one out of every five of the twenty thousand Ethiopian Jews who reached Sudan in the last two years has died. We don't want to believe that this special community has paid the highest price ever paid by any community anywhere for their ardent dream of aliyah to Jerusalem.

Yehoshua asked for flights to be operated every single day in order to save as many people as possible. He received a positive response. In spite of the disbelief about the numbers that he presented, all parties are interested in hastening the exodus. From our viewpoint it is important to save lives, even the life of one single child, while the Sudanese want to get rid of the Jews as quickly as possible in order to obtain the American assistance that they have been promised.

Yehoshua is now on his way back to Gedaref to organize the *olim* who leave for Khartoum tomorrow and arrive in Israel the day after.

DECEMBER 21, 1984 – OPERATION MOSES TRANSITION AND PLACEMENT CENTER, ASHKELON

Today marks one month that Operation Moses has been in action. In the last ten days, there have been five TEA flights plus two groups arriving via Paris, bringing altogether 1,233 immigrants.

People usually think that the head and the heart grow accustomed to facing terrible sights, but I've not yet become hardened to seeing the women who are still young but have deeply lined faces, and the children who are terribly thin but whose stomachs are swollen from hunger, and the old people whose legs are so like twigs that they can hardly stand on them.

The entire team at the Kupat Holim convalescent home in Ashkelon is working day and night. The home management advisers and translator/counselors care for the immigrants with love and devotion. There is fantastic enthusiasm and a feeling of exaltation, of cooperating together in a historic undertaking of which only the State of Israel is capable.

Today I was at the airport with Avi Mizrahi again, and again we were both gripped by the same feeling. It was as though this was the very first time that we had carried the tiny children in our arms, these infants saved from the abyss at the last moment. And once again, we were overwhelmed at the sight of the community elders prostrating themselves and kissing the ground; we cannot rush them to the buses as we do not want to disturb such a sacred moment. The airport is where we see the Israelis' true character, outwardly rough and tough, but weeping at the sight of an emaciated, barefoot child.

But in the transition center for absorption placement – where four buses draw up every two days with over two hundred immigrants – it is impossible to allow one's Zionist feelings to become overpowering. Avi and his people are faced with difficult decisions: to register a girl of fourteen as the wife of a man to whom she was given in Sudan, or not to register her as married to him at all? To operate strictly according to the law and send a child of ten to his parents, or to leave him with his grandmother, with whom he has lived since the age of two? And of course, the staff does not deal only with the registration but also with the distribution of warm clothing and with sending the *olim* to the various absorption centers which, in turn, are becoming so full that the people are being sent to hotels.

In Ashkelon, we witness heartrending scenes of Ethiopians who immigrated earlier and discover, in the course of a happy reunion with parents or siblings, that one family member is absent and immediately realize that the missing one died in Sudan. Such meetings touch us day after day after day.

Perhaps the cable that has just arrived from Sudan will save some lives. Jerry Weaver announces via Washington that the four buses that were ordered have arrived from Saudi Arabia, and that by working day and night, bodies have been fitted and tomorrow they can already be put into operation. If so, from tomorrow, over two hundred *olim* will be leaving every day and many Jewish lives will be saved. In light of the anticipated doubling of the pace, we must move from the convalescent home, which has accommodation for two hundred people, to the King Saul Hotel, as it has twice that number of beds. And so, the day after tomorrow, we'll exchange the lawns by the sea shore for the rather depressing concrete of the hotel. The pressure on us is also going to mount and I am already busy recruiting more staff.

DECEMBER 23, 1984 – BEN-GURION INTERNATIONAL AIRPORT

To date, 3,456 people have arrived here on fifteen flights. According to our estimate, a similar number of Jews are still in Sudan. Since there will be flights every day starting from today, we expect to finish the operation by January 6, 1985. The reports from Sudan are very reassuring. Everything is running as planned and following hard on the heels of the 207 immigrants who left yesterday, another group of 227 is leaving today and will land here tomorrow.

But recently, Yehoshua has been running into an especially tough problem that requires a fundamental decision. He has, therefore, asked his father, the incontestable leader of the community, to give him a ruling about the *bariya* – the slaves – who arrived in Sudan together with their masters.

Generally, in Ethiopian society, and to a lesser extent also in Ethiopian Jewish society, the institution of slavery has existed for hundreds of years. Usually the slaves were brought from the south, and they are nearly all of the Oromo tribe, known also as the Galla (meaning "dark-skinned"). They are indeed dark and, in contrast to the Amhara and Tigray tribes to which the Ethiopian Jews belong, the faces of the *bariya* are truly Negroid, as is written of the sons of Ham. Only a few Jews – the rich ones – could purchase men or women slaves. Before officially entering into their masters' households, the *bariya* underwent a conversion process according to the rules of Ethiopian Jewry. This meant that they were required to sit in a booth on the outskirts of the village and for a week live only on dry chickpeas and water. At the end of the week, when their digestive systems were purified from forbidden products, they had their heads shaved and were immersed in the river. After the immersion, they were each blessed by the *kessoch* and were even given a new name. This indicated that their past was erased and from now on they considered their master to be their father and the God of Israel their god.

The main social problem with the *bariya* is that their masters did not intermarry with them so they had no choice but to marry among themselves. They were Jews, but in Ethiopian society, they were second-class Jews with a separate status. Nonetheless, some of the women brought children into the world, fathered by their masters. These children did have a chance of being absorbed into society as more or less full members, that is to say there was the possibility of their marrying a non-*bariya* spouse. Therefore, the female slaves preferred to serve their masters and not marry.

Now we must deal with the problem of whether to bring the *bariya* to Israel. Until now, Yehoshua has turned down every attempt by the *bariya* to make aliyah, but he could not ignore their suffering. Faithful to their masters and to their new religion, they also made the trek to Sudan and they, like the other Jews, have buried their dead in Um Rakoba, Tewaba, and Gedaref. To help him in this dilemma, Yehoshua has turned to his father, who quickly arranged to meet with the chief rabbis, Rabbi Ovadia Yosef and Rabbi Shlomo Goren. The meeting will take place in the next few days.

Here in Israel, we feel increasing pressure from the local and foreign press and Avi, the director of the transition and placement center at the King Saul Hotel, is finding it difficult to prevent the journalists' gaining entry into the hotel. But there is no denying the fact that they are still managing to get information and also to photograph the *olim* through the fence. Additionally, today the military censor called a meeting of the foreign and local reporters and made them swear not to leak anything about the operation in order not to endanger it while it is in progress.

JANUARY 4, 1985 – TRANSITION AND PLACEMENT CENTER, ASHKELON

This morning gigantic headlines screamed out at us from the newspapers. In huge letters, the main headline of the mass circulation *Ma'ariv* reads: "By 'Ethiopian Magic Carpet Operation' the Lost Jewish Tribe Is Arriving in Israel." The article underneath states that in Operation Moses over six thousand Ethiopian Jews have been brought to Israel from Sudan.

Meanwhile, in Gedaref, the daily meeting took place between Yehoshua and the man from the Muhabarat, a Christian from the south who is an admirer of Israel. The Sudanese liaison regretfully announced to Yehoshua that there will be no more flights, saying, "It's true that in the past you acted negligently here and there, but in general, the secrecy was maintained until today. But now that the operation has been publicized in all the world's media, our leader, General Jafer el-Numeiri, is under pressure from all the Arab leaders. So, it's impossible to carry on. Unfortunately, we are forced to cease the flights."

There was nothing Yehoshua could do but to listen in silence. From what was said, he understood that the Sudanese knew that he was an Israeli. On leaving the room, he heard the man utter a short phrase that summed it all up, "What a pity."

And indeed, during the last two days, news of the operation has been appearing in media across the globe, as well as here in Israel. Under the headline "Most of the Ethiopian Jews Have Already Reached Israel," *Ma'ariv* reported on an interview that Yehuda Dominitz gave to *Nekuda*, the journal of the Gush Emunim movement. Dominitz said in this interview that "Most of the twenty-five thousand Jews of Ethiopia, who are known as Falashas, are now in Israel."

But the actual event that brought the Sudanese to announce to all concerned – first and foremost to the Americans – that no more flights would take place was the journalists' tour set up by the Israeli prime minister, Shimon Peres, in the transition center here in Ashkelon, where he held an on-the-spot press conference yesterday afternoon. I have never before seen Zimna so furious. He shut himself up in his room and refused to join the press tour. All he said, between clenched teeth, was, "Another three days; we just needed three days more. Why do they do this to us?" His face reflected how he identifies with the suffering of the Ethiopian Jews left behind in the refugee camps in Sudan.

Yehoshua's Sudanese liaison, who had informed him that the flights are canceled, asked him to leave Gedaref and proceed immediately to Khartoum. He offered him an escort as protection against the Muslim Brotherhood, who are rampaging in Khartoum. But Yehoshua asked to delay his departure till the next day, so that he would have enough time to give instructions to his people. At eight o'clock that evening, Yehoshua met with the Committee members. In a choking voice, he told them,

"Tomorrow morning I'm leaving for Khartoum and I don't know whether I'll be returning here. If I don't return, it's a sign that the operation is over. If that's the case, I want you to distribute the money that came from Israel yesterday to those still here. Be strong. Don't despair. We'll rescue you, as well."

He handed over the bags containing the money and medications to one of the Committee and quickly left the room. Outside, shielded by the darkness, he wept for those of his brothers that he had not succeeded in rescuing. During his six-week stay in Gedaref, he had sent 6,364 Jews to Israel. He had had the opportunity to continue his father's mission in life – the rescue of Ethiopian Jewry from spiritual and physical destruction.

While all this was happening, in the quiet resort town of Furlak in Austria, Jerry Weaver was relaxing. He had been waiting three days for delivery of a special rifle for hunting elephants. After downing several glasses of beer in the hotel bar, he went up to his room, stretched out lazily on the bed and switched on the television. Then, suddenly he shot off the bed as though burned. He could not believe his eyes and ears. Austrian television was showing the same pictures that were also being aired by the rest of the world's television stations. They were scenes of Ethiopian Jews who had arrived in Israel in the framework of the operation that the media were calling Operation Moses.

For several moments Jerry was rooted to the spot. He felt like a man who discovers that his wife is having an affair with his best friend. After pulling himself together, he decided he must return to Sudan immediately. He was worried about his assistants and about Yehoshua. He paid his hotel bill, got into the car and drove off toward Vienna's airport. Heavy snow was falling; however, Jerry paid no attention either to it or to the rules of the road and within a short time his car was stuck in the snow. Delay followed delay. He managed to reach a public telephone and ordered a taxi that took him to the airport. The next plane that could take him in the direction of Sudan was an Austrian Airlines flight to Athens, but he was forced to spend the night waiting in Vienna. Toward morning he managed to fall asleep, but he woke up an hour later and left for the airport.

JANUARY 5, 1985 – BEN-GURION INTERNATIONAL AIRPORT

This morning, Yehoshua went to Khartoum escorted by the Sudanese soldiers who have assisted him during the last six weeks. On coming down from his hotel room, he passed by the newspaper stand. In a locally published English-language newspaper, he saw a photo of an Israeli soldier hugging a young Ethiopian girl. Yehoshua felt as though a sword had pierced his heart and despair overwhelmed him. At that moment, he believed that the fate of those remaining in the camps was sealed. Weariness swept through his whole body. All he wanted to do was to sleep – to sleep and never wake up again.

Meanwhile in Israel, the last immigrants of Operation Moses arrived today – 214 in number. They were nearly all brought during the night from Kessela, the last camp holding Jews whose turn it was to go to Israel. This happened on instructions from Yehoshua's Sudanese liaison, in response to Yehoshua's request to get the people out of Kessela. They, like those who came before, are so thin that we fear for them. Even while embracing them, we cannot prevent our thoughts from turning to those still left behind. Will they ever manage to get out? What is going to happen to them now?

Jerry Weaver arrived in Athens in the afternoon and went straight to the American embassy. He wanted to get on a flight to Khartoum as soon as possible, but instead of giving him a flight ticket, the security officer called him in and told him that because of security problems, there was a ban on traveling to Khartoum. Ignoring these instructions, Jerry made contact with his friends in the Muhabarat and reserved a seat on a flight to Khartoum on January 8. Now he has to kill time until his flight, which is no easy task for a man like Weaver for whom sitting around twiddling his thumbs is the hardest thing of all.

General view of the Gondar region, Ethiopia, April 1984

A Jewish woman winnowing grain, Woleka, Ethiopia, 1984

Beta Israel girl carrying water in a special jug from the well, Woleka, Ethiopia, 1984

Jewish family in front of their hut, Woleka, 1984

Kes Tsegaye Beyene and behind him Kes Abebe Birhan,
Woleka, Ethiopia, 1984

Beta Israel members selling clay artifacts in the local market, 1984

Woman grinding teff (an Ethiopian grain) on a grindstone outside a hut

A *mergam gojo* (menstruation house)

Young Ethiopian Jew displaying pictures of relatives in Israel

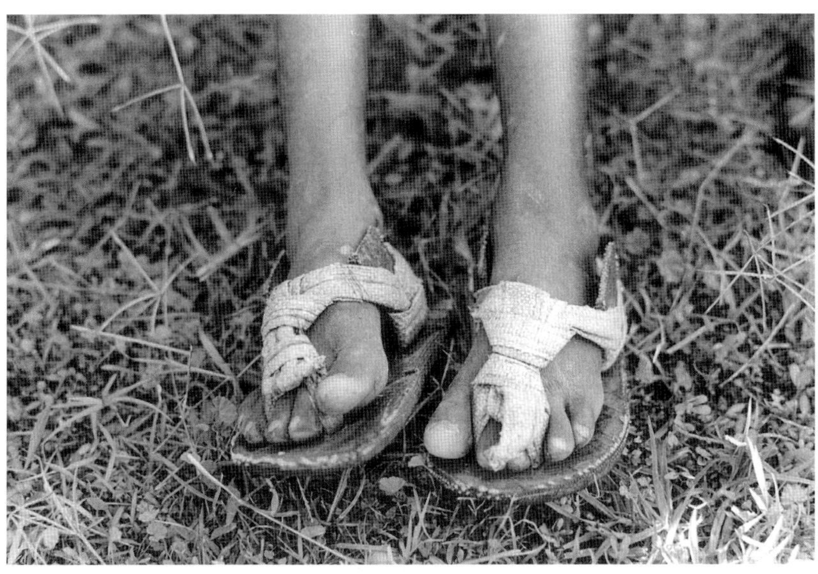

Sandals in the absorption center for immigrants of Operation Moses, after arrival from Sudan, Ashkelon, Israel, 1984

Reunion of brothers from Ethiopia who came in Operation Moses, at the absorption center in Ashkelon, 1984

Jewish children from Ethiopia on arrival at the absorption center in Ashkelon, 1984

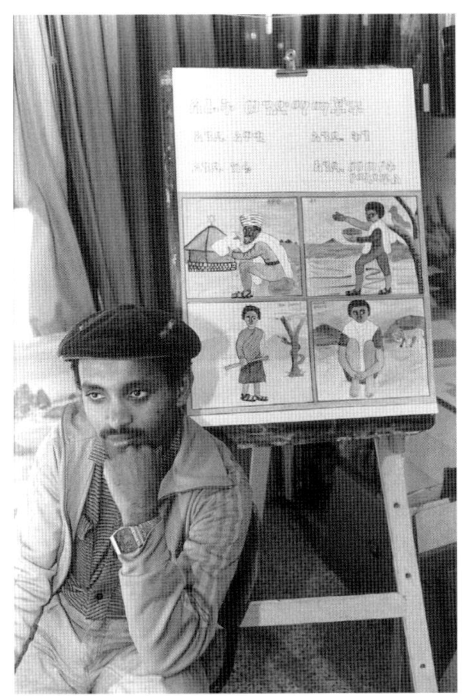

Painter Alemu Eshetie, Herzliya, Israel, 1980s

Registration of a new Beta Israel immigrant who came in Operation Moses at the absorption center in Ashkelon, 1984

New Beta Israel immigrants before changing clothes at the absorption center, Ashkelon

New Beta Israel immigrants after changing clothes at the absorption center, Ashkelon

New immigrant from Ethiopia, Jerusalem, 1984

Liat (on right) and her friend are crying after the many years of separation from their parents, Givat Washington, Israel, 1985

An absorption center in Pardes Hanna, Israel, 1985

Demonstration of Ethiopian Jews in front of the Chief Rabbinate, Jerusalem, 1985

Operation Moses: a young Beta Israel child

Demonstration of Ethiopian Jews in front of the Chief Rabbinate.
Jerusalem, 1985

JANUARY 6, 1985 – THE JEWISH AGENCY OFFICE, TEL AVIV

In Israel and everywhere else in the world, the fears are mounting for those who remain in Sudan. It's not certain how many there are – some say a few hundred while others claim it's several thousand.

On its front page today, under the headline, "Fears for the Fate of the Lost Jewish Tribe,: *Ma'ariv* has published Washington's official response: "If Israel had kept silent for one more month, it would have been possible to rescue all the Ethiopian Jews." Later in the article, one of the immigrants' leaders is quoted as saying, "There are some people in Israel who will be glad that this aliyah has ceased. It's a disaster. A terrible tragedy." I am trying to keep calm, but I am swept into the Beta Israel's pain. They feel so cheated.

Meanwhile, the truth has come to light. It wasn't Dominitz, but Arieh Dulzin, the chairman of the executive of the Jewish Agency, who first spoke publicly about the operation. His words were reported in the international press in December, when he was quoted in the *New York Times* and the *Boston Globe*. In fact, Dominitz has been the victim of a press conspiracy. What he said in an off-the-record background briefing was printed at the beginning of this month in a small, local publication – *Nekuda*, the settlers' periodical – and the next day became the main headline in a mass circulation newspaper. This flagrant disregard for the ethical pact that the media have traditionally upheld, to honor and not reveal off-the-record remarks, cost human lives. And for what? The "scoop," circulation? Their guilt is great, indeed.

JANUARY 8, 1985

The plane that brought Jerry to Khartoum later carried Yehoshua on his way home. The two did not meet; they are each wary of being seen together after the premature publicity about the operation.

When Jerry landed in Khartoum, no one was waiting for him from the American embassy. But while he was waiting for his baggage, he unexpectedly felt a hand on his shoulder. It was the head of the security services in the region, a good friend of his. They hugged each other and when the two of them sat down in the rundown restaurant of the airport, Jerry asked his friend the question that was to be expected under the circumstances, "What does the old man say?"

"Nothing."

"What does that mean?"

"It means that Numeiri, our president, is not upset. The only thing that he wants is for all the Jews to leave Sudan."

Jerry had not expected this reaction. He had expected to find people angry, desiring revenge for foreign interference in a Sudanese national issue. "Don't worry. I'll make sure that all the Jews leave soon," Jerry concluded the conversation, and proceeded to the embassy. In his head, he was already working out a plan to rescue the Jews still remaining in the refugee camps.

JANUARY 9, 1985 – TRANSITION AND PLACEMENT CENTER OF OPERATION MOSES, ASHKELON

Perhaps history is mocking us; two bitter adversaries have landed at Ben-Gurion Airport on this very same day. On one plane, Gedam flew in, together with another forty-two activists and their families, while Yehoshua arrived on another flight.

When they met, their inner emotions showed clearly on their faces. Yehoshua is angry with just about the whole world because he was prevented from completing his mission. In his first report to his controllers, he said that in his opinion about two thousand Jews still remain in Sudan, including the *bariya* – the slaves and their offspring.

Gedam and his people arrived at the King Saul Hotel, where an unpleasant reception awaited them – to put it mildly. This was the first time I'd seen Gedam for myself. When he entered the hotel lobby accompanied by his minions, some of whom are his relatives and some of whom are his adjutants, several of the counselors who were still on duty there confronted him. They would gladly have strangled him. Gedam didn't show any sign of fear, but somehow I felt it incumbent upon me to step in before tempers flared higher. I asked the counselors to assemble immediately in one of the adjoining rooms where, after they were all seated, I asked for an explanation of what was going on.

All the simmering fury built up in the community over the years boiled over when they saw these tyrants of the camps, these corrupt men who gratified their own whims and lusts, who possessed the power to sentence to life or death, who seized any beautiful girl against her will and even those betrothed or married to another. The counselors' chief spokesman, Desalign, rose. He didn't raise his voice, but his words were spoken with a hatred the like of which I had never heard before in my life, "These people, and most of all Gedam, only thought about themselves. They debauched themselves in the bars day and night; they dishonored our sisters and wasted our money. They are guilty of the deaths of thousands of our people. They had the means of rescue, but instead they stole the money that Israel sent for the Jews. Their suitcases are full of money and of gold."

The atmosphere in the room became ever more enraged, with some of the counselors ready to go out and avenge the blood of their brothers then and there. Clearly, I had to act quickly. Suddenly I had an idea how to defuse the situation. I thought of Desalign's last words, "Their suitcases are full of money and of gold." I soothed the irate counselors, saying, "I understand your anger and your desire for vengeance, but what good will that do us? You claim that Gedam and his people stole the money that we sent for the Jews in Sudan and it's in his baggage. So, okay, I'm going to confiscate the suitcases."

I quickly got up and went into the hotel lobby. The luggage of Gedam and his people was just being unloaded from the bus. I stopped them from claiming their belongings and instructed that the baggage be loaded into one of the vans that are at our disposal. Gedam tried to object but, perhaps because of the fury in the faces of the counselors, he gave up the attempt. I sent the immigrants to their rooms and the counselors back to work. I came to an agreement with Avi that tomorrow Gedam and his people will be dispersed to every corner of the country, wherever they have relatives. Then I personally transferred the suitcases to the absorption center's storage room in Ashkelon. After tempers have cooled, it will be possible to return their possessions to them.

And now, after the immediate danger has passed – at least for now – it is possible to prepare the final figures. We needed the help of Haim Halachmi who, even during the time of greatest pressure, insisted on maintaining an exact registration of the number of arrivals. It is apparent that within the last six weeks, the number of Ethiopian Jews in Israel has almost doubled. As of November 21, 1984, there were 7,088 Jews of Ethiopian origin in Israel. In the last few weeks another 6,870 have arrived, of whom 6,364 came on TEA flights, 475 on other flights via Europe, and 31 direct from Ethiopia.

A tremendous amount of work is now in store for us, especially with those whose relatives are buried in Sudan. The appalling facts strike us again: every family lost at least one of its members in the refugee camps, not to mention the permanent psychological damage to girls who were raped or given against their will to those in positions of power, and the harm suffered by children who worked twelve hours a day in order to support their parents.

I have now been working with the Beta Israel for almost two and a half years and it seems to me that the community possesses latent strengths that are perhaps not to be found in other groups. I believe that in spite of the terrible experiences that have marked each and every one of them, they will eventually succeed in overcoming them. But we should not be surprised if the weak falter, and therefore, we have to be ready to give particular care to all those in need.

JANUARY 13, 1985 – CLASSIFIED LOCATION

In a meeting that took place in a classified location, Yehoshua gave an extensive report on his work and his operators gave his achievements the praise they so richly deserve. At the meeting a cable from Jerry Weaver was read in which he reported on the condition of those remaining behind. According to him, the people are broken and have lost all hope of being rescued, but they have the means of subsistence.

Regarding the number of Jews still left in Sudan, an argument arose between Zimna and Yehoshua. Zimna agreed with the number given by Jerry in his cable – six hundred – while in Yehoshua's estimation, there are around two thousand people. The actual number is of crucial importance, since we could evacuate six or seven hundred by ourselves in two air operations, but if indeed there are two thousand, then only the Americans are capable of getting them out. In the end, Yehoshua's opinion was accepted, since he has just returned from Sudan. We subsequently agreed, despite Zimna's opposition, to apply to the Americans and request their assistance to get the Jews out of Sudan.

MARCH 22, 1985 – THE VACATION VILLAGE OF VA'AD L'MA'AN HACHAYAL (THE ASSOCIATION FOR THE WELLBEING OF SOLDIERS), ACRE

According to foreign press reports, sixteen gray Hercules planes bearing the symbol of the US Air Force have landed at the Ramon Air Base in the Negev. Our air force personnel, who were observing events, could not believe the quantity of equipment and supplies that was unloaded from the planes. There was the best of everything, starting from prepared meals and drinks of every kind and ending with enough spare parts to meet the needs of our Air Force for a whole year – and all this for an operation lasting only a few hours.

We have recruited sixteen translator/counselors who will act as liaisons between the Americans and our own staff with the *olim*. The Jews in Sudan have been assembled by the Sudanese in accordance with an agreement reached with Jerry Weaver. Toward morning, the planes took off, but only six of them landed in Sudan. Another three circled in the air and returned empty, while the other seven did not take off at all. It turned out that Zimna and Jerry were right in their estimate of the numbers, and that only several hundred Jews were left in Sudan. In the end 494 new immigrants landed at Ramon Air Base, and were bused from there to the vacation village in Acre.

When they got out of the buses, we saw immediately that most of them were much darker than other Ethiopian immigrants and had Negroid features similar to the natives of Kenya or Nigeria. When I called Zimna's attention to this fact, he said, "You remember I told you about the *bariya* – the slaves that were brought from southern Ethiopia, from among the black tribes. These people have been converted according to Ethiopian Jewish rites, then, after the ceremony, they were each given a new first name, and, instead of their father's surname, they were given the name of their master. And so, their past was rubbed out and they started a new life."

I have to admit that I don't understand how a person rubs out his past and becomes a new person when he is already an adult, but Zimna told me this in such a decisive way that I have to accept it.

While I'm still watching the group, I see another group of immigrants, originally from the Tigre region, who spent many years in Sudan. They did not make aliyah within the framework of Operation Moses, but now they, too, are here with us. Tigre is one of the northern regions of Ethiopia and the language spoken there is called Tigrinya. The Jewish communities in Tigre and Gondar developed separately and Tigrean Jews claim that those from Gondar received more assistance. That may indeed be true, but it was not done out of any deliberate intention to discriminate. Quite simply, the access roads into Tigre are more difficult and dangerous than those into Gondar. However, it is not clear why refugees from Tigre were not included in the original framework of Operation Moses.

As evening approaches, Zimna tells me that in the next few days another 106 *olim* will be arriving via Europe and then only a few dozen will remain in the refugee camps in Sudan. If we add the number of those who arrived today to those who are en route, we reach a nice round number – six hundred – which is the exact number that Zimna and Weaver cited when Operation Moses came to its abrupt end.

At night, alone in my room, I am desperately tired. It is as though the strenuous labor of over thirty months is crushing me in one fell swoop. This has been the most intense period of my whole life and though absolutely exhausted, I am exhilarated by the part I am playing in the absorption of Beta Israel. My hope is that someday I will see all the Jews from Ethiopia – each and every one of them – here in Israel.

Part Three

A Living Bridge

SEPTEMBER 5, 1985 – THE JEWISH AGENCY OFFICE, TEL AVIV

Today we learned that hundreds of immigrants from absorption centers all over Israel went to Jerusalem yesterday in order to demonstrate opposite Hechal Shlomo, the seat of the Chief Rabbinate, against its rulings.

My heart is with the *olim*. I understand their outrage at the Rabbinate's demands for a *hatafat dam brit*, "drop of the blood of the covenant" (as a symbolic re-circumcision) and for immersion, in order that they should be considered as full Jews by the religious establishment. It is especially difficult for me to come to terms with the demand for a drop of blood. I imagine how it would be if some rabbi were to come to me and say, "*Nu*, pull it out of your pants." And I – thunderstruck – pull it out and he gives it a painful jab. The physical pain would disappear, of course, but the mental trauma would remain forever.

I want to be with them, to express my solidarity, but Ora Donio, the director of the welfare services division in the Immigration and Absorption Department of the Jewish Agency, has imposed an absolute ban on any meeting with those on strike. At the present moment, she has not said anything else on the matter, but all the same, if the strike continues for long, I will go up to Jerusalem.

SEPTEMBER 15, 1985 – OPPOSITE HECHAL SHLOMO, JERUSALEM

It's only now, ten days after the strike started, that the striking Ethiopian immigrants have caught the attention of the general public with photographs of the strikers – elderly people with sad eyes – on the first page of *Ma'ariv*. Today is the eve of Rosh Hashanah, the New Year, and I feel I must go to encourage the strikers despite the ban that was placed on our doing so. I drive up to the capital. At first, I just drive past the strikers, hoping not to be recognized. Out of the corner of my eye, I see the *kessoch* assembled beneath one of the trees opposite Hechal Shlomo, and impulsively, I reverse the car and park it near the site of the demonstration.

Now I am with them. I feel like a thief in the night because I have been forbidden to be here. But I don't care. To me it's important that the *olim* know that I identify with them. Some of them are pleased to see me and greet me with bright faces, but there are some, especially the youngsters, who toss out at me, "Where have you been? We've been here for ten days already!"

I don't get into an argument and I go to the *kessoch*. They greet me with kisses and I sit down among them, feeling that I belong there with them. Kes Eshetu Mihret, from Ashdod, places his hand on my shoulder and says, "It's good you came, it's good that you are here."

After an hour, I'm ready to depart. After all it's the eve of Rosh Hashanah, but something holds me back, preventing me from leaving. Maybe I ought to spend the festival with them. Nevertheless, when I get up to go, I see that some sort of meeting is being organized. I see Addisu Messele and Moshe Rahamim. They are busy and don't spot me. The people are standing up and conversing in Amharic. I gather that they intend to bring all the children from the absorption centers and start a hunger strike. Using a particularly loud tone of voice, I interrupt, saying, "*Shalom*. This strike of yours is also my strike. I agree that you certainly have the right to strike, but please don't involve the children in it."

I wanted to add a few more words, but Addisu attacks me. "You! Who gave you the right to interfere? Who invited you to come here at all?"

I impulsively say that the *kessoch* are the people who invited me (even though they didn't), and I begin to make my way toward them. But those same *kessoch* who received me with such warmth a short time ago turn their backs on me, shaking their heads in denial when Addisu asks them if they did, indeed, invite me. I leave the area. Someone else calls out a hasty greeting to me and I wish him a good year, but I don't dare raise my eyes. The tears begin only when I am sitting in my car. I am cut to the quick by the insult. Apparently, in spite of my love and our long, close connection, I still don't fathom the mentality of the Ethiopian Jews.

OCTOBER 3, 1985

Yesterday, exactly one month after its start, the strike of the Ethiopian Jews opposite the Chief Rabbinate ended. The strike has proved effective and the Rabbinate has moderated its demands. But it is hard for me to believe that Ethiopian Jews are going to be able to marry and divorce like other Jews.

I am full of admiration for these *olim*, who sat quietly for a whole month opposite the Chief Rabbinate. It would seem that one can also win a strike by doing it their way. However, the embarrassing encounter twenty days ago still rankles. I wonder how my next meeting with the *olim* will be, especially my next meeting with the *kessoch*.

NOVEMBER 21, 1985 – BEN-GURION INTERNATIONAL AIRPORT

It's as though history is mocking us, again. Exactly one year ago we received the first plane of Operation Moses, with 283 immigrants aboard, while today only two immigrants arrived from Addis Ababa. During Operation Moses, almost seven thousand *olim* arrived in Israel and when it was over, the population of Ethiopian Jews in Israel had doubled. Meanwhile, since Operation Queen of Sheba, which the Americans implemented in March of this year, only 105 immigrants have arrived, all members of "important," long-settled families who have some connection with American organizations. When the aliyah operations were over, we thought that our main occupation would be the immigrants' absorption problems – problems of housing, employment, and education –

but the question of aliyah still hovers over every meeting we have with the *olim*, except when the conversion problem sometimes takes precedence.

There are many cases of youngsters who arrived during or before Operation Moses who come to my office and tell me, with tears in their eyes, that they are abandoning their studies in order to work and earn some money to send to their parents in the villages of northern Ethiopia. When they arrived in Israel a year ago, these kids were debilitated from hunger. When they arrived at the Youth Aliyah boarding schools, it seemed they had reached a haven to rest and feel safe. At long last, they would have regular meals, excellent medical care and the most important thing of all for them: a proper place in which to learn. For most of them, it was their first opportunity to study in a school.

In my visits to the boarding schools, especially in the absorption centers for youth in the north of the country, it is difficult for me to identify these children with those skeletons we received a year ago. Their clothes are clean, their faces are healthy, but their eyes – alas, their eyes are still so sad. And the eyes tell the true story. Two years ago they set out on their weary trek. Their parents said to them, "Go to Sudan. From there you'll reach Jerusalem. And soon, we, too, will arrive." And now, a year after the rescue and perhaps two years since they left their villages, many of the kids cannot concentrate on learning.

A few days ago, a boy came to my office and showed me a letter from his father. The father wrote, "My dear son, you know how happy we are that you have reached Jerusalem, but sadly, our situation here is very difficult. This is the second year that there is almost no rain and so we are on the verge of stravation." Then, toward the end of the letter, the father writes, "Our neighbor, Avraham, received a letter yesterday from his son in Jerusalem and there was fifty dollars in it. Have you forgotten us? Are we not your parents?"

A youth of about fifteen who receives a letter like this one is devastated. Such a boy cannot go on sitting in the classroom. He forsakes the Garden of Eden that he has at long last reached and is transformed from a student in school into a porter in the wholesale market or a laborer in agriculture, working from morning to night, so that he, too, can send a little money to his parents.

I was visited in my office by a girl who is studying in the boarding school at Givat Washington near Ashdod. With sobs racking her whole body, she showed me a letter she received from her parents, after she had sent her family a photograph of herself on the boarding school's lawn. And what does her father write? Not words of encouragement to pursue her studies, but rather, "I see that you have settled down well there in Jerusalem, you already have a car and a beautiful home. Have you forgotten us, your parents in the village in Ethiopia?"

This girl, too, like other youngsters, told me that she intends to leave the boarding school, even though she knows that by doing so, she is, in fact, throwing away the key to advancement in life. If I did not know the Ethiopian culture, I would be angry at parents who are capable of writing such letters to their children. If it were me, I would starve rather than write letters like that to my own children. In our culture, the child is positioned at the center. But in the Ethiopian culture, the central figure is the elder, the *shmagelie*. He is society's and the family's focus of concern. The child has to worry about his parents, and not the other way around.

So now, just when these children are benefiting from life's blessings – lessons, food and clothing – their conscience attacks them. If the boys were still in the villages, it would be they, and not their fathers, who would be following the plow harnessed to two bulls and furrowing their land, while the girls – not their mothers – would be grinding the millet into fine flour, and it would be they, and not their mothers, who would be carrying the water jugs on their backs from the river.

I understood these youngsters' distress, but I could not agree to their giving up their studies. So I went to Ami Bergman of the American Jewish Joint Distribution Committee (JDC) and together we set up a sophisticated system to assist Jewish families in Ethiopia. Before then, JDC was assisting forty families, while

Haim Halachmi, of HIAS, was helping another seventy families – usually relatives of old-timers in Israel who had arrived in the seventies and at the start of the eighties. But now the demands from the immigrants have increased and there is definitely a need to send assistance to hundreds, perhaps even thousands, of families.

Ami decided to lay some of the responsibility on Kobi Friedman, a young, energetic, rather noisy social worker. With him, we recruited two more people from among those Ethiopian immigrants who made aliyah two years ago – Asnakew Sendeke and Yosef Zevadia – both of whom had graduated from Kfar Batya in the fifties and had gone back to Ethiopia, where they taught in the largest Jewish village in the Gondar region, Ambober. They were both given the job of writing letters on different kinds of paper, using different pens, and dealing with different subjects, sometimes addressed to "My dear brother," and sometimes to "My dear father," or "My dear parents." The contents were usually, "I am happy to be sending you a little money…" and so on.

These letters were transferred to England and the USA. Then, after fifty-dollar checks were attached to them, they were sent to Jewish families in Ethiopia. Some of the Jews receiving the letters were not asked to acknowledge receipt because they lived in remote villages. This meant we did not know whether or not the money had reached its destination. And meanwhile, a growing number of complaints were received in my office that no money had been attached. At the same time, pressure mounted from other youngsters wanting to assist their families. Since it's impossible to transfer assistance in this way to over one thousand families, Ami has made contact with a Swiss company that has been given the job of transferring a standard letter to Ethiopia, written in English and Amharic, stating, "Your relative has asked us to transfer fifty dollars to you. This money is waiting for you in the branch of the Commercial Bank of Ethiopia in Gondar. Please confirm receipt of this sum in the attached postage-paid envelope."

Perhaps in this way we will manage to assist the Jews who remain in Ethiopia, as well as the youngsters who made aliyah and feel it is their duty to help their parents and relatives even at the cost of damaging what they cherish so dearly – education.

JANUARY 13, 1986 – IN AN ETHIOPIAN AIRLINES PLANE

My heart is pounding. For the first time in my life, I am in Ethiopian skies. A plane of Ethiopian Airlines is taking me from Nairobi to Addis Ababa.

Four days ago, exactly one year after Operation Moses ended, I left for Nairobi. My trip to Ethiopia, which is part of a mission of the North American Conference on Ethiopian Jewry, was authorized by the head of the Jewish Agency's Aliyah Department, Chaim Aharon. Based in New York, NACOEJ is supported by contributions from all over the United States and is headed by the journalist Barbara Ribakove. It maintains a direct link with Ethiopian Jewry. I am anxious about what is likely to happen after we land as I do not yet have a visa for Ethiopia, though the organization's representatives have promised me that I'll get a visa on arrival.

My main objective will be to study the condition of the Jews in the villages and to act as a living bridge between them and their families in Israel. In order to do this, I am in possession of a great many greetings, as well as a little money, which I have been asked to deliver to relatives in Ethiopia. I've written them all down in Hebrew in my diary. I wrote the telephone numbers in *gematria*, using letters as numbers, which is also how I've noted the sums of money that I was asked to hand over to relatives. I feel like a secret agent setting out on a mission in a hostile country. I only hope I can carry out at least part of the mission that I have undertaken.

Looking down through the plane's window, I see villages – villages with round straw huts, and beside each group of villages, a round building with a shining roof, surrounded by trees. It must surely be the church.

The Ethiopian pilot makes a perfect touchdown, but my anxiety was justified because no visa is waiting for me at the airport.

For about an hour and a half, the drowsy woman clerk checks through heaps of paper, to see whether some kind of message has been received from the Ministry of Tourism. Eventually, I am obliged to deposit my Israeli passport and take in its place a slip of pink cardboard, as a sort of temporary ID.

I go by taxi to a hotel that has known better times but is still tolerable. At the entrance, one of the staff tells me that this hotel was the finest hotel in Addis Ababa forty years ago and it was not for nothing that it was given the name "Ras," which means "The Top." I set down my baggage in the room, pick up the new ID, take my encoded lists, and leave the hotel.

In Israel, when they were preparing me for this trip, they all warned me about the Ethiopian secret police and the many people it employs. So, contrary to my usual habits, I stop every so often in order to see if I am being followed. In spite of the warnings, I do not detect any sign of surveillance. I walk around the streets of Addis like an excited child, peeking into houses and being shocked by the poverty, the dirt, and the disease. There are beggars in the streets, some with twisted bodies, some walking on their hands, and children carrying their brothers on their backs. It is difficult to describe the painful sights that meet my eyes in the streets of the capital city. Yet in spite of it all, I feel affection for the city's inhabitants – people with bright, smiling faces – beautiful people entrapped in destitution and distress.

JANUARY 15, 1986 – GOHA HOTEL, GONDAR

We flew in a small, seventeen-seater plane to Gondar via Bahir Dar. Once again, from the plane's windows, I gazed down on the roofs of the round huts and the shining roofs of the churches. After landing on a dirt runway at a rural airfield where the villagers had brought their cattle and merchandise, we flew on to Gondar, a city of eighty thousand inhabitants, which was the capital of Ethiopia from the seventeenth to the nineteenth centuries.

The hotel in Gondar is built of local stone and the rooms were pleasant. We were given a very nice reception and felt welcome.

After putting our belongings in our rooms, we immediately set out for the Jewish village that is nearest to the city, Woleka. Within a few minutes, we left the asphalt road for a dirt road. There were children in school uniform walking to school, but when they saw us in our car, they turned back and started to run. It was only later that I understood the reason. They were Jewish children from Woleka who realized that we had come to visit their village.

It seemed to be a sleepy siesta time in the village, but when the sound of our vehicle was heard in the straw houses, the women came out and displayed their wares – sculptures with Jewish motifs – all along the route leading to the village.

Meanwhile, the children who had spotted us on the way in joined us. They greeted us in Hebrew. One girl with pigtails, big brown eyes, a very dignified walk, and just totally beautiful, put her hand in mine and went with me to the synagogue. On the way, she told me that she is the daughter of the *kes*, Abebe Birhan, who was visiting in Addis Ababa at the time, and that her name is Rivka.

I was not the only one with a companion. The others in our group were all accompanied by children speaking in Hebrew. The synagogue is the only stone building in the village. It has a tin roof with a *Magen David* (Star of David) on top. When we reached its courtyard, we found standing there – with burning eyes and a head-covering tied with bands of white cloth – the last of the Jewish monks of Ethiopia. In the past, there were many such monks. This came about when, four hundred years ago, a Christian monk converted to Judaism and introduced the concept of monasticism to Ethiopian Jewry. From that time, monks were at the forefront of Ethiopian Jewish life and have kept the religious flame burning. Until a few years ago, the monks lived in the Semien Mountains, but now this monk is the only one left. He is a *kes*, named Beyene Demoze. He received us very graciously and gave us his blessing with a nodding of his head, but he refused to shake the hand of anyone in our group.

There were mats strewn over the floor of the poor synagogue and there were a few benches along the walls. A simple table stood in the center and in one of the corners there was a small and simple holy ark. Through the sole window, the women, with their small children on their backs, peeped inside. The children who had escorted us to the synagogue stood in a line beside the table and started to sing. At first I didn't recognize the lyric, but after a few moments, I realized that they were singing – a little off key – "Mizareh Yisrael Yekabtzenu" (He who has scattered Israel will gather us in) – perhaps the most suitable song of all for this occasion. After hearing a few more of their songs, including "Hevenu Shalom Alekhem," we gave the children small gifts – notebooks, pens, and erasers – while the *kes* received several notes in local currency for distribution to the poor.

When we left the synagogue, the sculpture market once again came alive. Each one of our group bought a few sculptures and then we were on our way to the waiting car, accompanied by all the people of the village. We were already sitting in the car when someone knocked on my window and said in Hebrew, "I am Alebachew Asefa, the brother of Tova Meshesha. She lives in the absorption center in Netanya. Please tell her that I want to come to her." Then, his expression turning serious, he added another sentence that sounded as though it was carefully rehearsed in advance. "I want to make aliyah to the land of our fathers."

When the car started to move off, Alebachew ran after it as though he had something else to say and again knocked on the window. I opened the window and then he shouted with a deep, panting breath, "When?" I didn't know what to answer. "When the time comes, we'll inform you," were the words that slipped from my lips. The disappointment in Alebachew's eyes stayed with me for a long time. He was expecting a signal that it was time to leave for Sudan, but in Israel, I had been instructed not to even mention that name.

When we arrived back at the hotel, I could devote some time to the landscape seen from the hill on which the hotel stands. Right below the luxury hotel, Gondar was spread out before me. Its houses are fenced in without any order, the roofs are made of galvanized tin, and the trees in the yards are turning green. The columns of smoke, which rise up from the fires in the houses and the yards, join into one cloud that hovers over the city.

JANUARY 16, 1986 – GONDAR

This morning we went to two villages, Ateye and Aba Antonis. After an hour's drive on a dirt road going westward, we stopped beside a small village whose most prominent building is a kerosene-operated flour mill, but it is not actually operating because no kerosene has been available for a long time. It was a Christian village called Gerargye. Now, as I prepare this diary for publication, I am aware that it was a village of Christian converts.

Very suddenly, a Jewish man appeared before us. He led us on the twenty-minute walk to our destination, the village of Ateye. As we walked along, more and more Jews joined us, summoned by our escorts. When these escorts, who were mostly barefoot children, discovered that I speak Amharic, they started to ask me about their relatives in Israel. Even if I didn't know their particular relatives personally, I told them that they are all fine and satisfied in Jerusalem – in other words, in Israel.

I told the local people that I did not want our official escorts to discover that I speak Amharic and so, when someone comes near us, they should say one of two words: *shevet* (tribe) if the person is Jewish, or *goy* (gentile) if not Jewish. When we reached Ateye, we already had over a hundred escorts who had come hurrying down from their houses or the fields around. We got to the synagogue and again it was impossible to err. Just as in Woleka, it was the village's only large and imposing building. Standing and awaiting us were the majestic figures of the three elders who are the spiritual leaders of the village. By then, we were surrounded by a crowd of hundreds, some of whom rushed home in order to return with pictures of their loved ones who had succeeded in making aliyah during Operation Moses.

Over and over, I photographed mothers dressed in traditional garments and holding in their hands pictures of sons and daughters in one of the youth villages in Israel. I wanted to stay longer in the village, to sit down with the elders, to hear more about their condition than only my eyes could see, but the Ethiopian Ministry of Tourism guide pushed us onward. I did at least manage to write down the names of twenty-four families sending regards to their relatives in Israel. They were mostly parents, wanting to know about the well-being of their children. I also managed to transfer the money that I'd been given in Israel for relatives in the village. And it was all done while avoiding the eyes of the official escort, even though he had said that we could give the people as much money as we wanted.

From Ateye, we journeyed to Aba Antonis, stopping en route for a light meal. What we didn't eat we gave to people who chanced to be passing by on the road, who thanked us with deep bows.

A dirt road led us to a hill beyond which, on a higher hill, Aba Antonis is situated. I decided this time, even before we got there, not to go with the rest of the group but to concentrate on my own affairs – which included giving the money I'd brought and writing down greetings. I had run down the hill and already started to climb the hill opposite, while the rest of the group were still getting ready to go down the first hill. At the village entrance, I met an elderly *kes* who had come for medical treatment in Gondar and was using the opportunity to visit his niece in Aba Antonis. I spied him from afar, sitting on a rock at the village entrance like Abraham sitting at the tent entrance when visited by the three angels. I told him that I was from Israel and he immediately started to say the Shema prayer: "Hear O Israel, the Lord is our God, the Lord is One," and then added the sentence, "How goodly are thy tents, Jacob, thy dwellings, Israel." He said that he had learned these Biblical verses as a youth. Unfortunately, I could not tarry with him because the group was coming nearer and nearer and I still had many things to do. I begged the *kes*'s pardon, after writing down the names of his children and siblings in Israel whom he had asked about.

As is the local custom, one youngster carried my bag and another took my hand and led me to the synagogue. The *kes* who had the key had gone to a funeral in the village of Gayna, about four hours' walk away, and there was no chance of his getting back that day. We sat under the *succa* in the synagogue's courtyard and talked, with me busy writing down greetings most of the time and answering questions about the circumstances of relatives in Israel. I managed to record regards from twenty-five families in Aba Antonis for their relatives in Israel.

Once again, the guide started pressuring us, and again we didn't want to leave these brothers to whom we had so quickly become attached. We had only been there an hour, but it felt as though we had always known each other. It is truly amazing how people who look so different can feel such great closeness.

I remembered that my friend Rahamim Yitzhak's mother lived close to the synagogue. At the entrance to her home, we met another of her sons leading a cow from the pasture. He called to his mother, and a woman, elderly but still beautiful, appeared. I said to her in Amharic, "Your son in Israel sent me to you and asked me to tell you that everything is fine and he misses you."

Rahamim had spoken with me many times about his mother and had also mentioned that she adores coffee. When we were inside her home, I hugged her and she kissed me several times, as though I were her beloved son. He had been forced to flee from Ethiopia five years before when the ORT educational network, where he had a senior position, was closed down by the government. I then put some money into her hand and said, "Your son sent you this money so that you could buy coffee."

When the guide came to call me, I felt I was leaving a friend, so great was the warmth between us already. I silently prayed that one day I would see her in Israel. In the car, on the way back to the hotel, I did not join in the general conversation. My thoughts were still in the countryside with all the poverty and distress. In my thoughts, I was seeking a solution for these people's tremendous desire to make aliyah. I decided that on my return to Israel I would meet with everyone possible and that I would present my written report to anyone who could possibly do something so that these people might be with us.

JANUARY 17, 1986, FRIDAY – GONDAR, NORTHERN ETHIOPIA

In spite of our repeated requests, the security authorities have not agreed to permit us to visit Ambober, the largest Jewish village of all. Having no other choice, we have used the time for shopping and to tour the city. In the evening, we sat down for a formal Friday evening dinner and the Sabbath candles were lit. I made the Kiddush over the wine and again, as on similar occasions, I emphasized the words "in remembrance of the Exodus from Egypt." It is only at times like these that one can fully feel the significance of those words.

JANUARY 18, 1986, SHABBAT – WOLEKA, NORTHERN ETHIOPIA

We returned once more to Woleka, going immediately to the synagogue, where the prayers had already started. The cantor was Adane Mihret, the brother of Zehava Aragay, who was one of the first Ethiopian immigrants in Israel. Adane is also the grandson of the elderly *kes* of Woleka. The service was conducted in Hebrew with Adane leading the prayers, joined each time, according to a fixed sequence, by the other children and youngsters. When the Torah scroll was taken out of the holy ark, there was silence. The *kes* monk came to me and said, "You are from Jerusalem; you will read from the Torah." I couldn't refuse and the scroll was opened at the portion of the week, which was Bo, one portion after Va'erah, which was my bar-mitzvah portion. The Torah cantillation, which I had learned twenty-nine years before, came back to me. Excitement gripped me on reading the portion that recounts the last plagues of Egypt and the Exodus from Egypt. Many of those in the congregation who understand Hebrew were crying and I wept with them.

Strange things happen to me in Ethiopia. There I was, standing in the shabby synagogue at the heart of a village deep in Africa, and reading with black Jews about the Exodus from Egypt. For a moment, the thought crossed my mind that perhaps the Pharaoh in this week's portion is Mengistu Haile Mariam, the president of Ethiopia, who will not let these people go until the time comes that he, too, will be forced to allow them to leave for Israel.

When we made the Kiddush, many loaves of bread were offered to the elderly *kes*, Adane's grandfather. The day before Shabbat, every family prepares the special Sabbath bread – *berekete* – and it is presented to the *kes*. He blesses it, then distributes two pieces to every person in the community, not just the same bread to the family that brought it. To me, it tasted like ambrosia. The *kes* monk came over to me and said that having us here on this Sabbath gives him strength to carry on and he is most grateful to us. I wanted to shake his hand, but he refused to take it. Neither would he allow me to enter his small hut. I still don't understand why.

We parted from the people with heavy hearts. They accompanied us to the car, waving farewell. The children ran after us a long way, until we could no longer see them.

***

In the afternoon, we went down into Gondar to watch the Timket, the festival of baptism. The way this festival is celebrated in Gondar is famous throughout Ethiopia and people come from all over the country to take part in it. The multitude of celebrants emerges from all the city's churches, becoming a flood of humanity that twists and turns toward the river on the city's outskirts.

I also went along with the crowds. I did not want to be swallowed up in the mass but to stand out by doing things that would catch the attention of any bystanders who might be Jewish so they could approach me. I soon picked up two of the festival songs and even danced the celebration dances with the young revelers. And, sure enough, I was joined by one of Alebachew's brothers, who introduced himself to me by his Hebrew name, Natan. His Hebrew was excellent, almost without any foreign accent, and each time he smiled, his splendid teeth bedazzled. While we were still walking among the mass of holiday makers, Natan told me about the condition of the Jews and about their strong desire to make aliyah. He spoke of the assaults by the governor of Gondar, Major Melaku Tafera, who imprisons innocent people and even kills people with his own hands. I'd heard of Melaku from Asnakew's stories and, judging by the heat with which Natan described Melaku's atrocities, it was clear that he, like Asnakew, would be prepared to assassinate Melaku personally.

I wished I could take Natan with me to Israel, but obviously I had to part from him. After he had gone some distance, he turned around and cast a quick look at me, leaving me with the indelible memory of his brilliant smile.

JANUARY 20, 1986 – TANA HOTEL, BAHIR DAR, NORTHERN ETHIOPIA

We left Gondar today. It is difficult to tear myself away from these brothers, the beautiful, suffering, believing Beta Israel. Never have I packed so many experiences into such an incredibly short time. During the brief flight from Gondar to Bahir Dar, the pictures crossed my mind again of Rivka and each special person I have met. I want to pack them all up and bring them with me to Israel, but instead, I have to leave them all behind. I have made a vow that I will not forsake the community. I will work on their behalf until every last one of the Beta Israel leaves Ethiopia and arrives in Israel.

After we arrived in Bahir Dar, I went out to search for Beta Israel, but I did not find any.

JANUARY 21, 1986 – ADDIS ABABA

This morning, too, we didn't manage to find any Jews in Bahir Dar – not even one family. If I have the opportunity to return there, I'll make sure I'm furnished with addresses beforehand. This evening, after we got to Addis, I went with two of the Americans to the home of Hailu Desta. It was there that David Zevadia held his meeting with representatives of the Jews from the northern region at the end of 1983.

Hailu is about seventy-five years old, with hair that is still black though there is just a tiny frosting of white here and there. His eyes are perceptive and he looks like a man who acts wisely. He seemed particularly happy that I was there, perhaps because I spoke to him in German and knew about his connection with Dr. Faitlovitch. More than once he said, "I see that you know my history."

Another man and two women were present. The man was Kes Barkew, one of the *kessoch* of Ambober, the biggest Jewish village with the greatest number of Kessoch. The *kes*'s eyes glow and he speaks with passion. When food was offered, he did not touch it because of *kashrut* sensitivities. I parted from those gathered there with great goodwill, and again I feel as though I am abandoning them, especially the *kes*. Once again I vowed to myself that I will not rest until the last of the Ethiopian Jews is safe in Israel.

At the hotel, a welcome message was waiting for me: Hiwot, Asnakew's wife, has arrived in Israel.

JANUARY 26, 1986 – ON BOARD THE EL AL FLIGHT FROM NAIROBI

I have prepared a report on my visit to the proud Jews exiled beyond the River Sambatyon. I have written that in Ethiopia they do not feel the same kind of anti-Semitism as that known in Europe, but there is abject poverty and a strong desire to make aliyah. I hope that this report will reach the highest levels and, in the same way that we rescued the Ethiopian Jews from Sudan, we will likewise rescue them from Ethiopia itself.

I have so many greetings to pass on to relatives in Israel, I feel, indeed, like a living bridge between Ethiopia and Israel. At least, this is one task that is within my power to fulfill.

MAY 26, 1986

Today marks four months since I returned from Ethiopia and I have just been informed that I am to go again, sponsored by the same American organization that I went with last time. I am so excited about this that I have been telling everyone who chances to be passing by that I am going to Ethiopia again, and perhaps this time to other villages. Zimna brought me to my senses when he remarked that not everybody needs to know about my trip. I didn't quite understand what he was getting at, but I think he was afraid that too many people getting information about the Ethiopian aliyah might harm future operations. I promised him that I would keep it to myself from now on.

MAY 28, 1986 – THE JEWISH AGENCY OFFICE, TEL AVIV

Within two days, the rumors of my impending trip have spread throughout Israel. The Ethiopians have been coming to me – standing or sitting, on the benches and on the floor, young and old, filling the corridor outside my office. Because I understand their need and because I sincerely want to help, I have received them all. Some wanted to send greetings to their relatives, but most of them came with dollars in their hands. I have started to write down the details of the family members in Ethiopia to whom I have been asked to transfer money, as well as the greetings, and I have promised also to take photographs of the people there.

Once again, Zimna asked me to stop right then and there. I believe he was uneasy about my delivering money, fearing I could get into trouble if any of the people would later claim that I didn't deliver it, etc., but I decided that I had to transfer the money, having seen the terrible poverty with my own eyes.

JUNE 18, 1986 – AT HOME IN RISHON LEZION

The torrent of people coming to see me with requests for Ethiopia has swollen continuously in the last three weeks and the money that has been handed over to me is now over $8,000. It's a bit dangerous to wander around with such a sum, but I can't undo what has been done and the Ethiopian immigrants are depending on me to see that the money, which they have been at such pains to save, reaches its destination.

I have prepared a list of people according to their location and a list in *gematria* of the various sums of money, so that should my notebook fall into the wrong hands in Ethiopia, they will not be able to make anything of it because everything – including the sums of money – is written in Hebrew letters.

JUNE 22, 1986 – NAIROBI, KENYA/ ADDIS ABABA, ETHIOPIA

I have spent two days at David Siyum's apartment. He is an Ethiopian Jew who used to work as an agricultural counselor for ORT until he was forced to flee to Sudan. In 1981, he made aliyah and worked for the Jewish Agency. Since 1983, he has been the local representative of the American Association for Ethiopian Jewry (AAEJ) and assists with the departure of Jews to Israel. At eight o'clock this morning, I left Nairobi for Addis Ababa. The skies were gray and the reception at the airport in Ethiopia was also chilly. Again, no visa was waiting for me and I had to cool my heels for three hours until I was issued the pink ID card that I remember so well from my previous visit.

I have already had so many meetings with Jews here in the hotel, it's as though my arrival was announced on the news. I hardly have a minute to myself – I had just said good-bye to two sisters and another entire family was waiting to see me. One of Dr. Faitlovitch's students also came. It was he who told me that there are still thirty thousand Jews living in Ethiopia.

JUNE 24, 1986 – ADDIS ABABA

More and more meetings. The most painful of all was with Yeshi Moges, the wife of Moges Rahamim, who made aliyah three months ago. He had given me money for his wife and I was happy to pass it on to her. Yeshi is a beautiful woman. She was wearing her festive clothes, the traditional white garments and a scarf with purple embroidery on the edges. The whiteness of her clothing emphasized her lovely skin and the delicacy of her features.

"It's hard for me without Moges," she said. "The children miss him." I understood what she has been going through. I knew Moges from the absorption center in Lod. He is dark-skinned, almost black, with narrow lips and kind eyes that are a mirror of his heart. All I could do was to promise Yeshi that her case will be taken care of as speedily as possible. Although I have no authority in such matters, I will raise it with the Americans who are dealing with her aliyah.

JUNE 26, 1986 – ADDIS ABABA

A girl called Yealemwork Derso, a relative of Natan, my friend from the village of Woleka, told me that he is in Addis. I asked her to tell him to get in touch with me and then arranged to meet him at the main entrance of the Hilton Hotel, where I am staying. I met him there with one of the Americans in the group. Out of the corner of my eye, I saw a group of soldiers and decided to head in the opposite direction to avoid them.

We had walked about twenty meters away when Yealemwork came out of the shadows and joined us; immediately one of the soldiers called, "Stop!"

We stopped.

A soldier of the civil guard came up to us and said, pointing at Natan, "This man is dangerous. You have to watch out for him; I've known him for two months already." In communist Ethiopia, every person not known to the authorities, and especially someone meeting a stranger, was suspicious.

I answered innocently, "Okay, I'll watch out."

But the soldier stood there, repeating, "Dangerous."

And I stood my ground, repeating, "I'll watch out."

This was repeated at least five times and meanwhile the group of soldiers surrounded us. Suddenly, their officer came up to us and, without any word of warning, slapped Natan. His pain seemed to burn my own cheek – I felt as though I had received the blow. I said firmly to the officer, "Now listen, I'm a tourist here in Ethiopia and this man is my guest. I ask you not to harm him."

This initiative did what it was intended to do and the pompous officer seemed to shrivel. In order to preserve his dignity, he asked Fentahun/Natan to show him his identity card. After inspecting it, he spat out, just as the soldier had done, "Dangerous," to which I again responded, "I'll watch out."

And then the officer turned his attention to Yealemwork and after scrutinizing her, he asked me, "Do you know her?" I had no idea what he was planning to do, so I responded in the negative. The officer asked her for her ID, too, but she did not have it with her. The officer drew his conclusion, "To the police station!"

Once again, I took the initiative and surveyed Yealemwork from head to toe as if seeing her for the first time. After a short silence, I took the officer aside and, placing my arm around his shoulder as though wanting to confide in him, I said, "She's a beautiful girl. I want her for tonight." The officer responded immediately, "No problem: twenty birrs." I quickly pulled two ten-birr notes – less than five dollars – out of my pocket. And that was how I rescued the girl from prison and from certain abuse.

When I hugged her, I felt how she was trembling. She and Natan will have difficulties falling asleep tonight. How cheap human life is in this country.

JUNE 27, 1986 – WOLEKA, NORTHERN ETHIOPIA

I am back in Woleka and once again the same excitement suffuses me on hearing Hebrew songs being sung in the depths of Africa.

The children are truly special. They are so beautiful and so friendly. Once again, I felt that I am the bridge between these people and Israel, but this time I was as powerless as before, unable to answer the question repeated over and over: "When? How long? When can we finally make aliyah?"

In the afternoon, we drove to Aba Antonis. Many of the people there recognized me and, unlike the previous occasion, this time the *kessoch* were present in the village. Together with the village elders, they received us at the entrance to the synagogue, each wrapped in a *tallit*, and recited a prayer that I did not understand, as it was in Ge'ez.

Youngsters here are conspicuous by their absence. However, nearly all the village's inhabitants swarmed around me, asking about the welfare of their children, some of whom are known to me and some not. I said that all the children are fine. More than that, I decided to assemble all the people and asked them not to write any more letters describing how pitiful their condition is. I explained that these letters depress the children terribly and even make some of them want to stop their studies in order to work and send money to their parents. Truth to tell, it seems to me that the conditions in Aba Antonis are not so awful. The fields are plowed and some of the people own cows, bulls, and sheep.

Anyway, I have done what I could. I have given the money to the people in Woleka and Aba Antonis, but the real problem is not money but aliyah. I could not answer the question: When?

JUNE 28, 1986, SHABBAT – GONDAR, NORTHERN ETHIOPIA

Shaharit – morning prayers in the Woleka synagogue. Although we had a rabbi from the USA with us, the same Ethiopian youngster, Adane Mihret, stepped in front of the holy ark once again and lead the prayers, with the children gradually joining in. Their prayer shook my soul to the core.

After the Kiddush, we went out into the synagogue's courtyard. The whole village assembled, with the women carrying in their hands the *berekete* – the special bread for the Sabbath. The *kes*, who is Adane's grandfather, wanted to start distributing the bread, but another *kes* asked me to first read the portion of the week aloud while he translated it. It is the portion Beha'alotkha, and everything went smoothly. However, when we reached the part where Aaron and Miriam argued with Moses about the Ethiopian wife he had taken, the *kes* hesitated in some confusion. In retrospect, I think he did not want to touch on the question of a "mixed" marriage.

In the afternoon, we visited Aba Antonis again. Once more there was the same frustrating encounter with those wanting to know when they could make aliyah. They see me – a man from Jerusalem – as their savior, while I can only feel how little influence I have.

JUNE 29, 1986 – GONDAR, NORTHERN ETHIOPIA

This morning was exciting. This time, we received permission to visit the largest Jewish village in Ethiopia, Ambober. In addition to the guide and driver, there was an official security man with us. The road there is outstandingly beautiful, passing between lofty mountains, sometimes traversing rivers, but the most amazing thing of all is the location of the huts. Never in my life have I seen huts set on mountain heights in such isolated locations.

As we entered the village, we were received with greetings of "Shalom," and one of the children, Babu Barkew, the son of Kes Barkew, took my bag with all its envelopes full of money from relatives in Israel. At my request, he took me to his mother. We walked between two small huts to a relatively large hut, in front of which a cow was grazing and children were playing among the hens. After giving her the money that her children in Israel had sent, I mentioned the names of each of them in turn and said that they all were well. She embraced me and cried. I hugged her in return.

Ambober's synagogue is especially prominent because of its contrast with the straw huts around it. The walls are stone and on its high roof is a wrought-iron Star of David decorated with bells. The *kessoch* assembled and the official meeting commenced.

I used the opportunity to slip away to Avraham Kehati's home. Avraham went to Israel in the fifties as a youngster, studied there for some years, returned to Ethiopia and became a teacher in a Jewish school. In the early eighties, ORT was running all the Jewish schools in Ethiopia. When its activities were shut down by the government, the teachers who did not manage to escape were arrested and charged with spying for Israel. Avraham escaped to

Sudan and from there made it to Israel. His wife and children remained in the village. Her parents and siblings moved in to be with her. His whole family was happy to see me and to have the greetings I brought them from Israel. I decided to turn this house into my base for distributing the money I'd brought. Babu, my adjutant, became my runner, and, following my instructions, brought family after family. I quickly distributed the envelopes and passed on the greetings from relatives in Israel. I did not even have the time to share their joy. Within a half hour, I had given out most of the envelopes, but then an uninvited visitor entered. I had been warned about him back in Israel. Former Ambober residents said that when he was a child he used to steal pens and food from the other kids at school. He has not changed since and has turned into a government informer and collaborator.

I acted promptly. I grabbed the guy by his shirt collar, with my hand in a tight fist, brought his face close to mine, and rasped between my teeth, "If one hair falls from one person's head because they met me here, I'll kill you." I accompanied the last two words with a movement of my left hand on his neck. I felt his body shake, but I didn't leave it at that. When I had only one envelope left to give out, I went again toward the synagogue. The *kessoch* and the American guests were already on their way out. I asked Babu to show me the guy's mother and he pointed to a short, delicate woman.

She looked so fragile that for a moment I thought of abandoning my idea, but I didn't. I took her hand and pulled her inside the synagogue until she stood by the holy ark. Its *parokhet* (curtain) is brown and embroidered with an inscription in golden letters. I forced the woman to touch the *parokhet* and repeated what I had said previously to her son: "If one hair falls from one person's head because your son saw me with that particular person, I'll kill your son," and as I said this I repeated the threatening movement. I saw the horror in her eyes. I was not at all comfortable behaving in this way, but I know I did the right thing. I would soon be leaving, but the Jews would have to go on living here. And then, as we were departing, the same young man came to me to say that he always helps people. I told him that if that were true, my long arm would reach him, not in order to kill him, but in order to get him to Israel.

When the guide announced that we only had five minutes left before our departure, I remembered that there was still one envelope with money in my pocket. I asked those around where I could find the woman that the envelope was for. They pointed eastward, to the outskirts of the village, but somebody ran to call her. Often, a curious crowd gathers around us, but this time the opposite happened. When the woman approached, all the village people stood in a formation like two human walls between which the woman walked. Suddenly, the voice of one of the *kessoch* was heard behind me, telling the woman to stop. I wanted to meet her, but the *kes*'s hand stopped me. He instructed me to leave the envelope on the nearby stone and to go away. I did what he instructed and left the place, and all the village people went with me. With a sidewise glance, I saw the woman picking up the envelope and extracting the money that her son had sent her from Israel.

Babu, who was escorting me to the car, explained that she was in the menstruation house and for that reason separated from the rest of the village.

When we left the village, the children ran after us, skipping barefoot over the sharp rocks and waving their hands to us.

After a short picnic in the midst of the stunningly beautiful scenery of the Ambober region, we went to another village, called Kosheshelit. We walked for about half an hour, being greeted by wide smiles the whole way. The people of Kosheshelit seemed particularly pleasant.

Our route ended in the courtyard of the *kes* where four people were standing around the fire. One of them was wielding the bellows, while the *kes* himself – with the traditional white fez on his head – held some sort of tongs grasping white-hot iron, and two other people were striking the iron with hammers in a rhythm reminiscent of an Ethiopian melody.

When they saw us, they stopped their work. I shook the *kes*'s hand and felt how hard his palm was, the hand of a farmer, worker, and blacksmith. In Israel, *olim* explained that sometimes, in Ethiopia, Jews are referred to as "Buda." They explained to me how it reveals the Ethiopian form of anti-Semitism. It is a derogatory term, based on the Jews' traditional employment as blacksmiths. Their gentile neighbors are dependent on the Jews, who forge axes, scythes, knives, and even plows for them. But they also believe that the Jews' ability to forge tools from raw iron comes from Satan. Furthermore, they believe that the Devil also turns the Jews into hyenas at night and they then go out on expeditions to their Christian neighbors, to eat their souls. So, when a peasant is stricken by illness, he sometimes calls out the name of the Jew who ate his soul and that same Jew is then brought to the gentile's sick bed and asked to recite the incantation that will return the person's soul to him. In such cases, the Jew faces a tough dilemma – if he recites some sentences and the gentile recovers, it proves that he is a Buda, meaning that he has the power of the "evil eye," while if he says nothing and the gentile dies, he is likely to be killed. This is the Ethiopian form of anti-Semitism.

In the village of Kosheshlit, too, I handed over the money that I had received. I also gave a sum to the *kes* in order to finish construction of the synagogue that they started building a few months ago. The people of Kosheshlit are the poorest that I have seen up to now, but, for some reason, they also seemed to me to be the happiest.

JUNE 30, 1986 – GONDAR

Today, I had an extraordinary experience. While touring around the city, I asked the guide to take us to the market, which I have heard is extremely colorful. At the entrance to the market, a tall, thin man, about fifty years old, was standing. He had a gold tooth and a bald head. When he saw us, he said in Hebrew, "Shalom, I've been waiting for you. I walked for two days so that I would meet you at this time and in this place." My amazement must have shown clearly on my face, so he repeated his words, and said, "I knew you would come and so I waited for you."

"How could you know two days ago that we would be here today, this afternoon, if I didn't know it myself until two hours ago?"

"I knew," he said simply, without any further explanation.

His name was Mengistu Avraham and he was from the township of Benker, about forty kilometers north of Gondar. I felt ill at ease, as though someone were directing my footsteps and my fate, but books that I have read about Africa mention that such things do, indeed, happen here.

In order to ward off unwanted attention, we went into a Jewish house inside the market. There, Mengistu told me about the condition of the Jews in the area of Wogera and Semien. The seven thousand Jews who live there are quite cut off. Some of them even sold their possessions a year ago, but in the end they did not reach Sudan. They set off for the border but were caught by the Ethiopian military and forced to return. Now, they have neither homes nor land to farm and the government does not assist them in any way except to tell them to apply to world Jewry for relief. Mengistu also told me that since Operation Moses, the government has been restricting the Jews' movement because of suspicions that they are going to flee the country. A Jew who wants to go from his village to the neighboring village or to the market in the nearby town is unlikely to receive the permit that allows him to do so. Therefore, the Jews' condition has been made much harder. On the one hand, the government does not help them, but on the other hand, they are not allowed any freedom of movement even near home, much less the possibility of leaving Ethiopia.

Toward evening, we went for a last visit in Woleka and saw the same sight as on the previous occasions. The children once again clasped our hands, the adults asked about the welfare of their relatives, and we bought everything we could, in order to leave money behind in the village. When we were already seated in our car again, Alebachew, Natan's brother, came to the window and once again posed the same question that he had asked half a year before: "When?"

"I'll let you know when it is time," I replied.

But he would not let go. "When?"

The driver started the car. I opened the window but did not manage to answer, and I heard Alebachew calling out to us, obviously choked by tears, as he disappeared from our sight, "Don't forget us."

JULY 3, 1986 – ADDIS ABABA

Back in Addis, I used the time for a meeting with Kes Dawit. He lives in Zimna's former house, the same place that Zimna left twenty years ago when he decided to go to Israel. The house has seen better days. Its walls are now cracked, the roof is rusty, and the wooden floor is broken. I went inside. It was almost bare of furniture, with only empty spaces and, in one of the corners, a bed and a few broken chairs. A very old lampshade hung from the ceiling. The *kes* was lying on the bed. He is obviously sick and coughs ceaselessly. His wife was sitting beside him and in another corner, on the floor, his wife's niece sat with a barefoot girl next to her. Here, also, I handed over money that I had been given for them. At long last, I saw Kes Dawit smile. To encourage him, I promised to deal with his aliyah.

Evening had already fallen on Addis Ababa. The city's randomly scattered lights can be viewed from the crest of the hill where Zimna's house is situated. I left the house depressed because I felt that the *kes*'s end is near and that there is hardly any chance of getting his aliyah addressed quickly enough so that at least he will be buried in Israel.

I hurried off to pay one more call before leaving Addis and returning home. This visit was to Aba Getie, the father of David Zevadia, who was sent to Ethiopia three years ago in order to encourage the Jews to leave for Sudan. We reached a large iron gate and the home of a Christian called Kassa Gideon. Several Jewish families live on the lower floor of the house and the first person to receive us was Kes Barkew, who remembered me from my previous visit. He led us to Aba Getie's room. And there on the bed, with the covers pulled up over his head, lay Aba Getie, the man who bears the title *lika kahanat* – the head of the priests. Aba Getie is an expert on Ethiopian Jewish prayers and deeply versed in Torah. At the end of the fifties, he was chosen to be the community's representative to the emperor, Haile Selassie, to request lands for the Jews. However, he had to wait a whole year until he was received by the emperor. Now, he can hardly see and the lower half of his body is paralyzed. I sat beside him and held his hand for several long minutes. I tried to cheer him up, saying that surely his torments would soon end and he would reach Jerusalem.

I left there with a heavy heart, feeling helpless. Why is it impossible to take these old people to Israel and let them die in peace? What advantage does the Ethiopian government gain from a few more old people's lives in a land where people's lives have no value anyway?

On the way to the gate, some of the youngsters accompanied me, most of them Aba Getie's grandchildren. They arrived a few days ago from Sudan after they had despaired of any possibility of our bringing them on aliyah from there. I did not have time to learn about the present situation in Sudan from them and their only request was that we should not forget them. That same sentence has been repeated over and over in every place where I have been here: "Don't forget us."

No doubt that same sentence is written in each one of the three hundred letters that I am taking with me to relatives in Israel from the villages and from Addis Ababa. I placed the letters in the bottom of a cardboard box, packed on top with all sorts of souvenirs that I bought here. But of all my belongings, it was precisely this box that the security people at Addis airport decided to inspect. I was the first of the group and I was asked to open all my suitcases, including the box with the letters inside. The woman inspector stared at me with penetrating eyes. She picked up one of the letters and started to read it. A cold sweat broke out on my back and each passing second seemed like an hour. In the end, she put down the letter and said curtly, "You can close the box."

NOVEMBER 21, 1986 – THE JEWISH AGENCY OFFICE, TEL AVIV

Today marks two years since Operation Moses, and only a few of us remembered what happened on this date. But it was on this morning, of all mornings, that I found a letter on my desk from a young boy whom I remember particularly well because I drove him from Safed to Rishon Lezion when he arrived in Israel three years ago and we chatted a bit on the way. We enjoyed each other's company on that drive and I had promised myself – a promise I regret I didn't keep – to follow the progress of this chunky, talented youth.

And now he has done what I did not do – in a letter written in very creditable Hebrew for one so young and in the country for so short a time.

MONDAY, MARHESHVAN 8, 5747, NOVEMBER 10, 1986

To Micha,

Dear Micha, how are you?

Micha, you know all the problems of the Ethiopian immigrants, meaning that you are very close to them and you know all our problems, each of us one by one, since one has no parents and another one has no father and another has no mother, and yet another misses his brothers and sisters. All this happened because the families, or the parents and the brothers and sisters, were left during Operation Moses two years ago and more. And then lucky ones succeeded, and I also, as a child, succeeded in arriving here. On the other hand, my parents did not manage to make aliyah to the Holy Land, Eretz Yisrael, and so I too am one of the children without parents and without brothers and without sisters, and I am alone here. I only have cousins and several families who are alone like me. And I hardly have any help; you could say that I am managing almost by myself. But nevertheless, without help from someone nothing will happen, and that says something. And what I want is to ask you, at the Jewish Agency for Israel, to help my parents who are still in the land of gentiles in Ethiopia, and then I here will not feel that they are beside me, but that they have someone too. And if you can also refer me to someone else who is responsible for foreign affairs, that is to say if you cannot give me help for my parents, to refer me to someone else who will be able to help me. But I assume that you will accept my request, also because I do not have anyone else to apply to and so I am applying only to you. And also eight or nine months ago, I think, I asked help for my parents in the name of Yehudit, the social worker in my religious youth village, but no response was received. It seemed to me that you would receive my request, but to my regret no help has been received. And so I am now asking too, as a pupil who is learning in the Land of Israel while his parents are in the diaspora, and then you will help me with help for my parents, because my parents have no one helping them. And also, I, as a child who is studying here, cannot help them and I will also not be able to help them because I am studying. And if you help them, I will feel that I can study while they are not here in Israel, because they brought me up and they are flesh of my flesh, and they fed me and gave me water in the evening when I was thirsty and hungry and did in every way what was possible to do for raising a child, and on the other hand, I, the son, did not succeed in recompensing my parents, because I am an immigrant here and need to learn the language and also to know my new land, Eretz Yisrael. Because of this, I cannot help, and also, from the aspect of knowledge, I am little and will not be able to help them, and I ask you again to give me help for my parents who are still overseas in Ethiopia. (Thank you).

The person asking help: Shimshon Kebede
from: the Kfar Hassidim Religious Youth Village
Haifa 20494

I read this letter over again and decide that JDC's assistance network has to be improved, so that we can achieve a 100 percent success rate in the assistance we send to Ethiopia.

DECEMBER 1, 1986 – TEL AVIV

Today, the festival of the Segd is observed in Ethiopia, as well as in Israel. It is the unique festival of Ethiopian Jewry, based on chapters 9–10 of the Book of Nehemiah, which describes the renewal of the covenant between those who returned to Zion and their Lord. Most of the Jews – men, women and children – in Ethiopia celebrate it. They all assemble in the large villages and, dressed in festive garments, ascend to the peak of one of the mountains, in a long line, like a long, white snake. Those climbing carry on their shoulders or on the backs of their necks a stone, which is a symbol of their request for forgiveness. The *kessoch* lead, dressed in their robes of office and with the books of the Orit, the Torah of the Ethiopian Jews. The Orit is written on parchment in Ge'ez, the ancient Semitic Ethiopian language, and is bound in pages, rather than rolled like a Torah scroll. The books are carried on boys' heads and they are guarded from the sun's rays by parasols that are interwoven with golden thread. At the designated place on the mountain top, the *kessoch* stand, with the people standing below them, and they pray to the God of all living creatures to expiate their sins.

Everyone present feels the sanctity of the day. The people all fast and ask from the King of All Flesh that He renew the days of Ezra and Nehemiah – the time when the exiles returned from Babylon and the Covenant between Israel and God was renewed. The whole community asks for pardon and calls upon Him to redeem them from their agonies and to take them up to the Holy Land.

I was longing to be there in Ethiopia, to celebrate this major festival with those who remain there, but here, too, I did not join the celebrants because I do not want to get involved in the argument that has broken out among the *kessoch*. Those who identify with the Rabbinate are celebrating at the Western Wall while their opponents, who are being organized by the Beta Israel Organization, are celebrating the festival in Talpiot, which was chosen because it has the best view of the site where the Temple once stood.

DECEMBER 26, 1986 – RAMAT RACHEL GUEST HOUSE

Today it is possible to sum up this year's aliyah and the numbers are depressing. A total of only 207 *olim* arrived from Ethiopia during the whole year, all of them via Addis Ababa and most of them, again, with the assistance of American organizations that operate in the field. The condition of the youngsters who have been separated from their parents is especially difficult, but we do not have the resources to assist with family reunifications. We have such a limited presence, at this time, in both Ethiopia and Sudan that all we can do is to send assistance and collect data about those who remain in Ethiopia.

For the last month, I have been engaged in a census of those still in Ethiopia. Since I have visited the villages in the Dembia region and know some of the Jews there, we decided to start with that area. This morning, toward the end of the census of that region, a problem came up that I was not aware of before. One of the elderly men, who had been invited to the guest house to augment our information, used the term *Felesmura*. Heavy silence fell. Some of those seated around the table lowered their eyes, as though someone had uttered a dirty word.

Working on the survey with me is Yair Feuer, a staffer of the Ministry of the Interior. For the last three years, he has been monitoring the community – in fact, devoting all his time to it. To him, too, this was a completely new expression. I asked what it meant. After some hesitation, one of those present started off by saying, "Felesmura means a convert to Christianity." I had read in Faitlovitch's book *Journey to the Falashas* about his meetings with the apostates, but this was the first time that I had heard the term *Felesmura*, which is the usual name by which Ethiopian Jews designate their relatives who have changed their religion.

In recent generations, there have been many cases of conversion. The Christian missionaries were very active among the Jews even in the last century and won over many souls, mainly in the Dembia area. The question arose whether the converts should also be registered in our census. Even though it is, after all, only a census, there is no doubt that a decision on this matter will have significance. I asked those there to concentrate only on the Jews remaining in the region and not to register the converts to Christianity, since, in the census of the Jews of Ethiopia in the seventies, the converts were not registered. In addition, the aim of the census is to determine exactly whose aliyah has to be our concern in the coming years, and obviously the Law of Return, which automatically gives Israeli citizenship to Jews making aliyah, will not apply to converts.

Just when I was leaving the office, a tiny man appeared whose whole appearance was so diffident and self-effacing that he almost seemed to be saying, "Don't bother about me. I don't want to disturb a busy man like you." Apologetically, he asked if he could speak with me in private. I sat down opposite this visitor, who appeared to go on shrinking in front of my very eyes, and he proceeded to tell me one of the most shocking stories I ever heard in my life.

His name was Mirkuzie Worku and he was from Upper Nazareth. He left a married daughter behind in Ethiopia. She recently sent him a letter that he was now holding in his trembling hand. In the letter, the daughter wrote that one morning people whom she had never seen before came to her house. It so happened that at the time, she was alone with her children, including her eldest son, a boy of ten years old. Her husband was working in a field an hour's walk away. The strangers grabbed her son and left. The woman ran after them shouting for help, but none of the neighbors paid heed to her cries and the child disappeared right in front of her eyes. Now she does not even know where they took him.

I asked Mirkuzie if his daughter is rich, thinking perhaps the kidnappers wanted a ransom for him. A weary smile glimmered on his face, "No. My daughter and her husband are not rich. They barely have enough to exist on. Their son was kidnapped by the gentiles because they fear that after all the Jews leave, there will be no more blacksmiths left, because, after all, that is the Jewish profession."

"And what good is a ten-year-old boy to them?"

"You and I know that he won't be any good to them at all, but they believe that all the Jews have connections with Satan and it is he who gives them the ability to forge iron. They don't understand that the profession has to be learned. So the Christians call us by derogatory names such as *Buda*, meaning 'people of the evil eye.'"

With tears in his eyes, Mirkuzie gave me a sum of money that had certainly taken him many months to save. He wanted me to transfer it to one of his relatives in Ethiopia who would be fairly easy to locate and who would take it upon himself to find the grandchild and get him released.

Even as I write these lines, I do not want to believe that such things happen in our world.

JANUARY 5, 1987

Two years have passed since Operation Moses and we are still dealing with the damage that Sudan caused our people. Over and over again, we discover how deep the wounds are, especially in children. Workie, a girl of eight, arrived in Israel with her uncle, her mother's brother. The mother died before the family left Sudan and the uncle took charge of the girl and cared for her until they made aliyah.

The day after they arrived in Israel, we sat with them in the large hall of the King Saul Hotel in Ashkelon and interviewed the uncle's family. The girl sat opposite us with downcast eyes and did not utter a sound. From time to time, she nodded her head. Only once could her pain be seen in her face – that was when her mother's name was mentioned and the uncle told us of her death in Ethiopia. Then I could see the tears on the cheeks of this fragile little girl. The uncle also told us that the girl's father had died while they were still in Ethiopia, and again the girl nodded her agreement with the story, but no sorrow could be discerned on her face.

In the end, the girl was sent to a family-type group home that was set up by Youth Aliyah in the Hofim Youth Village near Acre. All the children there, ranging in age between three and twelve, grow up together as a sort of family whose home is run with much love and devotion by an Ethiopian couple, Zehava and Uri Aragay.

This morning, two years later, Workie's social worker asked me to intervene in a family problem that has arisen, and has even worsened during these two years. It was discovered that the girl's father did not die. Not only is he alive, but he is living in Israel in Kiryat Haim, which is near the girl. The first meeting with her father took place in the office of the village's director. Zehava Aragay, the girl's housemother, was wary of arousing expectations in the child that could not be met. She required proof that the man claiming to be her father really was so. She received the proof when she overheard a telephone conversation between the father and the uncle, who cursed the father for everything he had done to his wife and for causing her death.

The father went to the group home and Zehava brought the father and daughter together. But this was no wonderful reunion of father and daughter finding each other at long last. The girl refused even to go near her father and wanted him to go away. The father did not reveal what he was really feeling. He tried to calm her and said, "I see that it's impossible for you now, so I'll come back in another week with your sister, so that you'll get to know her." A week later, when the father came with his daughter and his present wife, the staff understood why the father chose this method. The two girls are so similar that they look like twins.

And indeed, thanks to the immediate connection that the two girls felt, the father got his first daughter back. Now, after regular visits by the girl at her father's home, I got an urgent telephone call this morning from the social worker in Hofim. About a month ago, the girl said that she wouldn't go to her father's house anymore. So she went to spend the Chanukah vacation with the uncle who brought her up after her mother died. But the uncle's wife warned her that the uncle was going to beat her and it was better that she leave the house immediately. The girl had no other option but to return to Hofim.

The social worker wanted me to intervene since the child is torn between her uncle and her father. The social worker does not know why the girl has stopped visiting her father and why the uncle is angry. It was clear to me that the elders of the community have to be brought in to mediate between the sides and I suggested this to the social worker. The elders' status and wisdom in bridging gaps should be used more often and they should not be allowed to lose their prestige. In Ethiopia, they were the mediators in arguments between husband and wife, between relatives, and between neighbors. Usually, the mediation process is very long and drawn out, but the weight of their rulings is similar to a legal judgment. In Israel, their status, wisdom, and experience are not being fully utilized.

I am told that the differences are on their way to being ironed out: at the end of a meeting between the uncle and the father, the girl felt she could hug both of them without feeling that she is forced to give up her father for the sake of the uncle, whom she loves. The mediator was Yitzak Adge, a white-haired man of distinguished appearance, who delved seriously into the matter and succeeded in bringing about a reconciliation between the father and the uncle.

FEBRUARY 11, 1987 – THE JEWISH AGENCY OFFICE, TEL AVIV

In my normal fields of activity, the situation is not good. Unfortunately, I did not manage to persuade my department's director, Chaim Aharon, to give up his plan to withdraw the Jewish Agency sponsorship and support of several of the absorption centers. In my opinion, abandoning the centers means that we, ourselves, will be creating Ethiopian immigrant ghettos in Nazareth, Afula, Beersheba, and all the other places where they exist. When we remove the "Absorption Center" sign from buildings where the immigrants live, leaving them alone to manage by themselves, the building will, in effect, become an instant ghetto. A discussion on this topic has just been held in the large conference room of the Jewish Agency attended by representatives of all the agencies involved. The department head was not prepared even to listen to my objections to his plan and I walked out, slamming the door. The next day, I was deprived of all my authority and it was decided that I would be sent as a *shaliach* (emissary) to San Francisco for two or three years. It may well prove to be a pleasant exile, but I feel I am deserting the Beta Israel.

MARCH 28, 1987 – THE JEWISH AGENCY OFFICE, TEL AVIV

Yesterday, the operation to bring *olim* from Sudan ended. There are seventy-two new immigrants. Since I am being punished, I was not invited to the plane's landing, just as I was not invited to the previous landing on February 28, when sixty-seven new immigrants arrived. In any case, immigration has sunk to wretched lows. Since the start of this year, forty-seven *olim* have come direct from Addis Ababa and there is not much prospect of a change in the near future.

APRIL 17, 1988 – THE JEWISH AGENCY OFFICE, SAN FRANCISCO

I have now been here in San Francisco for over nine months. During that time, only 142 *olim* have arrived in Israel direct from Ethiopia. I heard yesterday that another fifty-five arrived from Sudan. They called me from the office and said that they miss me. If only they knew how much I miss the Ethiopian immigrants. The most hopeful note is that Israel and Ethiopia have begun negotiations on a number of issues.

I am trying to get back to Israel as soon as possible, but only on the condition that I am allowed to work with the Ethiopian community. I hope that the new department head, Uri Gordon, who has real affection for the community, will authorize my request.

AUGUST 8, 1988 – ISRAEL

We have returned to Israel after thirteen months in the USA. The department head did me great honor by coming personally to San Francisco to tell me it was more important that I return to Israel than stay in the USA. He also needed to persuade my children, who had just gotten used to their new schools, who were improving their English, had made new friends, and who wanted us to finish our *shlichut* (mission), which was supposed to be for two or three years.

In the meetings that I have already had with the Ethiopian community since my return, I have heard over and over again the sentence, "When you weren't here, there was no aliyah. Now that you're back, it'll start again." I tried to explain that there is no connection between the aliyah and my being here, but it didn't help. Somehow, in the community, I am considered to be the person who brings them good luck.

SEPTEMBER 15, 1988 – THE JEWISH AGENCY OFFICE, TEL AVIV

After five weeks of nerve-racking waiting, I have been informed that I have been appointed director of the Division for Ethiopian Aliyah. During my first days on the job, I actually did not deal with aliyah at all but spent my time checking the eligibility of people who are already here and about whom it has been claimed that they or their offspring are converts. It turns out that, over the years, many Felesmura have been brought on aliyah, and their relatives in Israel concealed from us that they are, in fact, converts. Family ties persist despite the conversions. Yet, in general, the two groups could even be said to hate one another. They did so in Ethiopia and the animosity continues in Israel.

An even more difficult issue is that similarly, during the last year, Ethiopian Christians have immigrated to Israel with the help of Jews with whom they had close relationships in Ethiopia. These were usually Jews who had status in the community, such as activists and members of prestigious families. The Christians are usually educated young people from Addis Ababa who were neighbors of the Jewish families and sought to reach Israel to study here, as Israel does not issue student visas for all countries, including Ethiopia.

It is hard to explain this to gentile friends, this insistence on saving Jews first. One has only to look at our long, painful history – and especially the Holocaust – to understand why. Israel's Law of Return, a central pillar of our state, was created to save Jews. It guarantees that Jews will never again be without a sanctuary should they need or want one. It was and is, first and foremost, intended to guarantee Jews a country of their own.

In another few weeks, it will be four full years since Operation Moses took place, and it turns out that the newcomers' absorption into Israeli society is difficult. The number of those who commit suicide is rising. Many of the *olim* still reside in absorption centers. Some are unemployed. But overshadowing everything is the problem of the cessation of aliyah. Since Operation Queen of Sheba, in March 1985, the total number of *olim* to have arrived is 806, and the news coming out of Ethiopia is terrible and depressing. Jewish houses in the villages are being set on fire and the people are being persecuted and forced to flee. It is clear beyond a shadow of doubt: the fewer the number of Jews, the greater will be the pressure on those who remain. In Ethiopia, only strong people survive, and the Jews are strong only when they are many in number, which they no longer are.

OCTOBER 14, 1988 – BEN-GURION INTERNATIONAL AIRPORT

For the first time since returning from the USA, I am welcoming a group of immigrants in the normal way. Among these *olim* are close family of Asnakew, including Tadese, his brother, and another relative, Koke Reta. Knowing how eager they would be to see the new arrivals, I invited Asnakew, as well as Tadese's two sons and Koke's son, to help me with the work. Dealing with the arrivals took a very long time, but it was worth waiting to see the joy on the faces of Asnakew and his nephews on greeting Tadese. With Koke, the situation is more much complicated. He is sick, apparently with TB, and also does not know that another son died a few years ago in Netanya.

OCTOBER 16, 1988, EVENING – AT HOME

Today, when I visited my mother at Assaf Harofeh Hospital, I found that Koke Reta is hospitalized in the same department. It was moving to see the concern of his relatives. His daughter, who is in the twelfth grade, is thinking of giving up her studies. I hope it will be possible to persuade her to carry on at school and not to put too much responsibility on her own shoulders.

OCTOBER 24, 1988 – KISHON PRISON, NEAR HAIFA
Today, I took the road to Kishon Prison to visit Sibhat. He has been arrested for beating his wife. This man has gone through many tragedies in his life. At one point, he made aliyah with his children, but without his Christian wife, who had a very senior job in Addis Ababa. His young daughter was then only three years old and, as was to be expected, could not bear the separation from her mother, so the family returned to Ethiopia. There, the older daughter died. After he made aliyah the second time – this time with his wife – his eldest son drowned when he went too far out to sea in a boat with a friend. And now, Sibhat is sitting in prison because he physically abused his wife.

I was led along long corridors. Sibhat fell on my neck and clung to me as though I was his last lifeline in an ice-cold ocean. When I managed to release myself from his grip, I saw a spent man, bent like a tree after a night of storms. The bare prison walls increased the feeling of gloom. This man has lost all his pride, that same pride that impelled him to walk the streets of Addis Ababa holding high the blue and white flag of Israel after the victory in the Six-Day War. When will he be at peace?

Now, I have to at least try to get him released. I know that the social worker has contacted his wife, asking her to speak in his favor at the trial tomorrow.

It turns out that even those of us who are close to the community and have been working with it for years have difficulties understanding how complicated the Ethiopian Jews' absorption in Israel is. When they feel down and depressed, the Ethiopians feel the sorrow in their stomachs, not their hearts, as Westerners do. That is why when something bothers the Ethiopian immigrant, he complains of pain in his stomach. The trouble is that sometimes the weight of distress bursts out and can become a criminal act.

Sibhat committed suicide in prison, shortly after my last meeting with him.

OCTOBER 28, 1988 – THE JEWISH AGENCY OFFICE, TEL AVIV

This morning I found a very touching letter on my desk. It was sent by a girl of thirteen, whom I have never met, who tells of her concern for her sister, brothers, grandfather, and grandmother.

WEDNESDAY, HESHVAN 15, 5749, OCTOBER 26, 1988

Dear Micha,

My big sister is still in Ethiopia, and I miss her very much. My mother reminds me of her often and she cries. That hurts me. She is fifteen, I'm almost thirteen. She is suffering from a very serious illness and so is my mother. I did not play with her much because she went from one hospital to another. As I am writing this letter I cry. Please understand in my heart. I miss my sister very much.

And my big brother was wounded in the war. His leg is short, he cannot work. I have only seen him once, I do not know him really. So when they sent us photographs I cried. I am little and do not understand anything, but now, when I heard about you, I am writing to you this letter – perhaps you will understand my heart and the heart of my family. They are always arguing. She says: "Because of you she was left in Ethiopia," and he answers "No." When I hear this, my heart breaks and I cry.

My big brother is thirty years old and he has one son and he lives with his family. Two weeks ago he sent a letter and said that this is my last letter. Because you are not sending money. Once he sent a letter and wrote that he misses us very much and sometimes he feels like strangling himself, and so when I hear the letter I cry. And because of this, in my classroom when I think about the things that he writes, I think about this and say, if my sister were in Israel she would certainly enjoy it very much, and sometimes I cry. My father is sick and also my mother. They are always sick. My mother does not receive money, only my father. They write to us and say send us money, but we have no money. It hurts.

When we were in the mobile homes we did not have food. Many times we stayed at home and did not go to school because we paid gas and water with part of the money and we sent part of the money to my brother and sister and it did not reach them. Please, Micha, help us and perhaps because you helped us, you will have much luck.

Please, I beg you that you will bring my brother and sister and grandfather and grandmother to me.

Shoshana, Ashkelon

She had carefully signed the letter, and given me her own name and address and the full names and address of her sister and brother in Gondar. I read this letter again and I am amazed at this thirteen-year-old girl's ability. I vow to myself that I will take care of the aliyah of her relatives and that I will get to know this girl personally because her letter gives such clear expression to the pain of separation.

DECEMBER 8, 1988 – AN AIRBASE SOMEWHERE IN ISRAEL

Today, 329 *olim* arrived in an air operation.

I greet the new arrivals and travel with them to Ashkelon. Afterwards, I am free to look for the family of Rachel Yalew, a young woman to whom I became very attached when she arrived here five years ago. Like many others who are almost at the end of their tether, she has contacted me several times recently and it has been very difficult for me to witness her pain.

Every single day, youngsters come to our office and break down right in front of our eyes. And these are the young ones who overcame the hardships of the way here and survived the refugee camps. And yet these youngsters, who achieved their heart's desire, are now collapsing under the strain of concern for loved ones. I can hardly restrain my own feelings, yet I am the one who is supposed to give them the strength to carry on.

Now, in Ashkelon, my eyes seek out people I should remember from my visits in Aba Antonis two years ago. After some searching, I find them: Rachel's three sisters and one brother. Their parents sent them and stayed behind in Sudan, saying they would arrive in the next aliyah operation. I look at them and the brother and little sister remind me very much of Rachel.

In my room, after a particularly hard day's work and before the excitement has worn off from meeting this family, I analyze the situation. In spite of all our efforts to bring people from Sudan and Ethiopia, all we do adds up to an insignificant amount. We are healing the wounds of very few and deepening the wounds of many.

DECEMBER 24, 1988 – THE JEWISH AGENCY OFFICE, TEL AVIV

Throughout this whole year, a total of 384 immigrants have arrived through Sudan and 220 direct from Ethiopia – 604 *olim* altogether. This low number and the overall situation are holding up the progress of the youngsters who are here. They express the problem very succinctly: "It is true my body is here, in Jerusalem, but my mind is still there, in Ethiopia."

MARCH 6, 1989 – THE OLD AGE HOME OF THE JEWISH AGENCY, ASHKELON

What a great, exciting day! I found Rachel Yalew's father. At the very moment that I identified him, he recognized me and we fell into each other's arms, hugging as though we were family. And truth to tell, that is just how it felt.

The number of *olim* who came today is 303. After they were sent on to their destinations, I hurried to the hospital. My mother has been sick for over five months now and her condition is deteriorating. But I am not alone. Many of my Ethiopian friends go to visit her and I can see how much this cheers her up.

APRIL 1, 1989 – SHARON HOSPITAL, PETAH TIKVA

I have spent a very difficult night at my mother's bedside. It is now clear that we will lose her within a few hours or, at the most, days. I asked the doctors to give her morphine, so that she will not suffer.

I sat beside her all night. I tried to get some sleep, but she was constantly wheezing. In the afternoon, my brother, Yohanan, took my place and stayed in the hospital while I returned home. I asked to be informed of any further decline in my mother's condition. At five o'clock this evening, the dreaded telephone call came: "Come quickly, it's the end." But when Ruthie and I were outside our apartment door, we heard the telephone ringing again. The commander of my army reserve unit – the one that deals with Ethiopian immigrants – asked me to come immediately to the hostel in Ramat Yosef where Chaim Getahun, who is on army reserve duty, was threatening to shoot himself. For a moment, I did not know what to do: whether to go and save a man's life or to be with the person who had given me my life during the last minutes of her own life. I felt I ought to be in both places. I decided to call the hospital and was told that there was no change in Mother's condition, so I knew that I had to do what my mother would want me to do.

Within twenty minutes, I was in Ramat Yosef. The police put me in the picture. Nobody knew for certain what had brought Chaim to the verge of suicide. I remembered Chaim and the smile on his face. He used to be known as "Gorgeous Chaim" by the staff in Ashkelon during Operation Moses. I also saw his father among the worried crowd. Everyone was jumpy and the feeling was that Chaim's life was evaporating even while we stood waiting.

I carefully approached the door of Chaim's apartment and told him that I was there. He greeted me with a voice choked with tears. Because of the trust between us, I felt that I had the power to save him. He asked me to get him a tourist visa to the USA. I never found out what caused his despair. Some said that his girlfriend had ended their relationship, but I told him that the American consul would give him the visa. He wanted to speak with the consul, but I persuaded him that there was no need and that my word was enough.

He yielded three-quarters of an hour later. He handed me the weapon through the window and opened the door to me. I arranged with the police that Chaim would stay with me and, in return, no complaint would be lodged against him.

I hurried home, collected Ruthie, and drove fast to the hospital. My mother was already unconscious. It pained me that I had not been able to say good-bye to her. Meanwhile, Chaim arrived at our home, so I hurried there to be with him. While we were discussing his future, the announcement came that my mother had passed away.

APRIL 3, 1989 – MY MOTHER'S HOME IN HOLON

We have buried Mother. There were a lot of people at the funeral, including many from the Ethiopian community, among them three *kessoch*. I told the rabbi of the *hevra kadisha* (burial society) that there would also be a burial prayer in Ge'ez. I saw the worried look that came over him – thinking perhaps that we were about to bury a non-Jewish woman or that we belonged to some strange cult. It was only after we explained our special connection with the Ethiopian community to the rabbi that his suspicions were allayed and he agreed to the unexpected addition to the ceremony.

The *kessoch* offered a very moving prayer, standing separate from the congregation, with their colorful umbrellas over their heads, praying with such a strange melody and in so strange a language. For those not from the Ethiopian community, it was certainly their first funeral according to Ethiopian rites.

After we recited the *Kaddish*, my mother disappeared into the ground – disappeared, never to return. How good it must be for those who believe in the resurrection of the dead and how difficult it is for one, such as myself, who does not believe in it.

Now we are in her home, sitting *shiva.*

APRIL 9, 1989 – MY MOTHER'S HOME IN HOLON

Today, we finished sitting *shiva* and went to my mother's grave. During this last week, we have had many callers – Mother's friends, friends of my brother, Yohanan, and friends of mine – but most of those coming to offer condolences were immigrants from Ethiopia. They came to honor my mother, as is traditional in the Ethiopian culture, where showing respect is a primary value, and especially during the mourning period.

During the *shiva*, there is a lot of time for thinking. I thought about the essence of life. I know that life is given to us as a gift and, therefore, we have to make proper use of the short time we are given. We have to be careful not to waste life. We must know how to enjoy it, but we must also occupy ourselves in important things and not in meaningless rubbish.

Memories of Mother keep popping up. It is difficult without her. Her spirit is here in every corner, even though she is not here physically. From time to time, I am struck by the realization that once a chapter in life is written, it cannot be erased.

APRIL 10, 1989 – THE JEWISH AGENCY OFFICE, TEL AVIV

It's good that we are under pressure at work. As I promised myself, I will deal only with important things and will not waste my time on marginal issues.

Today was particularly busy. There was a visit to Neveh Amiel, a youth village in the North which is home to many Ethiopian students, a farewell party for one of our veteran staff members, a graduation ceremony at the nursing school in Nahariya, and after all that, receiving new immigrants at the airport.

The newcomers are all members of one family. One of the young daughters has left an eight-month-old baby behind. When she was sitting in the arrivals hall, some milk dripped from her breasts. I took her to the Assaf Harofeh Hospital where she was given a pump for the milk. I said to myself, as on so many occasions in the past, that in spite of my knowledge of the Beta Israel, its culture and capabilities, I cannot understand how she could leave an eight-month-old baby behind her.

MAY 5, 1989 – THE RUNWAY OF AN AIRBASE SOMEWHERE IN ISRAEL

Another operation. This time 205 *olim* emerge from two Hercules planes of the Israel Air Force at the IAF airbase. With excitement and also with jealousy, I hug Zimna, who had the privilege of organizing these *olim* in Sudan.

This is the twentieth time that I have received immigrants at an airbase, but the exhilaration never abates.

AUGUST 8, 1989

Today marks one year since I returned from the USA, and what was prophesied by many of the Ethiopian community has indeed happened. This year 1,148 *olim* arrived, from Sudan and direct from Ethiopia. Obviously, I know that it was not I who did it, but many of the community believe that it was due to me. Even those who are not so naive think that my presence in Israel as director of the Division for Ethiopian Immigration somehow brings the community luck and increases the aliyah.

But the community members do not know anything about the underlying reasons for my return from the States. For over a year, there had been negotiations with the Ethiopian government, and now it is possible to see the fruits of those negotiations. More and more Jews are being allowed to leave Ethiopia.

We have been asked to prepare a list of fifty families who will be allowed to leave for Israel direct from Ethiopia rather than via Europe or other countries. This is because of the forthcoming visit of a high-level government delegation from Ethiopia a few months hence, headed by Kassa Kebede, who is considered the Ethiopian president's closest adviser; some maintain that he is his step-brother. Kassa has a very self-assured appearance and he exudes a superior air. He speaks Hebrew almost without an accent, as he was a student at the Hebrew University in Jerusalem in the fifties. He had the reputation of being a womanizer and it is said that he managed to lure quite a few college girls to his bed during his student years.

He will arrive in Israel in October in order to conduct official discussions on the renewal of relations between Israel and Ethiopia. As expected, Ethiopia requests military assistance while we want authorization for more Jews to depart and the lifting of the restrictions on youngsters so that they, too, can make aliyah.

My liaison is Haim Halachmi, whose contacts and personality have made him the confidant of nearly all the agencies involved.

It is difficult to prepare a list of just fifty families when there are over six thousand Jewish families in Ethiopia. In the end, we present a list of fifty-one families, marked List B-51.

Haim is optimistic and manages to infect us all with his optimism.

OCTOBER 27, 1989 – AT HOME

Almost six months have passed since the last *olim* arrived in the operation from Sudan. However, this morning 306 immigrants landed.

We were on our feet from five o'clock this morning, all of us very excited, but an announcement cast a pall over our joy: death is once again striking down our people in Sudan. Recently, sixty-nine have died, including some who are well known to me – Azanaw Bayuh Mehari, his son-in-law, and granddaughter. The sad news was given to us by his daughter. With tears spilling down her face, she told us, almost in a whisper, that her father, her husband, and her daughter died in Sudan during the long wait for aliyah.

As usual, we are maintaining secrecy about the arrival of immigrants from Sudan, but this time there is an additional reason for doing so. Kassa Kebede arrived here a few days ago to conduct the negotiations on the renewal of diplomatic relations. Nobody is interested in complicating these matters by announcing there has been another operation, since it might reach the ears of the Ethiopian negotiator and there is no way of judging what his reaction would be.

NOVEMBER 3, 1989, VERY LATE IN THE EVENING – AT HOME

What a strange day this has been. This morning the news broadcast opened by stating that an Ethiopian immigrant had killed his wife and four children in Kiryat Motzkin. They say that it happened during a sudden fit of madness. On the bus this evening, I felt as though all the passengers were looking at me, forgetting for the moment that obviously I do not look anything like an Ethiopian. But I understood how most of the Ethiopian *olim* must be feeling right now, even though most of them certainly are not acquainted with the murderer.

Then, I heard on the six o'clock news broadcast that the Ethiopian Foreign Ministry has proposed to renew diplomatic relations with Israel which were cut off at the end of 1973 after the Yom Kippur War. I called Haim and he told me that the talks with the Ethiopians had gone well and we can expect the departure of the families on List B-51 before long.

NOVEMBER 22, 1989 – THE JEWISH AGENCY OFFICE, TEL AVIV

Haim came here to my office. I saw that something was bothering him, but the reason for his gloom was revealed only when Yaffa, who has been my secretary for the last six months, left the room.

I met Yaffa for the first time at the home of her aunt, Ora, who looked after my mother. When her aunt introduced her, she said that she had just graduated from the secretarial curriculum at Kfar Batya. I then took a proper look at the pleasant young woman sitting there with head bent as though looking at something invisible on the floor. She looked very delicate, but what caught my attention was her sadness, which she did not express in words but which could be seen in her eyes. Since I had been without a secretary for several weeks, I offered her the job and she seemed very happy to accept.

Today, it was after Yaffa stepped out of the office for a minute that Haim told me that her mother died six days ago in Addis Ababa, at the age of thirty-five, and is survived by her husband. He must now care for many children, including a one-year-old baby. However, one of Yaffa's aunts, a sister of her mother, is with them in Addis and, since she also has a baby, she is now breast-feeding both babies.

It was clear to me that I had to act according to Ethiopian Jewish customs and not reveal this dreadful news to Yaffa there and then. When she came back into the office, I tried not to deviate from my usual behavior, but my hand fell on her head and stroked her black hair. In my heart of hearts, I hope she will not feel that I have been hiding the information from her. By the evening, when I got home, I was totally spent. I hope that within a day or two the elders will assemble and tell Yaffa and the other relatives what has occurred.

DECEMBER 3, 1989, EVENING – AT HOME

It was not one or two days but eleven whole days, with every day harder than the one before. It was so hard to be with Yaffa and pretend as though everything were normal. Whoever has not gone through such an experience cannot understand how terribly difficult it is. But yesterday, the signal was given and I was allowed to arrange with Yaffa that this morning I would come to pick her up from her aunt's house in Kfar Saba, on the excuse of our having work to do in Ashkelon. Yaffa was ready and waiting and we set out, but instead of driving to Ashkelon, we went to the home of another aunt, another of her mother's sisters, in Petah Tikva.

I looked in the car's rear-view mirror and saw that Yaffa grasped that something had happened. Judging by where we were going, she understood that it concerned her mother and not her father, who is actually the one she has been most worried about all these years. Walking along the paved path that led to her aunt's apartment, Yaffa grasped the reason even before any word was spoken. She threw herself on the ground and let out the most heartrending screams. And there she was, lying on the cold path. I tried to lift up this thin girl, but she was stuck to the ground as though chained by some hidden force. I could not manage to raise her until she rose of her own accord.

Inside, it was even more difficult. Yaffa went crazy, like a wild animal. This same quiet girl, who usually kept timidly in the background, let forth all her agony. She was nothing but one mass of pure pain, the pain of a girl wailing for her mother.

That evening, on my way home, I went via Petah Tikva. This time I found Yaffa wrung out and limp. As is customary, many people have come to console her and, as is the custom among the Ethiopians, they weep afresh with each new caller, until, in the end, the eyes are incapable of shedding any more tears and the whole body is totally exhausted.

I would have loved to be able to give Yaffa news that her father, who is on the list of the fifty-one families, was about to come to Israel, but in actuality, there has been no progress on the departures from Ethiopia.

DECEMBER 5, 1989 – AT THE HOME OF YAFFA'S AUNT IN PETAH TIKVAH

Today, I visited at the aunt's home, but I could not recognize my Yaffa. Yesterday, without anyone expecting it, she cut off all her lovely hair, so long and so black. It is a traditional sign of mourning for women to cut off their hair, and so that is what Yaffa did. It was the only way that she could fully express her mourning for her mother.

Even though it is difficult for me to see Yaffa suffering so much and behaving in this way, it is apparently the best way to mourn. I compare how we behaved after my mother's death to what happened just now in Petah Tikva, and it may well be that the Ethiopian Jewish ways are better. With them, the mourner gives vent to all his pain so that with every new person who comes to console him, he inches back closer to his normal life. But among us Ashkenazis, it is considered seemly to maintain a facade of "everything is normal" and to try to prevent the pain from rising to the surface.

DECEMBER 9, 1989, SATURDAY EVENING – AT HOME

After about seven and a half years of working with the Ethiopian community, I thought that I really had become an expert on all the issues, as well as all the absorption problems. And then, this morning, on a Shabbat excursion with my younger son, Kfir, I had a lesson that brought me back to reality.

On the lawn in the city park, several Ethiopian youngsters were sitting. I went over to them and said hello. There is no need to speak to them in Amharic; their Hebrew is excellent, as they have all graduated from Youth Aliyah boarding schools and are all now doing their compulsory army service.

One of them mustered up courage to ask me about something that has been bothering him – housing. He received an apartment with his mother, but recently his grandfather arrived and came to live with them. And he, out of respect for the elder, has given him his room, so now there is nowhere for him to sleep. Since I know their apartment, I suggested that he sleep in the living room. His reply stunned me. I never would have expected that a boy who has been in Israel for five years would give such an answer: "The living room is where we eat and drink and so I am afraid of sleeping in it. The *kole* might come, in order to eat and drink."

I know that the *kole* is a spirit who visits people that he controls, usually at night. He has human characteristics; in particular he loves food and drink. The person under the control of the *kole* has to placate him and then the *kole* helps him, but if he does not get the proper respect, he is likely to harm the person mentally or even physically.

Obviously, my face mirrored my astonishment at the response, but in the faces of the other young people gathered on the lawn, I only saw their agreement with this young man, who is serving in the Border Police and is ready to endanger his life in a battle with the enemy, yet still fears the *kole*.

Part Four

In Addis Again

DECEMBER 31, 1989 – THE JEWISH AGENCY OFFICE, TEL AVIV

The talks held during the last few months with the Ethiopian representatives have led not only to an announcement of the renewal of diplomatic relations but also to increased aliyah. While in the first half of this year only 133 *olim* came directly from Ethiopia, in the last six months 401 have arrived. Indeed, the number of immigrants in the last year equals the total for the three previous years.

I consider the increased aliyah as a satisfactory enough gift for my forty-sixth birthday tomorrow, but today I was given another present. I was called to the office of Arnon Mantver, the director-general of my department. Arnon worked in the Ministry of Absorption from its founding in 1969, serving as the ministry spokesman and as the head of the Students' Authority. Afterwards, he moved to our department in the Jewish Agency and was appointed director-general nine months ago. With a drama that is not at all typical of an old fox like him, Arnon informed me that in coordination with the Ministry of Foreign Affairs and other agencies, it has been agreed that I should be asked to go to Ethiopia to head the Jewish Agency mission there and to serve as the Israeli consul. I said yes immediately, even without consulting with my family, who will be the ones who have to pay the price. Although my official title was consul, I was actually to be the head of the Jewish Agency Mission to Ethiopia.

What a gift! To go to Ethiopia as the Israeli consul and to work to put an end to the exile there.

JANUARY 11, 1990 – THE JEWISH AGENCY OFFICE, TEL AVIV

Last week, two immigrants who are special to me arrived. Six days ago, Kes Beyene Demoze, the last of the Ethiopian Jewish monks, landed. And today, the sister of that thirteen-year-old girl who wrote me such a moving letter over a year ago finally arrived. That letter, describing her family's problems and how very much she longed for her older sister to be here, is never far from my thoughts. Since receiving it, I have used it constantly in lectures because it gives a powerful, very personal insight into the suffering of divided families.

I was hesitant about meeting the *kes* monk because I had not forgotten his aloofness when I visited Woleka, his village. I was hurt then because he would not even shake my hand. Since then, I have learned from *kessoch* in Israel that his behavior stemmed from his monastic vows, as he feared that any physical contact with me, even though it was the hand of someone from Jerusalem, would be likely to defile him.

And then he descended from the bus that had stopped at the entrance to the terminal in Ben-Gurion Airport. I focused my gaze on him and saw the happiness radiating from his eyes. To my surprise, he joyously came straight to me and not only did he shake my hand but he kissed me. I was thunderstruck. Perhaps it is the air of Eretz Yisrael that has caused this revolution.

The encounter with the girl was totally different. After all, we don't know each other. After I identified her, I went to her and greeted her with a kiss. As a good Ethiopian child, she allowed me to do so, but it was obvious that she didn't have a clue why she was getting this special attention from the person responsible for the whole group's reception. When we finished dealing with the *olim* and there were only a few minutes left before leaving the terminal, I tried to explain to her that we have a special relationship even though she is not aware of it, owing to her sister's letter. I don't think she really understood how a relationship could be formed between two individuals through a letter written by a third person, but a wide smile appeared on her face when I mentioned the names of her sister and parents. From that moment on, I felt the connection between us really gelled.

Relatives of the whole group were waiting outside and the joy broke all bounds. I stood looking on, trying to imagine what will happen after I arrive in Addis Ababa as the Israeli Consul, in another week.

JANUARY 20, 1990 – IN A PLANE OVER ADDIS ABABA, 9:45 A.M.

I am in an Ethiopian Airlines plane that is about to touch down at Addis Ababa's airport. Just like four years ago, I am very excited and this time my excitement is greatly enhanced because, after all, I am arriving as the Israeli consul and not just as a tourist. In my eyes, my mission seems like the most important thing in the world – to end the Ethiopian exile. I pray that I will be successful in this undertaking.

JANUARY 20, 1990, 10:30 A.M. – ADDIS ABABA

I have passed through border control. Unlike the previous occasions when no visa was awaiting me on my arrival, this time our people made sure that the immigration officials of the Ethiopian government would receive me with the honor due to the Israeli consul. And now we are already on our way to the Hilton Hotel, where I will stay until a permanent residence is found.

The streets of Addis are well known to me from my previous visits, and the sights, smells, and sensations take me back four years. This time, too, my job is to create a bridge between the Ethiopian Jews in Israel and their relatives here. But this time I will have the authority to send the exiles across that bridge until the need ceases to exist.

JANUARY 21, 1990 – HILTON HOTEL, ADDIS ABABA

My second day in Addis is coming to an end, although I feel more like I've been here a year already. It's a double-edged feeling: on the one hand, there is the feeling that I belong here, that I'm in the right place and that I will succeed in carrying out my mission, but on the other hand, I feel the separation from my family, even though my wife, Ruthie, has not complained and, indeed, has even encouraged me to press forward, in spite of the difficulties.

I spent most of the day at the new Israeli embassy making the final preparations for its official opening tomorrow. I've arranged and organized my small office, fervently hoping that it will be the focus of unceasing activity.

Perhaps tomorrow, I'll manage to see Kassa Kebede, who, according to our ambassador, Meir Yoffe, is the official in charge of emigration.

JANUARY 22, 1990 – ISRAELI EMBASSY, ADDIS ABABA

The big day has arrived. At 9:30 a.m., we assembled for the opening ceremony. Several Israelis, who are in Addis right now, came, as well as nearly all the Jews from Aden. The Adenite Jews, originally from the former British colony of today's Yemen, moved to Ethiopia some generations ago. There were also a few Jews from Gondar, headed by Kes Amaha Negat. Because the short ceremony was held in three languages – Hebrew, Amharic, and English – I was given the honor of conducting it. The locals, including three journalists, did not conceal their pleasure at hearing me speak in Amharic.

The flag was raised by the ambassador, who then spoke of the personal symbolism of the moment since, in December 1973, he was the person who had folded up the Israeli flag in this embassy when it was closed – and here he was now, as ambassador, with the privilege of hoisting the flag in the same location. After most of the guests dispersed, I stepped out of my room every few minutes, just for the pleasure of gazing at the flag flying at the top of the flagpole.

Some of the guests remained behind and I started to deal with them. I even had the satisfaction of stamping my first aliyah visa in

A group of *olim* who had just arrived from the north,
waiting in the courtyard of the Israel Embassy in Addis Ababa, December 1991

Tsehaye Elias, *z"l*, speaking with one of the community's elderly women in Addis Ababa, 1991

Waiting to be served in the embassy courtyard, Addis Ababa, 1990.
Center: Zimna Birhanie.

Every Tuesday at 4:00 p.m. a meeting is held with the community representatives in one of the classrooms of the Jewish day school located in the courtyard of the Israel Embassy.

The *kessoch* meeting in the embassy courtyard, Addis Ababa, 1990

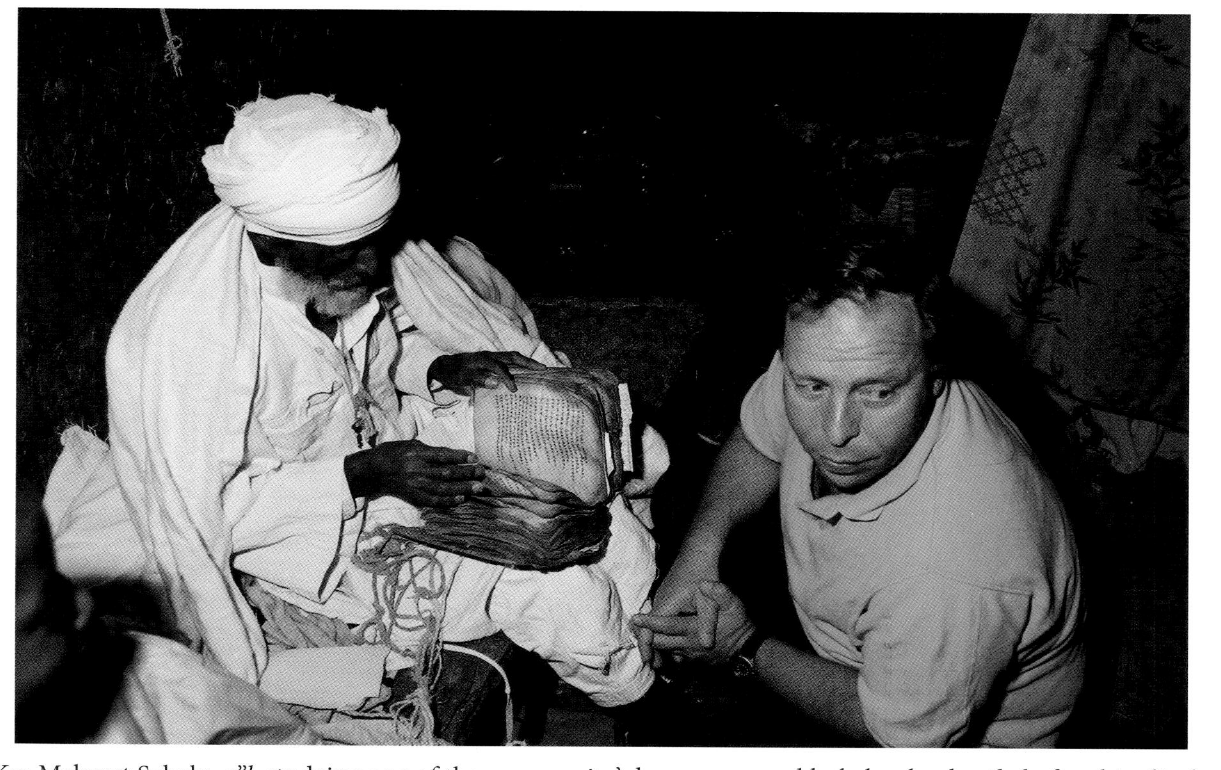

Kes Meheret Sahalu, *z"l*, studying one of the community's long-preserved holy books shortly before his aliyah, Addis Ababa, December 1990

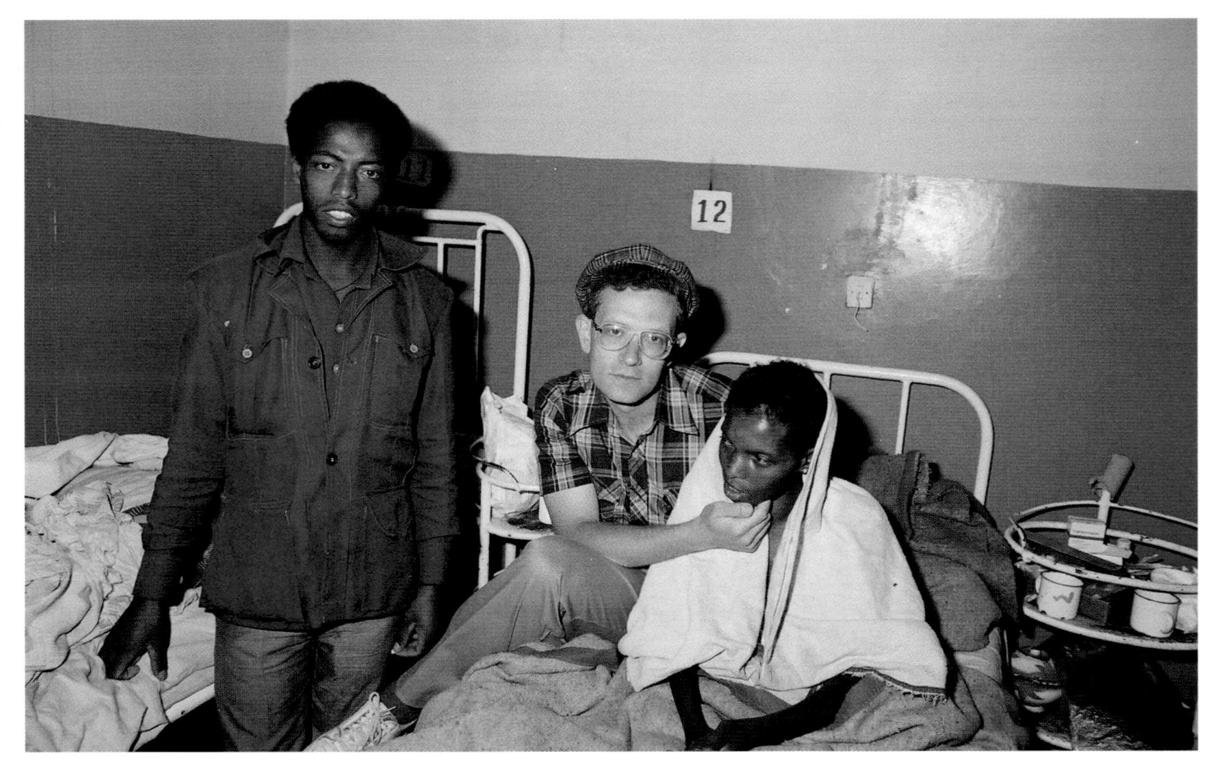

Dr. David Raveh examines one of the patients prior to the patient's aliyah, a short time before Operation Solomon, Addis Ababa, 1991

Building the roof of one of the classrooms of the Jewish day school, which was built in the courtyard of the Israel Embassy, Addis Ababa, 1990

Covering the roof of the classroom with straw, Addis Ababa, 1990

A Jewish girl in the courtyard of the Israel Embassy in Ethiopia, November 1990

Baking bread in the school's kitchen, housed in the courtyard of the Israel Embassy, Addis Ababa, 1991

Lunch break in the school housed in the Israel Embassy,
Addis Ababa, 1990

Benny Harel, a *shaliach* (representative) of the Jewish Agency, examines the *olim*'s documentation during Operation Solomon,
Addis Ababa, May 25, 1991

The soldiers and civilians involved in Operation Solomon on their way to Addis Ababa in a Boeing 707 that was emptied of its seats, May 25, 1991

Gathering for departure in front of the Israel Embassy in Addis Ababa during Operation Solomon, May 24, 1991

Yaakov Elias (Esnakow Sendake) examines *olim*'s documentation during Operation Solomon, Addis Ababa, May 25, 1991.

Operation Solomon, en route to Israel, May 25, 1991

the passport of the mother of Koke Reta, the immigrant who was hospitalized in the same ward as my mother during her illness.

JANUARY 26, 1990 – ISRAELI EMBASSY, ADDIS ABABA

Things here move so slowly. Even though today nine *olim* left, in Israel there are seventeen thousand Ethiopian immigrants who are waiting for their relatives. Here in Ethiopia at least another seventeen thousand are waiting to make aliyah. Nine immigrants do not solve the problem.

In the cable that the ambassador sent to Israel, he recommends meeting the Ethiopians halfway, since he sees Kassa Kebede's promise of providing a person who will work with me on emigration as some sort of progress toward solving the problem. The Ethiopians want assistance, but to me it seems that the only way of dealing with the problem is to respond to the Ethiopian demands only after there is some genuine movement on aliyah; this means, specifically, that some of the families on the lists we have presented have actually made aliyah.

JANUARY 27, 1990 – SHABBAT – ADDIS ABABA

In Israel it's raining, while here it's summer weather. It was a chance to walk from the hotel to the synagogue of the Jews from Aden. The way there crosses slum neighborhoods where women hawk goods. Everything is dirty and wretched, but the people greet us with smiles. One man came over to us to warn us not to pass through there at night since after dark it becomes a haunt for criminals and the only goods that women offer then are their bodies. In Amharic, this neighborhood is called Eri Bekantu – "Cries in Vain" – since crime rules there and no one hears or goes to the assistance of a person crying out for help.

The congregation in the synagogue included many who are waiting to make aliyah. At the end of the service, I met with the worshippers in the synagogue courtyard. I recognized most of them and was really excited by this meeting, but suspicion and fear hovered in the air, and the people were continually looking around to see who might be watching.

JANUARY 29, 1990 – ISRAELI EMBASSY, ADDIS ABABA

The new week started with a telephone call from Israel. Sarah Yaron, with whom I've worked for years, said that today she particularly misses me as a group of 425 immigrants – the largest ever from Sudan – has arrived in Ashkelon.

This operation had a lot of snafus. While the planes were still airborne on the way to Israel, those waiting to meet them were told that one of the two Hercules was carrying five corpses. The descent from the planes was not different from usual. The people descended in silence and proceeded slowly to the buses. Beside one of the Hercules, two military ambulances were parked. As usual, Haim Halachmi took the initiative and asked one of the officers, "Where?"

"In the jeep."

Haim realized that this must be one of the last operations from Sudan, since otherwise they would never have loaded the jeep on the plane. Our people have used it constantly in Sudan. After his eyes grew accustomed to the darkness in the plane's interior, he saw the jeep. There were only four stretchers in it, but from the side he heard a whisper, "There are two children on one stretcher." They were two tiny girls, each about two years old. The other three dead were a man of forty, a woman of twenty-four in the last months of pregnancy, and a girl of about ten.

The explanation was that too many Jews were waiting for the trucks at the assembly point. They swarmed over the vehicles and apparently these five were crushed to death under the pressure of those crowding into the trucks. It was only when they got off the trucks that the tragedy was discovered. Those commanding the operation decided, to the amazement of the immigrants, not to leave the dead behind in Sudan, but to carry them for burial in Israel.

This month, 189 Jews have immigrated direct from Ethiopia and another 425 from Sudan, making a total of 614 people.

Today I sent off my first cable to Israel:

Regular/Regular
To: Arnon Mantver, Jewish Agency, Jerusalem
c.c.: Moshe Gan, Haim Halachmi, Avi Mizrahi, Jewish Agency, Tel Aviv
From: Micha Feldmann
Re: Weekly Report

On Monday, the Consular Department was opened at the Israeli Embassy in Addis Ababa and the Israeli flag is flying here.

A. I have started organizing the applications of Jews, using the proper channels, and updating the data. Also, I have already issued visas to those who have completed the procedures.
B. In a meeting with Susan Pollack of AAEJ [American Association for Ethiopian Jewry], I clarified our policy regarding her organization's activity here. She made no objection to our stance that if and when there is a breakthrough in these matters, her organization's activities here will cease.
C. On Friday there was a meeting in the office of the Minister of Labor and Welfare, Mr. Shimelas Adugna, on handling the documentation for family reunification. I still have not received the name of the Ethiopian who is supposed to be my opposite number and work with me in the embassy. This seems to me like an exercise in deception by K.K.[1] I suggest that we play his game and not give him anything either – not just until he provides the name, but until at least the first family lands in Israel. For your information, the ambassador does not share my opinion on this.
D. In the above meeting, the Minister of Labor and Welfare suggested that JDC's activities in Gondar be expanded and also developed in the Shola neighborhood (where over 2,000 Jews in Addis live). All in all, I feel good and am still optimistic.

If no special problem arises, I will arrive in Israel on February 18th for a meeting with the organizations.

Sincerely, Micha

---

1. K.K. was the codename that we used for Kassa Kebede, especially in cables and telephone conversations, until in one of our conversations with him, he made it obvious that our lines were being tapped by his people and he himself suggested that we change his codename.

Toward noon, people started streaming to the embassy and over a hundred people thronged in, all asking to speak to me. I made a decision that twenty-five would be the top number I would deal with every day in order to give proper attention to each one. It is one week since the opening of the embassy and I have still not grown used to the sight of the poverty and the suffering in the streets of Addis Ababa – if, indeed, one can ever grow accustomed – but I notice that the Jews coming to the embassy look reasonable in comparison.

FEBRUARY 2, 1990 – ISRAELI EMBASSY, ADDIS ABABA

A tough day. Soon I will light the Sabbath candles, all on my own. I miss my family. It's hard.

However, it seems to me that we have made a little progress on the issue of aliyah. We have received the name of the man who will be my counterpart for emigration. He heads the Welfare Department in the Ethiopian Ministry of Labor and Welfare. Tomorrow, there is an appointment with the minister of labor and welfare and with his representative.

FEBRUARY 4, 1990 – ADDIS ABABA

Today would have been my mother's seventieth birthday. I feel such sorrow that she is not with us so that we could all celebrate her birthday, as well as my appointment in Ethiopia after twenty years of work, which coincides with this date.

It's Sunday today and we went on a trip to Sudere, one of the few recreation spots here, with a swimming pool and a lawn. On the way there, we passed by a fenced military camp. Gripping the fence from the other side were boys, some in uniform and others in normal civilian clothing. On the other side of the road, whole families were standing, dressed in their festive clothes. We were told that they are the relatives of these kids, who have been recruited into the army in the last few days to fight the rebels. I looked at these children. They seemed to be about fourteen or fifteen years old – years younger than my son, Amit, who will be drafted in another four weeks. The conversation between the two groups was conducted in shouts, since the families were not permitted to approach the fence and had to remain on the other side of the road.

On the way back from Sudere, we passed by a convoy of fifteen buses transporting these same kids. Knowledgeable sources say that the lucky ones will be those who return home with a foot or a hand amputated, but most of them will never return at all.

I think about Jewish youngsters, whom the headhunters in Addis Ababa do not exempt. The principle is simple: Ethiopian towns are divided into neighborhoods. In each neighborhood there is a *kebele* – a committee that manages it and receives its instructions from the ruling Communist Party. From time to time, each *kebele* receives its quota of youngsters that have to be supplied to the army. The headhunters go out at night and grab any youngster that they can lay their hands on. I am reminded of the horror stories of Jewish children who were kidnapped in czarist Russia. The Jewish families in Addis Ababa are prime candidates for such abductions, so I have decided to provide the families with the financial means to abort such attempts. Bribery worked in czarist Russia and it's a safe bet that it will work here, too.

FEBRUARY 9, 1990 – ISRAELI EMBASSY, ADDIS ABABA

What I feared has come to pass and, instead of expediting the departure of Jews, we see that the government is taking a tough line. I announced this by cable to Israel.

CONFIDENTIAL

To: Foreign Ministry/Arnon Mantver – Director-General, Dept. of Immigration and Absorption, Jewish Agency, Jerusalem

c.c.: Moshe Gan, Haim Halachmi, Zimna Berhanie, Jewish Agency, Tel Aviv

From: Micha Feldmann, Addis

Re: Change in Emigration Policy of Ethiopia

I call your attention to a change in the emigration policy in Ethiopia, which has recently taken place. In the last two-three weeks (since my arrival), it seems that the emigration office is implementing a tougher policy. This is shown by its authorizing the departure of adults, but not their children (including babies) even though they all appear on the same request form for family reunification. In the past, although they made it difficult for youngsters and children to leave, it was possible to "persuade" the emigration clerks.

Now it seems there is no way of persuading them. I have asked the ambassador to raise the issue in his meeting today with K.K. I shall report to you if there is a change.

Sincerely, Micha

FEBRUARY 13, 1990 – ISRAELI EMBASSY, ADDIS ABABA

At long last, the person who is supposed to be my contact has presented himself at the embassy. My excitement dimmed within seconds when it was made clear that he has not received any instructions on the issue of emigration and that, in fact, he came only because of the pressure that President Mengistu is exerting on Kassa to expedite military assistance, and because of the counterpressure from us for movement on aliyah.

Everything here happens at a snail's pace. There is hardly any aliyah at all. Only sixty-five people have left to date. I tried to make the situation clear in a cable that I sent today.

RESTRICTED/IMMEDIATE

To: Arnon Mantver, Director-General of Immigration and Absorption, Jewish Agency, Jerusalem

c.c.: Reuven Merhav, Director-General, Foreign Ministry
Haim Halachmi, Moshe Gan, Zimna Berhanie, Jewish Agency, Tel Aviv

From: Addis/Micha Feldmann

In the ambassador's meeting today with K.K., the latter put forward demands (I am not fully familiar with them) that are apparently due to the government's difficult military situation.

Among other things, he wants to make a trip to Israel in order to present the demands himself. In response, the ambassador told him that there is no point in such a journey unless it is linked to emigration.

In reply, K.K. made clear to the ambassador that he and his government are allowing the exit of Jews, and even mentioned the exaggerated number of 209 that left in January, adding that in February even more will depart. On the other hand, he claimed that it is impossible to be quick in implementing the project of family reunification using the forms. He also hinted that it is better to carry on in the present way without using the forms because using the forms would allow them to stop aliyah whenever they want by simply claiming to find mistakes in the forms. And, in fact, that is what they really did later.

In my opinion, K.K. is trying to avoid keeping his promises.

We should not abandon the principle that we, and not chance, make the decision of who has first priority for departure; and also, it should not happen that authorization is given only for parts of families (as is happening today – see my cable of February 9, 1990).

I am not saying that we must under all circumstances operate using the forms, but we must not abandon the above-mentioned principle.

I presume that in the next few days there will be additional developments.

Sincerely, Micha

FEBRUARY 14, 1990 – ISRAELI EMBASSY, ADDIS ABABA

This morning, Kes Amaha Negat, whom I met at the opening of the embassy, presented himself at my office. He is one of the most prominent *kessoch* and a very handsome and distinguished-looking man. He brought with him Wubnesh Mera.

Even though there was a long line of people waiting outside my office, a young woman and the *kes* with her passed by them all without any hindrance. I saw that the people in the corridor reacted as they would during the ceremony of consoling mourners. That was their response to this barefoot, distraught girl as she walked by them. She wore a dress so torn that her brown body was revealed in places. Her timid appearance said, "Don't pay attention to me. I don't want to bother you. I'm not important."

After they sat down facing me, Kes Amaha started by saying, "I've brought Wubnesh Mera to you. She will tell you about a thousand Jews who have been returned to Ethiopia from Sudan and are now awaiting rescue in the north."

WUBNESH'S STORY

Nine months ago, I went with my children to Sudan. My husband had managed to reach Jerusalem through Addis Ababa but I was left behind with my three children. My husband told me that the Ethiopian authorities were not allowing children to leave, only adults aged fifty and above.

I went with my brother to Sudan and for many months we waited there to make aliyah. We lived with all the Jews in Sufuha. Every few months, people would disappear from their homes, and then after a few days it would become clear to us that they had made aliyah to Israel in a secret operation. We waited for our turn to come, but fate was against us.

Four weeks ago, on January 11, Sudanese soldiers escorted by people of the Tigrean underground movement arrived at the place where we were living. They wrote down the names of all the Jews. We cooperated with them and even directed them to houses that were slightly distant, where we knew that Jews were living. We thought that they were about to renew Operation Moses and we did not want any of our people to be left behind.

When darkness fell, the Sudanese and the Tigreans left and then we gathered in small groups and whispered to each other about the assistance that we were soon going to receive from the Red Cross and about our chances of being reunited with our families in Israel. At eight o'clock that evening, about twenty trucks arrived driven by Sudanese drivers. We all left our houses. Adisu Reta, a very brave man who has been helping Jews to reach Sudan from Ethiopia for years and now helps to arrange aliyah, stepped forward and asked the Tigrean soldiers why the trucks were there. They answered that they were taking us to Um Rakoba where we would get care from the Red Cross.

We asked the Sudanese for permission to bring our belongings from our homes, but they did not allow it and started to put the people into the trucks by force. That was when we understood that it was not a rescue but a disaster. Some of the people fled, but most were trapped by the Sudanese and lifted into the trucks. I saw Adisu running away, but then he came back and whispered to me, "Don't worry, I'm with you all." His presence calmed me down.

Within an hour and a half, the Sudanese and the Tigreans packed over a thousand people into the trucks. Crying could be heard on all sides. That was when we realized just how enormous the disaster was. Many women had left behind their husbands or children who were working some distance away and so were not at home at the time of the raid. After we traveled for an hour, it became clear that the Sudanese were not taking us to Um Rakoba and in the trucks there was more and more talk that we were going to be executed in the desert. At midnight, the trucks stopped and the soldiers threw us out of them. We were in total darkness; only the ridges of hills could be vaguely seen on the horizon. The children asked for water but we didn't have any to give them. Because of exhaustion, the children fell silent and we, the adults, waited for dawn.

When the sun rose, the children started calling out for water again and Adisu set out at the head of a group of men to search for water, but they looked in vain; we couldn't find any.

The old people told us to pray and walk. We didn't even know in which direction to walk, but we believed that God would direct us. So we started walking, a long column of about a thousand people, like a long snake twisting among the hills. After four hours of very difficult walking, with the children crying for water, we reached a road. Even though we could not see anyone on it, we were as happy as if we'd run into an old friend since the road meant that we would find water and maybe even food. After walking a short way along the road, Adisu suddenly let out a shout. He realized that he knew the road and even remembered that there is a water source not far from where we were. He took about eighty people with jerry cans and immediately set out.

When we saw them on the horizon coming back, a murmur of joy passed among those of us waiting and even the children, who were crying the whole time, fell silent as though they understood that soon they would have water to drink. It was around noon and people were so thirsty they were ready to grab all they could, but it was measured out in the lids of the jerry cans, one measure to each person. Some people did not even get that, but anyway within an hour we reached the water source. It was a swamp full of muddy water, but who cared? We all swarmed over the water and drank as much as we could. The results were not long in arriving, and some of the people fell ill because they had drunk too much.

The next day we set out with full jerry cans that would supply us for seven hours until we would reach the next water point. On the way, a baby died and so did a woman. We buried them at the roadside. What else could we do?

After walking four days, carrying our sick and elderly on stretchers that we'd made, we reached Derek Ambo. Twenty of the sick and elderly remained there and we went on walking for another day until we reached Tebari where Adisu lives.

Adisu entered the village first and was showered with kisses from his neighbors. There was great rejoicing, but within a short time it turned to tears, when the gentiles discovered the long column of people, who had collapsed to the ground from exhaustion at the entrance to the village. But the people of Tebari provided us with food and drink and took the elderly and the sick into their homes. We knew that we could not stay there for long, so the next day we left for Tikil Dengay, a little town that is near Gondar.

Luckily for me, my father and brother came two days later and took me to Gondar, and from there to Addis Ababa. You can imagine how happy I was to see them, but at the same time I was sorry that it was impossible to take all the people and bring them here.

I hope that now, after you've heard this, you can help us.

When Wubnesh finished telling me her story, she burst out crying. I tried to soothe her and asked her to come back tomorrow when I would be able to give her some money so that she could buy clothes for herself and her children and find a suitable place for her family to live. I promised her I would let her husband in Israel know that his wife and children were safe and sound.

FEBRUARY 15, 1990 – ISRAELI EMBASSY, ADDIS ABABA

I had difficulty falling asleep last night. For many long hours, I saw in my mind's eye the long line of people winding among the hills and I could hear the sound of the children begging for water. It was only toward morning that I dropped off. At present, I am sitting in my office, waiting for Wubnesh to come so that I can give her the money I promised.

But my first visitor today was not Wubnesh but Lakech Mihret, a lovely girl, dressed in city clothes, with her hair in tiny plaits all over her head, large earrings, and a captivating smile.

When she entered my office, she did not come first to me, but ran to the flag on my desk and kissed it twice. Only then did she turn to me, introducing herself with a self-confidence that is unusual in an Ethiopian youngster, and said, "I am Zehava's sister. My name is Lakech."

Zehava Aragay works with her husband, Uri, in the Hofim Youth Village, where they serve as surrogate parents to a group of children. I am very fond of her and I know how much she worries, in particular, about her sister. When I heard Lakech's story, I understood why Zehava worries so much.

LAKECH'S STORY

When I reached the age of seventeen, after I finished six years of schooling in Gondar, I decided to leave the village and go to Addis Ababa in order to make aliyah to Israel. In our home and in our synagogue, where the prayers are in Hebrew, we spoke all the time about Jerusalem, and my desire to get there was as strong as it could possibly be. My brother gave me his protection and we set out together for Addis. We lived here with a gentile woman and paid her rent.

I was a beautiful girl and I felt men ogling me when I walked in the street. I knew that my brother would protect me from anyone bothering me. But nevertheless a tragedy happened. A relative who was friendly with a Christian soldier promised him there would be a relationship between him and me. I knew the soldier, since he used to visit us a lot. One day, when my brother was not at home, this soldier came by himself. From the first moment his behavior was threatening and when I served him a cup of coffee, he grabbed my arm and threw me on the bed. Within moments he tore off my dress and raped me.

I was frightened to tell my parents that I'd been raped and kept it secret. I knew how easily my father gets angry and I didn't want to be the cause of an argument between him and this same relative who had apparently made some sort of promise to the soldier. After a few months I could feel movement in my belly. I knew I was pregnant. I couldn't return to the village, since my father would be angry, and in the city I had no one I could rely on. I saw no way out, except suicide.

I made all the preparations for it, when suddenly my father arrived in Addis. The rumor of my pregnancy had reached the village and he'd set out immediately. When I saw him, I tried to run away but my father called to me and calmed me down, saying, "We can't do anything about it. It's already happened."

He persuaded me to come and give birth in the village, just as all the young women always do when it's the first time they give birth. So we left Addis, my father, my brother, and I. Two weeks after we reached the village, I gave birth and a month later we all left, the whole family, for Addis Ababa.

The first one to make aliyah was my brother. That was after a year and a half. After another year, my parents made aliyah and they were followed by my other brother. I was left alone with a three-year-old son and just a cousin with me. But my troubles were not over.

About a month ago I arrived home, but the son of the landlady and a relative of his – I used to call him the sportsman soldier because of his build – blocked my way. The soldier had a stick in his hand. "You get dollars and eat alone. You're arrogant," the soldier said, and made some sort of prearranged signal. The landlady's son then grabbed me and the soldier hit me twice. I fell and felt that I was losing consciousness, but I was still aware that the soldier was trampling on me and that two of my teeth were broken.

I was left lying there, I don't know for how long. In the end I came to, and crawled into my home. I shut the door and burst out crying. I didn't understand why they treated me so cruelly. Luckily, I met a friend who told me to go to the embassy. So here I am. Now perhaps you'll be able to help me to reach Jerusalem, where my parents, my sister, and my brothers are waiting for me.

I wish I could take Lakech with me tomorrow when I go to Israel to report on the situation to the Board of Governors of the Jewish Agency. Who knows how many months she'll be forced to wait here. I escorted her out of the office and asked her to come to me any time she has a problem; to look on me as though I were her father. When I got back to the office, I was sorry that I hadn't given her the flag that she'd kissed. I'll do it soon.

And meanwhile, Wubnesh Mera was waiting for me in the office. I gave her 300 birrs in order to buy clothes and rent an apartment. I then took down all her particulars in order to speed her aliyah.

Tomorrow I'm flying to Israel. It'll be good to be home. It's hard for me to be here alone, and it's so much more difficult when I see the people's great suffering without being able to provide immediate assistance of the kind they really want.

FEBRUARY 18, 1990 – BINYANEI HA'UMA CONVENTION CENTER, JERUSALEM

We landed at seven o'clock this morning. I didn't manage to go home to see my family. I had to go to Jerusalem immediately to give my report to the Board of Governors on the situation in Ethiopia. I stressed to them the plight of the one thousand people who were thrown out of Sudan, telling them Wubnesh's story. In spite of the slight progress on the aliyah front, I recommended to the Board of Governors that action to bring more Jews from the villages to Addis Ababa be set in motion. In any case, I think that there is going to be a breakthrough and we will manage to bring one thousand people a month on aliyah. Of greater numbers, I dare not think.

MARCH 1, 1990 – ARMY RECRUITMENT CENTER, TEL HASHOMER

After ten wonderful days in Israel, this morning I accompanied my older son, Amit, to the army recruitment center and said goodbye to him. Ruthie was very emotional and so it will be even more difficult to leave today for Ethiopia. But I cannot desert the Jews there. While I've been in Israel, I have been able to meet with many Ethiopian *olim* and I could feel the great trust that they place in me. This trust is accompanied by expectations for a solution to the main problem: family separations.

In February, 146 immigrants arrived, but I have not done anything for them, except for issuing visas and reserving plane seats. Most of them were actually dealt with by the American organizations NACOEJ and AAEJ.

MARCH 2, 1990 – ADDIS ABABA

The landing this time was more a routine matter. My heart didn't beat faster and I'm no longer anxious about border control or documentation. I know that Israel is a very important country for them and its representatives are considered, in a way, like relatives, or, as they say in Amharic, *zemed* – blood relatives up till the seventh generation, whom one is obligated to be concerned about and to defend. Indeed, I passed through the inspections quickly and without mishap and was soon on my way to the embassy, driving through the crowds of people who walk along the roads, seemingly without direction or purpose. My thoughts were abruptly halted when the car entered the embassy courtyard and I saw dozens upon dozens of people waiting, either to get a visa or a flight reservation or to register for assistance.

It is possible to differentiate immediately between the old-timers who are almost at the end of the process and those who have just arrived from Gondar. The former are dressed in nice clothes, some of them in Western clothing, and their children wear shoes. The newcomers are thinner and wear traditional garments that are old and sometimes torn. The women and children do not wear shoes on their feet at all, while the men have rubber sandals, made from car tires.

I know most of the old-timers, but my heart goes out to the scrawny newcomers, seeing in their eyes how much they wish for a word from the Israeli emissary. I greeted all of them with a nod of my head and entered the embassy's basement full of offices, one of which is my own little room, which so many people seek out.

MARCH 21, 1990 – ADDIS ABABA

Today, two young men arrived in Addis Ababa who made aliyah under false names, pretending they were Jewish. At the airport in Israel, three weeks ago, Zimna discovered their deception and today they were returned to Addis Ababa. By lying, they had taken the places of two Jews, desperate to get to Israel. We will have to beware of a repetition of such cases in the future, even when working under pressure. I know that it will not be easy since in Ethiopia people do not have ID cards – those are only used in Addis – and we rely on people to tell us their true names. Of course, they usually do, but sometimes someone will give a false name.

I had still not recovered from my anger about these impostors when a man with thick eyeglasses entered my office. He was well built and seemed very self-confident. He introduced himself: "My name is Addisu Wodaj and I just reached here from Sudan. I have to speak to you."

There was a certain something in his voice that made me put aside all my other work and devote my full attention to him.

ADDISU WODAJ'S STORY

I was born about forty years ago in north Ethiopia. After I got married and my first son was born, I was recruited into the army. I served five years and was wounded four times. When I returned to my village, it was clear that the Jews were starting to move to Sudan. As a wounded, demobilized soldier, I was given a job as a guard in the Gondar bus station.

I waited for the right opportunity and indeed, it arrived. I received authorization to go for medical treatment in Addis Ababa. I went back to the village, prepared my wife and parents to leave, and other relatives joined us. I loaded two of our children on my back and we set out, not for Addis but for Sudan. We walked for three weeks until we reached the first township in Sudan. I was arrested there because I'd forgotten to take off my army belt. Meanwhile, my wife and the other relatives went to Um Rakoba.

After two weeks of hard interrogations and torture, I was released and joined my wife. I found her with her parents and relatives in a large tent. Within two days, I transferred them all to Gedaref. Then, two months later – it was the beginning of May – the big day arrived. We gathered together with many Jews at the assembly point and surged, like everybody else, onto one of the two trucks that were waiting. It was our misfortune that our truck suddenly broke up and the ones who were on it, who did not manage to run away, were taken to the distant refugee camp, Wadihilu, us included.

I remembered the story of Zewditu and how, because she happened to be in the truck that did not break up, she arrived in Israel in May 1984, while her family remained behind.

> Immediately, I returned with two of my friends to Gedaref. I barely managed to avoid the police, but one of my friends was arrested. The next day, the police arrived at my home and arrested me, too. My friend had broken under police tortures and had given out the names of his friends and also told them that the government of Israel was helping Jews through a committee that transfers money to the families.
>
> In the prison, I was beaten and tortured as the Sudanese wanted to know the names of the members of the Committee. When it got dark, with both of us in the same cell and our bodies still in agony, I explained to my friend what he had to do: "They want to know who the Committee members are, so show them a few Christians and then when they try to arrest them, utilize the commotion and run away."
>
> The next day it all happened exactly as I had predicted to my friend and he did, indeed, manage to run away. In the end, they also released me. I went several times to Wadihilu and got all my family members out of there. After some time, I was recruited by the Mossad to work for them and thanks to that, my wife and family were sent to Israel. In Operation Moses, I worked with Yehoshua, but I didn't make aliyah and when the operation ended, I devoted my time to transferring people from Ethiopia to Sudan.
>
> On one occasion, all the fifty-three people that I'd brought were seized and placed under house arrest. I managed to get away and took care of transferring money and messages to them. In that way, I kept in contact with them for over two years. One day, when I was busy preparing documents for one of the activists in the camp, a man came to me whose father had a senior position in Ethiopia. He asked me to arrange documentation for him, too. I did not know that his mother was Jewish, so I told him that I could not arrange even half a document for him.
>
> The man went to the Sudanese police and told them that I was active in the exodus of the Jews. Again I endured torture, this time for seven days. They beat me terribly and accused me of being an Israeli. I said to them, "It's not true. Have you ever seen a black Israeli?"
>
> Throughout those seven days, I drank only tea and the only food I was given to eat was dirty and full of worms. In the end they took me to my home in a car. Fortunately, I was living alone then

and some time before I'd buried the money, the gun, and the list of people in the ground outside. They turned the house upside down, even knocking down the walls, but did not find anything. So in the end, they drove me to a desert region outside Gedaref. Suddenly, the car stopped and I was thrown out onto the sand. I pushed myself up on one foot, looked around and could not see a sign of a living being. The Sudanese officer started by saying, "If you tell us who you're working for, we'll release you. If you don't start talking, we'll kill you here on the spot."

I only knew that if I didn't reveal anything at all, they'd let me live, so I replied, "I don't know what you're talking about. All in all, I ran away from Ethiopia because I can't live there. I have no connection with Jews or Israel."

They did not kill me, but believe me, it would have been better to die. They kept me for a whole year in a cell, in solitary confinement. All I was given to eat and drink was leftovers from the meals of the Sudanese soldiers. I learned to keep food for the next day, since there were days when I did not get anything to eat. For a whole year, I never showered nor changed my clothes. My whole body itched. I combed my hair and my beard with my fingernails. I was fed up with life. I wanted to die.

One day, when one of the soldiers took me to the toilet, I hit him with my fist and cracked open his head. Blood was pouring out from him. I didn't run away but waited until others came. I expected them to kill me. Instead of the death I expected, a tall officer came. The soldiers said to him, "This is the Falasha who came from Israel to work here."

He took me aside. He had a pleasant face, and asked, "Are you a Falasha?"

"I don't know what a Falasha is. I've been locked up on my own for a year without any help. Without a trial. I want to die. Put me on trial or kill me. I've not had a shower for a whole year."

"A whole year?" The officer was shocked. He decided he would put me in the house with the group of fifty-three Falashas. I said to him that I didn't want that. I wanted a trial or death. In the end, the officer said to me, "If you don't go in with the Falashas, you'll rot here for another year. Go there, and in a few days you'll get an answer."

So in the end I agreed. At least I'd get a shower, I thought. But for four months my feet were shackled. Four months later the same officer returned for a visit and was amazed to see me in irons. When he asked why, the policemen answered that that is the punishment for beating up one of them. The officer took me aside and said, "If you don't make problems, I'll make sure you are released from the shackles."

I promised.

In one of the Red Cross's monthly visits, I told them that all the good food they sent us – such as rice and beans – was stolen and we were left only with rotten corn. Within an hour the Sudanese commander was dismissed, but my troubles had not come to an end. The brother of the same Sudanese commander was a police officer and I was informed that he had given orders for me to be killed. I decided to escape. At night, I slipped out of the house and found a merchant who used to smuggle goods from Sudan to Ethiopia. I agreed a price with him and went back to the house. I gathered the people together and proposed to them that they escape with me. They were afraid.

I said to them, "If you don't go, then I'll stay too, and then they'll kill me."

Eventually seven of the young people joined me. One of them stood up and said, "If you die, then we'll die too and if you flee, then we'll flee too."

The next night at ten o'clock, I took the seven of them, one by one, out of the house and led them to the merchant's car that was waiting for us nearby. At six o'clock in the morning we reached the Ethiopian border. But it took us several weeks more to reach Gondar. Now the seven of them are waiting for me in Gondar.

I was riveted by Addisu's story. I gave him some money so that he could quickly bring the other seven escapees to Addis.

MARCH 23, 1990 – THE PRESIDENTIAL PALACE, ADDIS ABABA

Today, the Israeli ambassador, Meir Yoffe, presented his credentials to the president of Ethiopia, Mengistu Haile Mariam. I was delighted that Meir chose me to accompany him. After we waited for some time in an anteroom, the chief of protocol led us to a very spacious room. From the ceiling, a heavy, enormous light fixture hung; immediately below it, in the center of the room, we were halted and waited until the president rose to receive us. We went forward and the ambassador presented a cardboard tube containing a photocopy of the ambassador's credentials. This had been agreed beforehand, since the original of the credentials has not yet arrived from Israel.

After presentation of the credentials, the president spoke of how the friendship between Israel and Ethiopia has lasted many years and of how both countries have common enemies – and so we are obligated to help each other. In the course of the farewell, I said to the president, in Amharic, that after what he had said, we feel like *zemed* – like relatives in an extended family. The emotion on the president's face was clearly discernible.

Perhaps it is the hand of fate, but today, of all days, the last rescue operation is taking place in Sudan, taking out 344 of those who remained after the thousand were expelled in January. The operations in Sudan, though laced with tragedy, are a glorious chapter in the history of our people and our country. Altogether, there have been twenty-five operations – eight of them by sea – bringing to Israel 3,948 immigrants. In addition, there was Operation Moses, in which 6,364 Jews arrived in Israel between November 21, 1984, and January 5, 1985. It was cut short prematurely, but in Operation Queen of Sheba the Americans transported another 494 Jews on March 22, 1985. So a total of sixteen thousand Jews have been taken to Israel from Sudan, of whom twelve thousand arrived by means of the various operations while the rest made aliyah through Europe with the assistance of the Intergovernmental Committee for Emigration (ICEM).

MARCH 24, 1990 – ADDIS ABABA

Three weeks have passed since I returned to Addis and I'm just not managing to cope with all the work. I don't have time for all the people coming to the office nor time for myself. I have to deal with all issues pertaining to *olim* – their eligibility; providing them with subsistence support; their receiving letters of invitation from Israel; assistance in various offices, such as the Ministry of Finance, the emigration bureau, the banks; and finally, issuing visas and organizing flights.

Since the bureaucracy here is massive, something must be done to get rid of some of the procedures. But meanwhile, I am using educated people from the Jewish community to help the Jews to surmount the hurdles in the various offices.

Now, I am waiting with the ambassador for a meeting with Kassa Kebede in the offices of the Communist Party in the center of Addis Ababa. After an annoyingly long wait, we are called into a long, narrow room in the center of which is a long table. While we are still standing, Kassa Kebede enters like a whirlwind, smiling, comes up to the ambassador, and shakes his hand warmly. The ambassador presents me to Kassa, who gives me a firm handshake. I get the impression that Kassa's eyes proclaim, "Don't worry, I'll fix you, too, and then you'll understand who runs things around here."

Kassa's assistant was also present, General Demeke Fenta, who is responsible for internal security in Ethiopia. At the end of the short meeting, it was agreed that the general will coordinate the registration process for family reunification and will set up another meeting for us with the minister of labor and welfare and the person designated by him to work as my opposite number.

I feel cheated for some reason. It turns out that Kassa is heading an Ethiopian delegation that is going to Israel the day after tomorrow in order to request military assistance – mainly arms. He set up this meeting so that he can show that the process of family reunification is moving forward.

The ambassador sees these meetings as progress, but in my opinion they are a sham. The forms that Kassa has invented, as though they were necessary for family reunification, are, in my opinion, nothing but a cover-up for the fact that nothing is actually being done.

MARCH 26, 1990 – ADDIS ABABA

This morning, I went with the ambassador to bid an official farewell to Kassa and his delegation. General Demeke Fenta, whom we met the day before yesterday, was there. After the plane took off, I hoped for a word with him, but apart from a cordial greeting, he did not say a thing.

Every Ethiopian citizen who wants a passport has to have authorization from the income tax authorities, the National Bank, and the mortgage bank stating that he does not owe any of them money. In addition, he also needs authorization from his neighborhood *kebele* stating that he is a law-abiding citizen. The Jews are not expert navigators in the Ethiopian bureaucratic maze and have a hard time obtaining all these permits. That is why I have decided to concentrate my efforts on getting these procedures canceled, and I have set up a meeting for today with the director of income tax. The meeting in his office started in an atmosphere of suspicion on his part, but changed when I began speaking in Amharic. He approved all my requests.

Now that this meeting is over, I realize that that's how I have to work. Although it's the government that sets policy, it is its officials who can either help or hinder the ordinary citizen. We agreed that Jews who have been in Addis Ababa less than two years will be exempt from the income tax authorization needed for a passport. I believe that other obstacles can also be removed, making the exit of Jews easier.

APRIL 1, 1990 – THE AIRPORT, ADDIS ABABA

I am waiting at the Addis airport for two colleagues: Shoshana Zinger, who has been responsible for computerization for the last two years, and Asnakew Sendeke, who in recent years has been employed by JDC to assist with Ethiopian Jews. I remember his sickening descriptions of the tortures he underwent in the Ethiopian prison after he was arrested on suspicion of spying for Israel when he was working here for the ORT educational network.

We sat together for a whole night, Asnakew and I, while he told me of his two years in prison, about the ghastly torments he suffered when his torturers beat his heels with a bull's dried penis, peeling off layer after layer of his skin until the bone was visible and he could not stand on his feet. He told me of the despair that gripped him when they hung him on a board with his hands tied behind so that all his body's weight hung from his back and hands, and the physical agony that produced. He described how in his heart he begged God to let him die, when his torturers forced his head into a barrel of polluted water and then did it all over again.

Now he is returning to Ethiopia. He must be apprehensive about what is in store. I wait outside the door at passport control since neither of them has a visa to visit Ethiopia. I see them coming and how worried Asnakew looks, but then I see a wave of happiness sweeping over him when he spots me. I take their passports and say, "Don't worry, we're here with you."

I spend about ten minutes in the airport's visa department. Since my first visit there over four years ago, nothing in their organization has improved. I think of Asnakew, whose worries must certainly be mounting, but it is just impossible to speed up the entrance permits. Ethiopia, like the rest of Africa, operates at its own pace. When I finally leave the room, I wink at the two jittery people waiting for me, and say, "Come on, let's go."

The customs inspection went quickly. Their suitcases were not checked at all when I said to the inspectors, "They're ours."

I decided not to waste any time and brought Asnakew and Shoshana straight to the embassy. At one point during the journey there, Asnakew asked that we slow down. As I did, we saw a car with a man and woman in it driving past us, with the occupants waving at us. Asnakew just managed to return their wave before they sped away. "That's my nephew, Ayanaw Alemeneh. He's a Kfar Batya graduate, like me," Asnakew explained. "He has an important job in the Ethiopian secret police. It's forbidden for him to be seen with us, but he wanted to welcome me on my arrival in Ethiopia."

With a minimum of ceremony, they both started working. People have arrived from Gondar and had to be checked for their eligibility for aliyah. This work was performed underneath the trees in the embassy courtyard. Shoshana and Asnakew turned into an investigation team, checking that the dozens of arrivals from Gondar indeed appear in the census of Ethiopian Jews that we have named “The Book of Jewishness.” This book contains the names of the heads of Jewish families, as they were registered between 1974 and 1976 by a Jewish-British organization, the Falasha Welfare Association.

It was only after night fell that we went to the Hilton Hotel. Asnakew joined me in my room and Shoshana has a room of her own on the same floor.

APRIL 2, 1990 – ISRAEL EMBASSY, ADDIS ABABA

Now we are three. Asnakew and Shoshana continue to receive the arrivals from Gondar in the embassy courtyard. Through my window, I heard excited voices and hurried outside. I saw Asnakew with tears in his eyes hugging a woman who was older than he. Shoshana explained, “It’s his sister.” My reaction was very rude: “So, finish welcoming your sister already. You’ll meet her tomorrow and there’ll be plenty of time in Addis for you to get together.”

I saw how angry this made Asnakew and how much he wanted to answer me back, but he was held back by his ingrained courtesy, as well as by his affection for me. That night, in my bed, I thought of apologizing, but instead I fell asleep.

APRIL 8, 1990 – LEONARDO DA VINCI-FIUMICINO AIRPORT, ROME

We’ve been very busy these last days, even though there are now three of us to do the work. Every day we have dealt with dozens of people arriving from Gondar. There have been attempts by Christians to pass as Jews, and yesterday Asnakew discovered just such an impostor. He asked him, “Do you know what Shabbat is?”

“Sure,” the man said. “On Shabbat, we get up in the morning, light the fire and prepare coffee and slice the bread.”

“Thank you,” Asnakew said, and asked the man to leave the embassy, knowing that Jews are not allowed to light a fire on Shabbat.

Tomorrow is the eve of Passover, Pesach, the beginning of the Festival of Freedom, and I am in a plane with a group of 121 *olim*, including many children. The women and children are all dressed in white, except for one woman and her child who are dressed in Western clothing and keep their distance from the other immigrants. After checking the list of passengers, I realize that they are the Christian wife and son of a young man whose mother is also a Christian. He is already in Israel.

We are met in Rome by Jewish Agency staffers and several security people. It is moving to see their deep concern for the *olim*, as though they were their own families. I sit in one of the corners and watch my *olim*; yes, they are mine, since most of them got their passports thanks to my intervention. I am proud that since I arrived in Ethiopia about two and a half months ago, over five hundred immigrants have gone to Israel, half of them in the first week of April. Who would have thought that in one week there would be 250 *olim*?

The satisfaction is great, but it's still not enough. I want to step up the momentum to five hundred *olim* a week, without the assistance of the American organizations. In order to achieve the American level of efficiency, we must have a better system of care and finance. Two American organizations have been active for years in rescuing Jews from Ethiopia and Sudan: the American Association of Ethiopian Jewry (AAEJ) and the North American Conference on Ethiopian Jewry (NACOEJ). We have sometimes had differences of opinion in our methods of operation and there have been occasions when they interfered with our people's work in Sudan. However, since Operation Moses, their primary efforts have been carried out in Ethiopia and they have reached a very high level of efficiency – and, of course, they've got almost unlimited funds. It's difficult for me to put people off and not deal immediately with their wishes and problems, but I don't have the resources to respond immediately to every request, while the Americans do.

In a few hours, we will land in Israel and celebrate the Passover Seder. But immediately after the holiday, I will go up to Jerusalem and present this problem to Arnon Mantver and Uri Gordon, and

I will not leave their offices until I have the authority to be more responsive to the people. It's the only way that we'll be able to prove to the Americans that we can do the job ourselves. I feel strongly that it is our responsibility, not theirs, to take care of Jews who are going to become Israeli citizens and are in need.

It's symbolic that I am arriving in Israel with 121 *olim* on the eve of Passover. I remember the service in the Woleka synagogue on Shabbat, over four years ago, when I read aloud from the Torah about the Exodus from Egypt. That night, I was forced to tell the youngsters that there was not yet a way for them to reach Israel, but today I am bringing my first *olim* to Jerusalem – to Eretz Yisrael on the eve of the Festival of Freedom.

APRIL 23, 1990 – IN AN ETHIOPIAN AIRLINES PLANE, OVER ADDIS ABABA

It was lovely being home with the family for the holiday, but somehow my heart was still in Ethiopia with my African brothers.

By the end of this month, 550 *olim* should leave, but one can't allow oneself to get caught up in any euphoria or complacency. The procedures have to be made simpler and the system has to be made more efficient. Only then will we be able to ask the American organizations to quit the field. Even so, we'll have to remain in Ethiopia for at least three years if the rate of aliyah stays at five hundred a month.

Once again, we wonder why the government does not allow all the Jews to depart. After all, they have fifty million citizens. Why should it matter to them if eighteen thousand people leave for their homeland, leaving them that many fewer mouths to feed? The only answer is that the Jews serve as hostages for the government. As long as there are Jews in Ethiopia – so the government believes – Israel will keep its promises to give aid.

MAY 1, 1990 – ISRAEL EMBASSY, ADDIS ABABA

Today the Communist world is celebrating its Labor Day. They are celebrating it here in Ethiopia, too. It's not a festival that we regard particularly, but today we have a reason to rejoice, as well. Today, almost two hundred Jews have arrived from the Gondar region. At four o'clock this afternoon, when in other embassies the workers are packing up for the day and getting ready to go home, a whole new workday is starting for us. On our internal communications system, the Ethiopian guard announces from the gate that families have arrived from Gondar. We quickly go down to the gate where a spectacle that is difficult to envisage meets our eyes. Toyota cars, painted blue and white, pull up one after the other and let out Jews from Gondar. They remind me of the Jews that we received in Israel from Sudan – the men dare to approach the gate while the women and children stay back, waiting to see what happens.

My heart goes out to these people, but I do not have time for displays of affection. Within two hours it will be night and we have to arrange somewhere for them to sleep. We agree with Susan Pollack, the AAEJ representative in Addis Ababa, to accommodate them in the compound where she has her office. To accommodate this number, she has erected two huge tents in the yard. She is happy to be able to help. I enjoy the cooperation with Susan. She is wise, charismatic, and energetic. It's true that she does not always work in cooperation with us, but everything she does is out of concern for Jews.

MAY 2, 1990 – ADDIS ABABA

I wanted to devote my attention today to the children who arrived yesterday, but it was impossible. Time presses. Today, too, many Jews arrived from the north.

MAY 16, 1990 – ISRAEL EMBASSY, ADDIS ABABA

The appearance this morning of the group of over fifty people that Addisu Wodaj brought from Woleka reminded me of the sights that we saw during the operations in Sudan. Their clothing is torn and their bodies gaunt, but more than anything else one notices their eyes...such sad eyes, taking me back to the meetings on the lawn in Ashkelon. But the stories of the Jews who were returned from Sudan to Ethiopia four months ago and are now arriving in Addis Ababa are even more alarming than the stories I heard during those operations. One has lost his wife, another one has lost two of her three children, this one his father and this one his sister. All the stories are ghastly.

Still, I cannot get caught up in melancholy; for one thing, I just do not have the time for it. During the last four months, we have come a long way. I managed to persuade Arnon Mantver, director of the Aliyah and Absorption Department, as well as Michael Schneider, executive vice-president of JDC, of how essential it is to give immediate economic relief to the refugees and they have given me the authorization and the means for it. Now I can respond immediately to any request.

I have also succeeded in streamlining the procedures in the Ethiopian government offices and today it is enough for a Jew to bring a letter of invitation from relatives in Israel, together with a *meshenya* – a travel permit – from Gondar to Addis, for the process of issuing a passport to start. Authorizations from the income tax office, the mortgage bank, the National Bank, and the *kebele* are no longer needed. Only the emigration bureau still presents a problem: the official who sits in room number four. His name is Kifle. He is very rude to the people and delays their appointments by weeks, but it is also possible that he is acting according to instructions from above. I'll deal with this in the next few days.

MAY 23, 1990 – ISRAEL EMBASSY, ADDIS ABABA

Today broke all records. More than five hundred Jews came from the north in an endless stream. More and more flowed in, some straight to the embassy and some to Susan's office on the hill.

This morning we dealt with the group that came yesterday, over two hundred people. We checked their eligibility for aliyah using the "Book of Jewishness." Most of them are eligible and, in fact, most of them are already registered on our computer since at some time in the past their relatives in Israel had sent them assistance through JDC. Sometimes details have to be corrected, to change some name or other, to add a child or two, or to alter the age that was previously noted. The details that the relatives in Israel gave are not always exact.

After finishing the registration and correcting the data, we send the families for a medical checkup and give them enough money for three months' rent and two months' provisions. However, I suspect that the families do not always rent suitable accommodations for unsavory reasons. Coming to the big city confronts them with many temptations like alcohol and prostitution, so, in some cases, they will spend the rent money on such things.

Fortunately, Ami Bergman of the JDC is here right now in his capacity as cochairman of Almaya – an organization established by JDC to assist Ethiopian Jews while they stay in Addis Ababa. Ami and I have worked together in close cooperation for several years and have always understood each other completely, thus we could usually get things moving without any waste of words. Ami has added an Ethiopian doctor, Dr. Melesse, to his team, and JDC is also responsible for the distribution of funds. That way the traditional division of labor is preserved – JDC looks after people's sustenance and welfare while we address aliyah.

A few days ago, I visited several of the Jewish homes and was shocked by the conditions. One family is living in a room two by two meters, which was formerly a toilet. They cannot be allowed to go on living there. Today I found fourteen families in a building that was formerly a cowshed, which its owners have turned into fourteen rooms, divided by partitions. It stinks of a mixture of garbage and urine, and the whole structure is full of smoke from the cooking fires. Tomorrow, I will find these families new accommodations.

MAY 24, 1990 – ADDIS ABABA

This morning, I evacuated the fourteen families from the cowshed. I really enjoyed seeing the place empty of people. I felt like picking up the garbage that was left and throwing it inside the landlord's door.

Immediately afterwards, I went up to what has become known as "Susa Compound" – Susan's office up on the hill – in order to deal with the five hundred Jews who arrived yesterday from the north. There are also some converts among them. The term *Felesmura* was often heard – a term I heard for the very first time four years ago. Others use another term, *Mariam Wodid*, meaning "those who love Holy Mary." But during the few minutes we give to each interview, there is no leisure to delve into the significance of terms. We had to explain to these people, who had arrived together with the Jews, some of whom are their extended family – *zemed* – that we cannot deal with them and they have to return to their villages.

In another few minutes, I will have to go out to a family of six people and tell them that they do not belong here and all because their father's father converted to Christianity about eighty or a hundred years ago. They look the same as the Jews – their clothing, their language and their features are the same – but I embrace the Jews and the others I have to expel. I put off going out to the convert family. How will I tell them that they have to leave this place? That they have to go back to the place they have abandoned? But I must do it, because if I don't, thousands of others like them will show up here, perhaps slowing the continuing aliyah of the Jews.

I mustered the strength and went out.

I amazed myself. The steely words that emerged from my throat were those of someone cold and impervious: "You are not eligible for emigration to Israel because you are Christians. You must go back to your villages. You must pack up your belongings and leave the courtyard."

To my surprise, the family did as I instructed – without arguments, without asking further, without begging, without raising a voice. They quietly packed up their few belongings and departed into the night. Only the youngest of the children dared to look at me, his eyes enormous. That night, in my room at the hotel, I hated myself for my toughness; I hated myself as though I were another person, not myself. It was difficult for me to fall asleep. The child's enormous eyes were pursuing me.

MAY 25, 1990 – ISRAEL EMBASSY, ADDIS ABABA

I kept myself busy all day, so as not to remember that child's eyes, but the picture of the family going away and the kid's enormous eyes stayed with me the whole time. I analyzed the situation with Susan and we agreed that she would send emissaries to Gondar to prevent the converts from coming to Addis Ababa.

I hope it works.

And again, in order to forget and keep myself occupied, I worked out the aliyah statistics for the previous months. Today, a group of seventy-one *olim* left and in another six days, 113 will depart, so that during April and May there will have been over one thousand emigrants to Israel.

JUNE 7, 1990 – IN AN ETHIOPIAN AIRLINES PLANE EN ROUTE TO ROME

A very hard week is drawing to its end today. On the one hand, we received over fifteen hundred Jews from the north and, on the other hand, I was told that my six-and-a-half-year-old son, Kfir, misses me so much that he is threatening to run away from home. My longing for him has also grown to the point that I can no longer ignore the cries of a son who misses his father.

I asked my deputy in Israel, Avi Mizrahi, to come to Addis Ababa right away and, indeed, he arrived the day before yesterday. I introduced him to the work and I think that he will cope with the problems, even if the flow of Jews to Addis grows.

A few days ago, I sat with Susan Pollack in her office on the hill. When we were alone for a few minutes, Susan showed me the official stamp that she bought from one of the senior officials in Gondar. It is used for stamping every *meshenya* – the travel permit that allows passage from one region to another in Ethiopia. That's how she is now able to provide to every family that has arrived in Addis without papers the right document that they need to begin the process at the emigration bureau. I have no problem with agreeing to the use of this stamp, since I am committed to the premise that every Jewish family who is here must be assisted, and none should be asked to return to Gondar in order to obtain some document or other; not only does that cost a lot of money, but it's also very dangerous, since a war is being waged in the Gondar region.

Yesterday ninety-four immigrants left, and another fifty-eight are sitting with me now in the plane. We are flying over Egypt and I am rereading *Mila 18* by Leon Uris. The first time I read it, I was seventeen years old and living in Germany. I regretted then that I was not old enough to have taken part in the struggle against Nazi rule and the establishment of the State of Israel. I wished I'd been born in the twenties or thirties. But now I feel that I, too, am playing an important part; at long last I have the opportunity of doing something that has historical significance. At present, there are about 8,500 Jews in Addis Ababa, half of whom arrived in the last month. Susan's plan is working. Most of the people arrive in buses that she hires, direct to the courtyard of her office. For the last two weeks, we have been receiving the people there, and that is where we check their eligibility for aliyah. However, we are now faced with a major problem because complaints have been sent from people in the Communist Party in Gondar to the party headquarters in Addis Ababa.

Kassa Kebede cautioned us yesterday. According to him, the Jews' exit from Gondar is causing disquiet there. The gentiles think that the organized departure of the Jews is a sign that the rebels will conquer the area soon. He said that he would no longer allow the Jews to leave Gondar for Addis and is even considering assembling all the Jews now in Addis and sending them back to Gondar.

We hope to get through this crisis peacefully, but we decided that meanwhile we have to keep our distance from the organizations operating here, and in particular from Susan, whose work we value highly. I told her about our decision to cut off contact, saying that we are doing it with a heavy heart, but for the benefit of the cause. She understood this and accepts it.

Another difficulty that is a source of constant worry is the problem of medical care. I have recently often witnessed the work of the Ethiopian doctors and nurses and I also paid a visit to Dr. Melesse's clinic; it is simply inadequate to deal with so many. Day by day, my opinion grows stronger that a team of doctors has to be brought as soon as possible to Addis Ababa to care for the refugees, especially for the children, whose condition is a cause for concern; some are likely to die.

Tomorrow morning, I'll deal with that as well, after I get to Tel Aviv.

JUNE 15, 1990 – THE JEWISH AGENCY OFFICE, TEL AVIV

In Avi's first cable, he reports that the stream of Jews to Addis Ababa continues. There is no doubt that Susan works very efficiently. Every single day, hundreds of Jews are arriving by bus and car direct to Susa Compound. However, no one can guarantee that this flow is actually a good thing. What will happen if the Ethiopian government tightens the screws and does not allow the Jews to depart? Who knows how many of them will pay with their lives?

I do not forget the gaunt children I have seen and I run around from office to office until I have obtained two things: Firstly, in the near future two doctors will go out to evaluate the situation. Secondly, I have acquired vaccines against meningitis and measles, two illnesses that can be fatal to children. On the day I fly back to Ethiopia, I'll take possession of the vaccines and carry them in an insulated thermal box to Addis Ababa.

With all my love for my family and my joy at being with them, I am pulled back to the Ethiopian Jews who are waiting to make aliyah. The time spent until my flight is difficult.

In the meantime, the aliyah is continuing and we hope that by the end of the month, about 440 *olim* will leave. In addition to those, another twenty-two have arrived via Kenya.

One problem that Avi has had to address is the converts. Day after day more and more of them are arriving via Susan's organized transportation. Her people are not familiar with the Law of Return and are not able – or do not see the need – to differentiate between the Jews and the converts. It is also likely that it would be impossible to dissuade these people, in any case. There seems to be an urge for anyone connected to the Jewish people to go to Israel. Our people in Addis, who must operate within the framework of the Law of Return, are forced to refuse the converts and ask them to return to their villages, even though these people have liquidated everything they own, left their villages, and now have nowhere to go back to. In addition, the Ethiopian social codes of honor do not allow them to return to their villages. A way has to be found to prevent the stream of converts from continuing to flock into Addis Ababa. But how?

JULY 15, 1990 – ISRAEL EMBASSY, ADDIS ABABA

I returned to Ethiopia five days ago, carrying the insulated box of vaccines. The staff of the Kenyan airline was no doubt amazed at seeing an Israeli carefully shlepping a large plastic picnic box everywhere, as though it were pure gold. The day before yesterday, I received authorization from the Ethiopian Ministry of Health to immunize the people and they also sent teams to deal with it. The work commenced right away and yesterday over one thousand people were vaccinated. Since everything was running smoothly, I wanted to take advantage of the fact that the people had assembled anyway to distribute blankets to them. The rainy season has started and the cold penetrates through all the holes in their dilapidated huts. At first, we decided to give one blanket to every two *olim*. And indeed, after the vaccination everyone proceeded from the immunization tent on the slope of the hill up to the embassy building, where every two *olim* received an army-type blanket. Those blankets bring back clear memories of Israel in the fifties and sixties.

I decided that the immunization campaign would continue during Shabbat, as well, which led to an argument between me and the *kessoch*. A delegation of *kessoch* came to me and in their usual pleasant manner asked me to postpone the campaign till Sunday. I was furious. How can such an operation be delayed when children are dying? After all, recently, in a short period, twelve people, including four children, have died. My position was clear: no delay. But the *kessoch* were not willing to relent and asked me why I am so insistent. I gave them the halakhic ruling that "Saving a life takes precedence over Shabbat" but the *kessoch* did not give an inch. One of the senior *kessoch* said, "We understand the concept that you have presented to us just now. We understand that you believe that it is permissible to desecrate the Sabbath when it is possible to save a person's life, but our belief in God is so great that we believe that if the Holy One, blessed be He, wants it, whoever needs a vaccination in order that his life be saved will live until Sunday. Therefore, there is no need to desecrate the Sabbath."

They did not persuade me. The *kessoch* are hurt, but, nevertheless, I did not yield. There will be vaccinations on Shabbat, as well. We have to save the children's lives.

The blanket distribution yesterday, however, has worked against us. When we arrived at the embassy this morning, our car could not get through. It was impossible to see the road and its wide, grass-covered shoulders. All along its length, for about half a kilometer, one could see only heads, heads, and more heads. I reckon there were about ten thousand people there.

It was impossible to vaccinate such a number and so I went to those waiting and asked them to return to their homes. They all nodded their heads, but not one of them made a move. I went back and repeated the request over and over again, but they did not budge. Even those who were vaccinated yesterday have returned today. They all wanted blankets. Not one of them is interested in the immunization, which in our eyes is so important. Finally, I started shouting, but that had no effect on the people either, so all the Jewish Agency and JDC people who were on the spot formed a human chain from one edge of the road to the other, and started to push the people back, in the direction of the neighborhoods where they live.

Even so, in the end, another three thousand people were vaccinated today, of whom about fifteen hundred are children. They have all, apart from pregnant women, been immunized against meningitis, and all the children up to age fifteen were also vaccinated against measles, and once again every two people received one blanket between them.

Kassa Kebede continues his requests for sophisticated weapons to fight the rebels while the Americans pressure us not to provide anything to the Mengistu regime. So, having no other choice in the matter, but also because of our own national interests, Kassa has been given a negative answer. The result is that for the last three weeks no more passports have been issued to our people. However, in discussions with the Americans, they promised us that they will bring pressure to bear on the Ethiopian government to release passports, as it did in the past. Meanwhile, it is difficult for us without any aliyah to Israel. Indeed, it is even more difficult as the stream of those coming to Addis Ababa is not decreasing; hence, the number of Jews in the city is continually increasing. Their situation is dire and there are many deaths. Even as I am writing these lines, the brother of a girl who has just died comes to inform us about it. He is just one of so many, but a very personal reminder.

Recently, we were joined by Mamuye Zerie, whom we call Mamush, meaning "tiny" or "cute." The name fits him like a glove, since he really is short, sweet, very modest, and never gets into any argument or quarrel. In light of the many cases of death, Mamuye, who is a social worker by profession, has been given the responsibility of visiting every family where there has been a death to examine its situation. Whenever considered necessary, especially when contagion is likely, such a family is moved to another apartment and the family members receive medical attention in order to prevent more deaths.

I watch Mamuye as he interviews a mourning family outside, and even though a closed window divides me from them, I can feel this family's grief.

Toward the end of the day's work, Addisu Wodaj arrives. He is very agitated. The forty-six Jews – and three gentiles wrongly considered to be Jews – who were under house arrest with him for over five years in Um Rakoba were brought a week ago to Addis Ababa, but yesterday they were all returned to Gondar because during their interrogation, they said that they were Christians. Nobody told these poor people that if they revealed the truth, they would be transferred immediately to the Israeli embassy. As it is, they have been sent back in buses to Gondar, where they are now exposed to the cold and the rain in one of the open yards in the town.

JULY 20, 1990 – ISRAEL EMBASSY, ADDIS ABABA

In the last few days, death has continued striking down the children, always more frequent during the rainy season. In my mind's eye I always see my son, Kfir, in the place of one of these barefoot children whom I see in reality day after day at the embassy. I am angry with the whole world.

I am angry with the JDC for not allocating more doctors and nurses to treat our people. In the JDC's clinic, there is only one nurse plus a doctor who visits twice a week for two hours. That's how they take care of a population of over ten thousand people!

I am angry with my superiors in the Jewish Agency who do not respond to my requests to send at least one pediatrician and one general practitioner immediately in order to stave off death's rampages. In response to my requests, I receive an answer that makes me even angrier: "Health is the responsibility of JDC and, therefore, we cannot interfere." *Cannot interfere?* When children are dying?! How is it possible?

I am angry with God Who allows these children to die.

I am angry with myself for not doing more to save the children.

I am angry.

Today another child died, but there might be a breakthrough on the aliyah front. Yesterday, we had a difficult but important meeting in Kassa Kebede's office in the building of the Communist Party. This building is situated in the center of Addis Ababa beside Arat Kilo Square. We were led along long corridors to the waiting room and, as usual – and perhaps it was done deliberately – we had to wait. Eventually, we were ushered into his room with its long table. We sat along the two sides of the table and Kassa started by saying that Ethiopian-Israeli relations are not normal relations and the State of Israel is maintaining relations with Ethiopia only in order to get Jews out. We assured Kassa that this issue is important but it is not the only one.

It was clear to us that Kassa was mouthing the president's words and that he is not pleased that his requests for sophisticated weapons have not had a positive response. But perhaps because we hinted that the American government might soon open itself more toward Ethiopia, one could see that we were once again going in the right direction and by the end of the meeting it seemed that they would renew aliyah. Indeed, this morning, Kifle, the man from room number four, called and asked us to tell eight families to report to his office.

In the afternoon, the Um Rakoba detainees arrived from Gondar, going straight to Susa Compound. I rushed over there. The sight of them was just ghastly. The first one I saw was Muchit Mekonen, the oldest woman in the group. She is about seventy years old but looks more like a hundred – nothing but skin and bones and her face with about the same number of wrinkles as the number of days she spent imprisoned. I went to her and kissed her, then did likewise with the other forty-six released prisoners.

JULY 21, 1990 – ISRAEL EMBASSY, ADDIS ABABA

I visited room number four today and saw some of the people I had told to go there. Let's hope things will start moving.

In the afternoon, more people arrived from the north, but it turned out that most of them were converts. The identification process took place in Susa Compound and was carried out by two of the Beta Israel, Esther Eyob and Moges Rachamim. Esther has managed to climb the career ladder in only a few years and is now an accountant in Magen David Adom. She deserves great credit for her success, especially as her life has not been at all easy since making aliyah. More than once she was beaten by her husband but she finally managed to get away from him altogether. Then three years ago, she lost her only daughter in an elevator accident in one of our absorption centers. I have felt particularly close to Esther and fully valued her ability, which is why I proposed recruiting her to work in Ethiopia. At Magen David Adom, they understood the need and authorized a year's unpaid leave for her.

In the last few weeks, since they arrived in Ethiopia, Esther and Moges have handled the identification processing of the new arrivals. Since this process is critical, sealing the people's fate, Avi and I devote a lot of time to helping them. It is tremendously difficult for them when they have to inform the converts that they must leave the courtyard and return to their villages. Sometimes they even have to say these things to their very own relatives, people whom they were so happy to see again.

Today has been the hardest day of all. We had to tell nearly all those who arrived that they are not entitled to make aliyah to Israel and that they must leave here. And today of all days, the sky is gray, it's raining cats and dogs and a bitterly cold wind is blowing. The people are frozen and the children shake from the cold. How is it possible to tell them to leave this place? How can we be so cruel to them? What an appalling job we have to carry out!

I could not ignore the distress of Esther and Moges and so I did the dirty deed myself. I gathered the people in the main hall. Outside it was getting dark. I explained to them that since they are converts to Christianity they are not entitled to make aliyah to the

Jewish state. But they refused to leave the area. However, we cannot give in. If we yield to this group, tomorrow thousands more will pour in and their suffering will also be on our consciences. So with steely firmness, which took great strength for me to muster, I announced to them that the decision is final. Kobi Friedman, the Almaya representative who, ever since he arrived here a month ago, has been working energetically and creatively for the people's welfare, came to our aid and together we did the unthinkable – we threw the converts' belongings over the stone barrier. The people went after their possessions, but still did not understand why we could not accept them. They do not understand the Law of Return.

In the evening, Kobi summed it up in one sentence, "We're tough during the day, but cry at night." And indeed, that night I cried. I barely recognize myself.

JULY 22, 1990 – AT THE HOUSE OF THE WOMEN STAFFERS, ADDIS ABABA

Today Moges Rachamim is winding up the first part of his mission here. Moges, like Esther, had to take a leave from his regular job (at Bezeq, Israel's main telecommunications company) to work here for a year, and it is great that he has been with us. Now, he is leaving behind a really depressing letter that sums up the difficulties that arise from encounters with the Felesmura:

> They say that all beginnings are difficult and that proved to be the case. My first months in this crucial work were the hardest of my life. I couldn't see the start or the finish. It was total chaos. Masses of people were entering the embassy courtyard without any control and without any identification papers. And each with his own story and requirements. For each person we had to provide an answer that would calm him down and relieve his distress. We had to work incredibly long hours in the open air without a break and almost without eating.
>
> I don't know whether I was successful in my work here but there is one thing I do know: it has been a very hard task to carry out. In particular, when faced with people who know you and some of whom

are related to you; this made the whole job even more difficult. It is not easy to tell a family of six or seven people to go to hell because they are not really Jewish, after they have left their village and traveled eight hundred kilometers, or even more, in the hope of reaching Jerusalem.

How would you feel when a family like that comes to you and asks helplessly, "What have I done to you that you tell me that I won't get assistance? When I heard that you work here, I was so happy because, after all, we are relatives. Your father was a good friend of mine. I never expected to hear such a thing from you; otherwise, I wouldn't have left the village, and ruined my own life and my family's life."

It has not been easy at all to carry out the policy of expulsion of the converts. In spite of the fact that legally it is justified, from the humanitarian point of view, it was not pleasant to look at barefoot, half-naked children, shivering from cold, who are forced to depart when it is pouring rain, because they are not Jews. In my mind painful memories are definitely imprinted that will never be erased....

Your colleague,
Moges

JULY 23, 1990 – ISRAEL EMBASSY, ADDIS ABABA

Today Haim Divon, who is substituting for the ambassador, sent off a cable to Israel in which he expresses superbly what we all feel. Haim is a lovely person, very warm, who behaves nothing like the typical image of an ambassador. We all love him. And now it transpires that his felicity of expression is one his most laudable qualities, as his cable to the Foreign Ministry in Jerusalem proves:

RESTRICTED/IMMEDIATE
To: The Minister's Adviser on Diaspora Affairs
c.c. Deputy Director-General African Affairs Desk
From: Addis/Divon
Re: Ethiopian Jews

If there is one issue that, at least from my point of view, will justify this short stay in Addis, it is the work involved in sending the Ethiopian Jews on aliyah.

Not one article in the newspapers, not even the best, can do justice to the sights and the feelings. Most of the aliyah sagas of the past are dwarfed in comparison with the events of the last weeks in Addis Ababa.

The climax was at the end of last week when almost ten thousand – I repeat, ten thousand – people assembled opposite the embassy's walls waiting for their turn to enter in order to obtain a vaccination, a few biscuits, and a blanket and to feel, inside the embassy – among the Israelis – a tangible fragment of their dream of aliyah to Israel.

Their wretchedness, their poverty, and their diseases are apparent in every inch of their bodies, but they wait patiently and draw encouragement from the truly sacred work carried out by the devoted staff of the embassy and the Jewish Agency (headed by Micha Feldmann – who, in my opinion, really deserves a medal), as well as the staffers in other Jewish organizations. None of them skimp on words of affection and encouragement, a hug, a handshake – all so vital to these Falashas. The expression "hardships of the journey" is totally inadequate to express what they have actually gone through since leaving Gondar. The work of the staff gets an enormous boost because we can see with our own eyes what just a few years of life in Israel have done for some of these same people who, only a few years ago, were broken reeds. As you know, a significant number of the staff here are of Ethiopian origin and it is not so many years since they suffered the same hardships. Now, compared with their brothers here, they are like people from another world – vivacious, healthy, easily operating the computers (used by the Jewish Agency). Only their fluency in Amharic reminds us that they are, in the words of the well-known song, "from the same village" and that the State of Israel, with all its problems and difficulties, will also succeed in bringing this remnant of the exile, who are now here, into the twentieth century. I am doubtful whether any other country would succeed in doing so, and I suspect that no other country would even try.

In order to appreciate the size of the present endeavor, I only have to look at the expressions on the faces of non-Jewish visitors who come to the embassy (foreign ambassadors and others) as they look with amazement at the groups of Jews sitting and waiting. They cannot hide their feelings of shock and wonder and complete lack of understanding. It is obvious from their expressions what they are thinking: the Israelis have gone crazy; what interest do they have in accepting these miserable wretches, clothed in rags, and infested with all sorts of diseases that we thought had disappeared from the civilized world? Indeed, neither they, nor any other country on the planet, would allow the feet of these people to even touch the ground at the doorway of their own embassies, and it is needless to add that they would certainly not allow them to set foot in their actual countries, not even as tourists.

I suspect that we are making a mistake in not documenting what is happening here day after day, and I intend to hire an experienced television crew to film it professionally. We owe this, first and foremost, to ourselves, but we also owe it to those who accuse us, among other things, of racism. To everyone at present in Addis, the accusations of "Zionism = Racism" sound completely evil. A film that will document this special aliyah of the nineties will nullify those accusations better than a thousand explanations and speakers, whether to audiences in Africa, the Third World, in general, the black community in the USA, or any other group.

JULY 24, 1990 – ISRAEL EMBASSY, ADDIS ABABA

This morning, once again, we were informed of further deaths – a child and an adult. Then, we received a telephone call from Israel that Esther's sister has died. In this case also, we acted in keeping with Ethiopian customs and did not tell Esther the sad news, but said instead that her grandmother is not feeling well and so she needs to be in Israel. Fortunately, the emigration bureau has provided forty-one visas for *olim* and tomorrow there is a flight, so Esther will fly with me to Israel.

I remembered how difficult it was for me to keep the secret of the news of her mother's death from my secretary, Yaffa, and I know it will be a difficult flight.

JULY 25, 1990 – ON AN ETHIOPIAN AIRLINES FLIGHT EN ROUTE TO ROME

Today we have heard of yet another death. Since the beginning of this month, thirty-six have died – of whom twenty-four were children aged fifteen and under.

In the afternoon we flew out with forty-one immigrants. Esther is with me. She is a great person – intelligent, beautiful, gentle. Why does she have such a hard life? First, there was her marriage and the terrible beatings and abuse that she suffered from her husband. Then, there was the death of her daughter. And now, her sister. Has she sinned or committed a crime that she should be condemned to such suffering?

JULY 26, 1990 – AT HOME IN RISHON LEZION

We arrived in Israel. This is the last group for this month. The number of those leaving Addis has decreased drastically: eighty-two *olim* – about a fifth of those who came last month.

When I saw Esther's family waiting for her, a heavy load was removed from my heart. But the news will be hard for her to bear, even surrounded by all her relatives and even though she has only too much experience of tragedies.

This time, I'll only be home for four days because I have received permission to take my family to Ethiopia, so that they too can feel the importance of the work that we are doing there. It's especially important for my son, Kfir, who resents the separation from me most of all.

JULY 30, 1990 – IN AN EL AL PLANE EN ROUTE TO KENYA

We are en route to Kenya – Ruthie, Yifat, Liad, Kfir, and I. Tonight, we will have a transit stop of a few hours and then we will continue to Addis Ababa. I hope that when my family returns to Israel in another two weeks, they will all understand why I am so passionate about working in Ethiopia.

While we are landing in Nairobi, the stream of Jews from the north is continuing unabated and there are now only a few Jews left there, but this should be matched by the number of those leaving Addis, which, sadly, is not the case. It is a major worry; nonetheless, in Addis, death is the overriding issue. When I was in Israel, I asked for doctors to be sent – and it does not matter who funds them or who will be their bosses. My request has gone unanswered. Once again I was referred to JDC as being the agency responsible for health issues. I just don't get it. Is it important who is responsible? The important thing is to save lives!

Since the beginning of this month, thirty-eight have died. I shall carry on the struggle.

AUGUST 10, 1990 – ISRAEL EMBASSY, ADDIS ABABA

There is still not much hope relating to aliyah. The emigration bureau is not summoning people, nor is it issuing passports. The urgency grows as death continues to strike; nearly every day another child dies.

The problem of the Felesmura also does not give us any relief. It is an especially difficult situation for our Ethiopian-born staff, some of whom have relatives among the converts. But the burden weighs heavily on the entire staff. We are now a team of ten people dealing with a population of sixteen thousand destitute refugees. They have abandoned all their possessions in their villages. The children are suffering from the most severe malnutrition – 75 percent are below the minimum on the scale of weight according to height. Many of them are sick – measles, TB, pneumonia.

The housing situation is also appalling. The non-Jews in neighborhoods close to the embassy rent out "holes" to the Jews, charging exorbitant rates. Sometimes there are over ten people crowded into the tiniest little room, with a low ceiling and no windows. The whole family sleeps on the cold, damp ground. There is one water tap for two hundred people and nobody can have a proper wash. It's better to relieve oneself in an open field and not in the filthy, smelly, overflowing toilets.

Yesterday, I went with my family to visit one of the better houses. Ruthie and the children were shocked. When we left there, Ruthie said that she realizes how important our work here is. I told her that I spared her and our children from a visit to a woman who lives with three small children in what was previously a bathroom where the owners have blocked up the hole and turned it into a "residence." Now that it is the rainy season, sewage water rises up and fills the room with damp and stench. I also spared them from a visit to an old blind woman: she and her daughter can only enter their tiny room by crawling in on hands and knees, as though it were a kennel and not a room.

Kobi deals constantly with relocating families whose lodgings must be changed, but death still continues to stalk us.

In a meeting that was held today with Michael Schneider of JDC and Michael Shiloh, the foreign minister's adviser on Diaspora affairs, it was agreed that the problem will be tackled in a variety of ways. First of all, JDC undertook responsibility for expanding and upgrading medical care. A large clinic will be set up in the center of the neighborhood that houses most of the Jews – Shola – and our health system will be headed by a doctor, sent specifically for that purpose from abroad, who will be in charge of the local doctors. The educational system – which today reaches only 240 children learning in four shifts – will also be expanded, so that it covers all the children, four thousand in number. The main aim is not the actual lessons, but the opportunity it will provide us to supervise the health situation. In the first stage, we will turn Susa Compound into an additional school, serving eight hundred pupils, and in the next stage, for which planning will start immediately, we will build twenty straw huts in the embassy courtyard. Each one will serve fifty children per shift.

I thank the Lord that Haim Divon is now directing the embassy, if only temporarily, and I am so happy that Michael Shiloh is here now. With them, it is possible to make this sort of decision which is, after all, a decision completely without precedent.

I imagine to myself four thousand children gathered in the embassy courtyard, all properly dressed and washed and healthy.

It has also been agreed that every Jew in the city will be given food. In addition, Eli Eliezri, the cochairman of Almaya, has promised to purchase fifteen thousand thin mattresses, made in China, so that most people will no longer sleep on damp floors. At this same meeting, it was also decided that we will evacuate the families whose living conditions are the worst, since one of the main reasons for people dying is, without a doubt, the substandard accommodations.

The problem of the Felesmura in Addis, now numbering three thousand people, was also raised at the meeting. Since these people are completely destitute and on the verge of starvation, it was decided to resettle them in the Gorgora zone of the Gondar region. Kassa has agreed to this, and JDC, through Michael Schneider, is ready to finance the project and help the converts to build homes for themselves there. He is also willing to provide them with crop seeds and cattle.

AUGUST 15, 1990 – ISRAEL EMBASSY, ADDIS ABABA
Today I returned from a short trip with my family and Ami's family to Kenya. It was great to get out of the pressure cooker for a short time but the distress quickly sucks me in again on our return. As soon as I entered the embassy, I was told that last night a five-year-old girl and a seven-year-old boy died.

I find some comfort in the work as today we have started to register the children for the new school in Susa Compound. The Almaya workers have managed to complete the renovations of the rooms in only a few days and even raised the height of the wall around the courtyard, in accordance with the requests of the security officer. Hundreds of people are standing outside the courtyard waiting to have their children registered. What a success! Maybe now we'll also succeed in halting the deaths.

AUGUST 21, 1990 – ISRAEL EMBASSY, ADDIS ABABA
Every day a baby dies. Sometimes adults die, too – especially women. The day before yesterday, one of the women who fled with Addisu Wodaj died. She endured five years of suffering in Um Rakoba, and then gave birth here to a son, but now she is dead.

Three days ago, an Ethiopian military mission returned from Israel, headed by their chief of staff and Kassa Kebede. Once again they had presented their requests for sophisticated weapons, while we only agreed to provide them with nonlethal equipment – such as night binoculars and so on. The Ethiopians propose the immediate exit of twenty-seven hundred Jews, to be followed by the departure of another thousand in another month, in exchange for our supplying the equipment they request. We cannot do this without American agreement. The waiting is nerve-racking. We fear that the deal will not go through, leaving some fifteen thousand Jews stuck here without any hope.

And meanwhile, we continue trying to fight off death. JDC has already set up a large clinic in the center of the Shola neighborhood, distributed blankets to nearly everyone, and has started setting up a network of health coordinators – men and women from the community – who visit homes to see if anyone is sick and then direct them to the clinic.

For some reason, Susan does not like this setup and, backed by the heads of her organization, has decided to set up a parallel health system that is not needed and will only confuse people. Once again, the wars of the Jews are being fought at the expense of the wretched.

This morning, I was at the cemetery for the funeral of one of the community's distinguished personalities, a man of eighty-two, as well as for the funeral of a boy of five. There was a large crowd and much grieving at the first funeral, but at the second, the burial of a little boy, hardly anyone was present. In Western society, it is easy to come to terms with the death of an old person but the death of a child is more painful. But that is not how it is in Ethiopian society, where honor has precedence over life and it is the elderly person who is most honored.

I walked around the cemetery. It was difficult to bear the sight of the small mounds – the graves of children who did not even reach bar mitzvah age. I said Kaddish for them and cried.

I have decided to fast each day that I hear of another child dying.

AUGUST 27, 1990 – ISRAEL EMBASSY, ADDIS ABABA

Today I am fasting. I sent off a cable to Arnon in Jerusalem, reporting on the opening of JDC's large clinic. Susan is continuing to run her own clinic. I asked Arnon to immediately send an Israeli pediatrician and it is not important whether the funding comes from us (the Jewish Agency) or from JDC. Today also brought a ray of light. The ambassador reported that, in a conversation with Kassa, he was informed that the number of *olim* will increase to five hundred a month, and that Kassa himself will visit room number four to examine the situation there. Also today, we received over sixty passports, without any connection to Kassa's announcement. The number of immigrants this month will total 128 – an improvement on last month, but still only a drop in the ocean.

AUGUST 28, 1990 – ISRAEL EMBASSY, ADDIS ABABA
This afternoon, I went with Esther and Yehiel Eran (of JDC) to visit Esther's cousin Belete Direb at the local hospital. He has returned from Sudan very ill, and the doctors have diagnosed malaria, anemia, and pneumonia. He looked like those Jews who were found alive in the death camps at the end of the Holocaust – elongated face, enormous eyes sunk in their sockets, protruding cheekbones, ears sticking out, and bald head. He was lying on his bed, unable to move his body or his head, with a completely expressionless face. Not even a look of pain. An IV was attached to his arm.

There are another seven patients in the same room, some of them with their families clustered around. Belete's father has not moved from his son's bedside and his mother brings her husband fresh food every day. The room is dilapidated, the walls are flaking, the faucet in the corner of the room leaks, and there is a pool of water gathering on the floor underneath. The situation in the corridor and on the stairs is even worse – the marble stairs are broken and what was once a splendid wall is now peeling.

Throughout the whole hospital, and especially its courtyard, one sees patients with amputated limbs sitting or wandering, while the visitors run in and out at all hours.

When we returned from the hospital, I had a word with the ambassador and he is willing to intercede with the authorities in order to receive documentation for Belete to be evacuated to Israel quickly. Tomorrow, I'll try to get a medical certificate recommending that he be treated in Israel.

In the afternoon, we – Esther, Yehiel, and I – donated blood for Belete at the Red Cross center. I was pleasantly surprised by its efficiency and sterility and the strict screening for AIDS.

Soon, the construction of the large synagogue in the embassy's courtyard will be complete. We intend to hold prayer services there during the High Holy Days. At the same time, construction of the school has also started. Getu Yitzhak, who is coordinating all the work, is truly admirable. Kobi, Avi, Yehiel, and I all give him various jobs to perform, with each one of us asking him to put up some different structure or other, or to repair here or there, and he smiles and nods his head and somehow manages it all. I don't understand where he gets the strength to do the work under the difficult conditions that prevail here, but he does so without ever losing his calm.

Since the primary aim in constructing the school is to save lives, not only are twenty-five or thirty large straw huts being erected, but also a big kitchen to supply the children with nutritious meals. Sanitary toilets and showers are also under construction, so that each child will shower at least once a week. We will no longer see children standing beside one faucet that serves hundreds of people, throwing water over themselves from rusty cans.

I also have a vision of a sports ground where the kids can play and forget their misery and crowded living conditions. I see them gathering on the festival days in the planned amphitheater, presenting plays before an audience.

AUGUST 29, 1990 – ISRAEL EMBASSY, ADDIS ABABA

In Jerusalem, Ami (Bergman) is worried about the health care situation, too, and so he has asked the Foreign Ministry representative here, Michael Shiloh, to send a letter to Michael Schneider of JDC, asking that there be no delay in sending us a pediatrician who is expert in infectious diseases. He finished his letter to Michael Schneider with, "Please, ask Ami Bergman of JDC in Jerusalem to find an Israeli pediatrician and send him out within the next few days. It may be that from the statistical viewpoint, six doctors are enough to serve fifteen thousand people, and we here believe that the Ethiopian doctors are very professional, but it is always preferable to do 20 percent more than is necessary rather than 20 percent less."

Professor Ted Myers, who has been appointed by JDC to supervise health arrangements, is also under the impression that the situation here is serious and I hope that he, too, will press for a speedy solution to the problem.

This afternoon, Esther and I managed to take Professor Myers to the hospital where Belete is lying. As soon as he saw the living skeleton, he said, "This boy has Leishmaniasis. I saw hundreds of similar cases in the refugee camps in Sudan. It's a disease that proved fatal to many of our people there and we must not let it kill anyone else."

The Ethiopian doctor agreed that the diagnosis was likely, but when Professor Myers suggested the patient be transferred to Israel, the polite smile vanished from the local doctor's face. We did not discuss it any further. I think that the ambassador will receive authorization from Kassa to move Belete to Israel and then I'll cope with the doctor.

At the entrance to the embassy, an unpleasant surprise was waiting for us. The Felesmura have decided to demonstrate opposite the embassy gates. In my innermost heart, I admit that they have courage to demonstrate in a country like Ethiopia!

In the evening, we said goodbye to our Mamush. Over these last two weeks, the state of his health has deteriorated, maybe because the burden we placed on him was too great to carry. In these last few months, he has gone out nearly every single day to houses of mourning in order to understand the reasons for the deaths and to send the survivors to the clinic. It's a mission requiring superhuman strength and it was apparent to all of us that Mamush's naturally sunny disposition was turning dark and sad.

SEPTEMBER 3, 1990 – ISRAEL EMBASSY, ADDIS ABABA

Death is perhaps relenting. In the last three days, "only" one child has died and in the whole of last week, we lost three children. The week before, there were eleven deaths. It may be that we are seeing the fruits of the comprehensive medical examinations that have been carried out on all the children. Kobi uses money as a strong tool to get what he wants: the monthly allocation to each family is given only after all its children have been brought in for a medical examination. This has also led to incidences of cheating being uncovered, with the same children being registered as belonging to several different families so that they would all get more money. A few days ago, I saw Mamush smack his forehead and cry out, "I don't believe it, I don't believe it; they've registered a child who hasn't even been born yet!" The family had declared a nonexistent child in order to get another allocation and, of course, was not able to bring the child in for a medical examination.

I believe the drop in the incidences of death is also due to the opening of JDC's clinic and the new school for eight hundred pupils in Susa Compound.

SEPTEMBER 5, 1990 – ISRAEL EMBASSY, ADDIS ABABA

I have had three meetings with the Felesmura in recent days. I suggested rehabilitation for them in the Gondar region, but they would not agree. I spoke to them with respect, expressing my concern for their welfare and the welfare of their children. Yesterday, I heard that they are asking for rehabilitation in the Addis Ababa region, no further than fifty kilometers from Addis, in the hope that one of these days they will be allowed to make aliyah.

Kassa formally announced to the ambassador today that passports will soon be issued to sixty people. I hope so, but I have My doubts. Meanwhile, I am fasting again. Since the beginning of this month, three children and two women have died.

Abie Nathan spent three days here and had a three-hour meeting with the president. As soon as he arrived, he announced to the press that all the Ethiopian Jews would depart for Israel by Yom Kippur. This morning, he phoned me from Cairo to tell me that he was promised that tomorrow Belete will be allowed to leave. Let's hope it's true.

SEPTEMBER 13, 1990 – ISRAEL EMBASSY, ADDIS ABABA

It's been a hard day. Three more deaths. Among them was a youngster of seventeen who arrived in Addis a few weeks ago with his sister after his parents and eight of his siblings died in Sudan. Yesterday evening, his head started hurting and his sister rushed him to the hospital, but during the night he died and now she is alone. We have to get her to Israel as soon as possible.

And more bad news. We hear that now the Ethiopian government does not intend to issue more passports to Jews and that next month a sharp drop is expected in the number of *olim*. It's clear to all of us that the Jews are being used as a tool to extort assistance from Israel and the USA.

At the same time, I successfully moved matters forward so that by tomorrow Belete will be receiving treatment at Tel Hashomer Hospital in Israel. He will be saved.

Since early this morning, I have been running around to get a passport for him. At half past five this afternoon, there is a flight to Israel and I reserved a place for him in first class because the other tickets were already sold out.

I went first to the hospital. Belete's father greeted me and helped me to position his son so that I could photograph him for a passport. With the photo in my hand, I rushed over to Colonel Salomon, the head of the emigration bureau, who had meanwhile certainly received instructions from Kassa to be helpful in issuing this passport. I presented the colonel with the photograph and saw his expression change. He said angrily, "A passport cannot be issued with this sort of photograph." From previous experience in Ethiopia, I knew that there was no point in arguing. I rushed back to the hospital. We covered the bed's headboard with a sheet and once again positioned Belete with his father and mother supporting him at each side. And once again, I presented myself to Colonel Salomon with a photograph in my hand. He instructed his people to issue the passport on the spot. According to him, the ambassador came to an agreement with Kassa on this matter. However, Abie Nathan claimed that he is the one who made the agreement and it was with the president. It's not clear who could actually claim credit for the youth's departure but the main thing is that he was leaving here for Israel.

Within two hours, the passport was in my hand and I was on my way back to the hospital. Climbing the broken stairs, the stench of urine in my nostrils, I made a wish never ever again to see this hospital or any other hospital in Ethiopia. In the corridor, with Belete in my charge, I bade farewell to the doctor who had cared for him and rushed over to the airport.

The staff of Ethiopian Airlines was already busy distributing tickets to the sixty-five *olim*, who were dressed in their best finery. Among the green tickets, there was one red ticket, a first-class ticket, for Belete. But when the staff person saw Belete, she refused to hand over the ticket. He sat there in a wheelchair, looking like a heap of bones surmounted by a big head, his sad eyes sunken in their sockets, not understanding what had already been made clear to me: Ethiopian Airlines was not prepared to fly him.

I went over to the smiling girl and explained that if the boy didn't fly today, he might very well die. I added that I was ready to sign any document they required of me in order that he should be allowed to fly. The girl's lovely face expressed understanding and distress but inwardly she must surely have been thinking that these Israelis are crazy, worrying about a heap of bones in a wheelchair. The minutes ticked past. From time to time, I stole a look at Belete. In the background, I saw that the senior airline officials were having a consultation. Suddenly, the one in charge of the flight came over to me, shook my hand and quietly said, looking at Belete, "He cannot fly."

"What?" I shouted.

"The company cannot fly such a sick person."

And once again I found myself shouting, "You want him to die? This boy will fly!"

The eyes of everyone in the departure hall were now fixed on me. Such shouts have never been heard in the Addis Ababa airport. But the flight manager quietly asked, "Do you have a medical certificate from the company's doctor?"

"I'll bring you a certificate," I answered. I knew the company doctor. He speaks Hebrew, since he graduated in medicine at Hadassah University Hospital in Ein Kerem, Jerusalem. But it was already four o'clock in the afternoon and he was not in his office. Again, I found myself shouting, "Why didn't you tell me yesterday that you require that sort of permit? Now it's too late and I won't manage to get it."

I saw a change in the man's expression. He was under pressure. I exploited this and shouted louder. The man asked me to go with him to the office behind the passenger departure counters. There was tremendous activity in the office with staff running hither and thither. We sat down at a large table and the company's manager joined us. They both calmly explained to me that they did not have the authority to allow a sick person to fly without a doctor's certificate. But I responded, calmly, "I have a doctor who is escorting the patient. He is outside and is looking after him now; his name is Dr. Melesse." I rose from the chair, but the two of them remained seated at the table and the senior one said, "But in any case, we cannot fly him."

I completely lost my cool and shouted, "I guarantee to you that he will fly!"

I rushed to the telephone and called the airline's regional supervisor, with whom I have developed excellent relations. Unfortunately, he was not in his office. For a moment, I was stumped, not knowing what else to do. The plane was due to depart in another half hour. The *olim* had already handed in their baggage and they were all excited, while I was there with Belete. I was not prepared to give up. Suddenly, one of the airline staff appeared with a thick book held in his hands – he was running with the book open. He pointed out a paragraph in this book to the flight manager, which is the company's official book of instructions, where it says in black and white, "It is permitted to fly a sick person only with that person's own signature, the signature of a person who takes responsibility for the sick person, and a doctor's signature."

Immediately, I ran to Belete and announced to him that he would fly. I asked Dr. Melesse to sign in his own name and to get Belete to sign, and naturally I was the third person who signed. Everything was arranged. The *olim* went out to the plane and I pushed the wheelchair in front of me. I pointed, showing Belete the plane, and the tiniest vestige of a smile flickered over his face. I left the wheelchair at the foot of the steps to the plane and carried him up in my arms through the door of the plane and seated him in the last row, even though he had a ticket for first class. He was barefoot and I did not want to embarrass the airline company. The main thing was that he was on his way to Israel.

I felt as tired as though I had just run the marathon and as happy as a marathon runner who has completed the course.

When I returned from the airport, completely spent, a new struggle was awaiting me. In my weekly meeting with the *kessoch* and community representatives, Addisu Wodaj rose and accused me of not caring enough about aliyah. As proof of the fact that we are not interested in aliyah, he cited the construction of the synagogue and the school in the embassy courtyard. Similar opinions are being voiced in Israel where they are also citing the construction as proof that we want the Jews to stay in Addis to ensure our own jobs for many years to come.

When the atmosphere cooled down, I answered Addisu with a declaration that I am not prepared to speak with a man who does not believe that the State of Israel is making every effort to bring all the Jews of Ethiopia on aliyah as fast as possible. I refused to discuss it any further with Addisu and his friends – how can they even think such things?

SEPTEMBER 17, 1990, MONDAY – IN AN ETHIOPIAN AIRLINES PLANE EN ROUTE TO ISRAEL

Now that Avi Mizrahi has arrived in Addis Ababa with his family, I can go to Israel. With me are seventeen *olim*. It's a small number, but nevertheless these people will be in Israel for Rosh Hashanah.

In Addis Ababa meanwhile, Getu Yitzhak and his people have managed to complete construction of the synagogue. Next Wednesday, the eve of Rosh Hashanah, the *kessoch* will consecrate it and from now on, festival and Sabbath services will be held in the embassy courtyard. But two matters continue to trouble me: the emigration bureau is issuing hardly any passports at all so there is hardly any aliyah, and worse, death continues to strike down our people.

I hope this time I'll manage to persuade the various agencies in Israel that dispatching doctors immediately will solve the problem. Infuriatingly, this stupidity about which agency is responsible continues. While they argue, people in Addis are dying.

OCTOBER 7, 1990 – THE JEWISH AGENCY OFFICE, TEL AVIV

Today, a detailed report was received from Avi. Its overall tone is very pessimistic. Last week only two passports were received. There is no doubt that this is a matter of deliberate policy. In the whole of September, there were 177 immigrants to Israel. The reception he got from Colonel Salomon, the head of the emigration bureau, was extremely chilly, which means that the latter has received instructions to put a brake on aliyah.

Avi thinks that I must return to Addis and in his cable he writes, "I came here with my family for a relatively long period and one of the aims was definitely to ease Micha's workload here in Ethiopia and certainly to substitute for him when he is in Israel, but I was not meant to replace him here. Micha has built up a system and has developed relationships with various agencies. These ties must not be allowed to wither and it will be difficult for any of us to form similar connections. It is very important that Micha be here, playing an active part in all matters connected with the lives of our people in Ethiopia and, above all, issues of aliyah. However important the role of a senior official in Israel may be, the crucial work and activity are here in Ethiopia and Micha's place is here with us."

I am encouraged by Avi's cable but I am worried that somehow I will not be allowed to return to Ethiopia in the near future.

OCTOBER 11, 1990 – THE JEWISH AGENCY OFFICE, TEL AVIV

I am crushed.

Arnon has made his position clear to me. As long as Avi is in Addis, I am to stay in Israel. It is important that the Ethiopian issue be properly presented here. And it's true that at the meeting that was held four days ago in the office of the chairman of the executive of the Jewish Agency, Simcha Dinitz, I described to those present the situation of the seventeen thousand Jews who are now in Addis Ababa. I emphasized the incidences of death, especially among the children. At the end of the meeting, it was agreed that the Jews in Addis would be considered a population in transition to settling in Israel, which means that the Jewish Agency, and not JDC, is responsible for looking after them.

Immediately after the meeting, I told Ami Bergman in Addis about the decision. Ami has been pressing his superiors in New York for several weeks to send doctors from Israel, but no one there has been in a hurry about it. And now, today, Ami tells me that permission has been received to send doctors and a team of nurses from Israel. And this is all because the Jewish Agency threatened to appropriate the initiative.

However, I still haven't seen any change in the medical situation and am in a very black mood. Meanwhile, I am visiting my patient, which is what I call Belete. There has been a tremendous improvement in his condition. He is standing up now. The doctors and nurses praise his family's devotion – his two brothers who have lived in Israel for a long time never leave his side, even for a moment.

Avi reports that the *olim* are organizing in Addis and are requesting to meet with him. This has been done at the urging of the American organizations and maybe that of the Ethiopian Israelis there. We must on no account forget that there has been no aliyah for three weeks; children continue to die and the pressure is mounting. In the end, Avi decided, wisely, to hold separate meetings with the *olim* and with the Israelis of Ethiopian origin. Last Tuesday, a forum was established of teachers, *kessoch*, and neighborhood representatives, and it will continue meeting every week. This forum is considered as representing the community and all important topics may be discussed by it.

Part Five

Ready, Set, Go!

OCTOBER 14, 1990 – THE JEWISH AGENCY OFFICE, TEL AVIV

I never thought things could change so quickly, but people who are usually well informed have been calling me, one after the other, hinting that I am going to Addis tomorrow. In the afternoon, I sat at home and waited for Arnon to telephone. The call eventually came through late in the evening. Arnon told me that Uri Lubrani, who is leaving tomorrow for Ethiopia at the head of a diplomatic delegation, wants me with him.

OCTOBER 15, 1990 – ISRAEL EMBASSY, ADDIS ABABA

The diplomatic mission aboard the El Al plane to Kenya is a very diverse group, but the main figure is Uri Lubrani, who, in the past, was Israel's ambassador to Ethiopia and Iran and is now the government coordinator in southern Lebanon.

Uri is pleasant to those around him, but never lets personal relationships distract him from his goals. I watch him talking with people and I see how seriously he treats their words. From what he says, I gather that the prime minister, Yitzhak Shamir, has sent him to Ethiopia in order to expedite the aliyah of the Jews, and the sooner the better. Uri does not reveal what the Ethiopians expect from us in return, but I am interested in anything that will improve our chances of getting the Jews out. Uri says that he feels that this mission will succeed and his optimism also infects me. I am happy that I have been given the opportunity to be part of this process and I'm also happy that Haim Divon, who is 100 percent behind the aliyah efforts, is also part of Uri's entourage.

OCTOBER 19, 1990 – ISRAEL EMBASSY, ADDIS ABABA

The last days have been full of action and Uri Lubrani orchestrates the proceedings with sensitivity and wisdom. One can see how much he enjoys the negotiating game, planning his moves like a chess player. From time to time, he gathers us together and reports on what is happening. It looks like things are moving in the right direction and soon aliyah will be resumed.

There has also been an improvement in the health situation and for the last eight days, not one death has been reported.

I feel good here in Addis Ababa and it's as though I've not been away at all. I feel good with the Ethiopian Jews and with our staff. I feel good that death is on the wane and I feel good that apparently there is light at the end of the tunnel, again.

OCTOBER 21, 1990 – HILTON HOTEL, ADDIS ABABA

Uri summoned me this morning to prepare for a working meeting that he is having this afternoon with Kassa and his people. It has been agreed that in exchange for assistance, civilian as well as military, five hundred to six hundred Jews will be allowed to leave every month.

The Ethiopians also held a preparatory meeting this morning, chaired by Kassa and attended by Mersha Ketsela, the deputy minister of the interior, as well as representatives of the internal security apparatus. Kassa planned to open the meeting with an attack on the staff of the Jewish Agency, and above all on me, saying that we are interfering in internal affairs by encouraging Ethiopian citizens to abandon their villages in the north of the country and relocate, without suitable preparation, to Addis Ababa. He is also going to suggest to the president that an Ethiopian delegation go to Israel in order to evaluate the condition of immigrants who have arrived there in recent years.

His strategy in the meeting with Uri is based on the assumption that from now on it will be up to Israel to give something in exchange for Jews, and such compensation must be, first and foremost, military.

So it looks like we can expect many more things to go wrong since the Ethiopians are expecting compensation that we will not be able to give.

Uri leaves at two o'clock for the appointment with Kassa. He asks me to wait in the embassy in case I should be called to join the delegation. And indeed, half an hour later, the telephone rings and I am summoned to take part in the meeting. On the Ethiopian side, in addition to Kassa, there are also the deputy minister of the interior and Ethiopia's ambassador to Israel. In the end, they decide to go back to using the family reunification forms, but in a different format which will, in Kassa's opinion, speed up the process.

I leave the meeting with mixed feelings. On the one hand, I want to believe that aliyah will be accelerated but, on the other hand, I suspect there will be delaying tactics because obviously we cannot provide the Ethiopian government with the military assistance they need to help them defeat the rebels. At the meeting, we brought up the problem of a hundred forms that have already been handed in, but Kassa ignored the issue.

In the evening, in the apartment of the women staffers, which we call "The Girls' House," we set the operational priorities, so that we will be able to deliver the first forms to the deputy minister of the interior without delay. It is very pleasant to have a working meeting with such a superb team. Not one of them complains about the long hours they work, seven days a week. They all give their best and each one draws strength from the others. The team in Addis proves how the whole can be greater than the sum of its individual parts.

OCTOBER 22, 1990 – THE AIRPORT, ADDIS ABABA

Uri Lubrani is now returning to Israel and we feel more optimistic. The other mission members are staying here to make tours of inspection and contacts concerning the civilian assistance to Ethiopia. In their opinion, the agricultural and medical assistance requested in the next two years will amount to five to six million dollars, which seems feasible. We are sure that this assistance will bring about the departure of Jews. The acid test of Ethiopian seriousness will be November's aliyah, when we expect five hundred to six hundred Jews to be allowed to leave.

OCTOBER 25, 1990 – ISRAEL EMBASSY, ADDIS ABABA

I received an unexpected telephone call. Kassa wants to know whether all the one hundred families whose forms were handed in two months ago have actually departed as the emigration bureau claims. I answer that not all of them have left and that within a few hours I'll give him lists of the families who have left and of those who are still here. He, on his part, promises that the deputy minister of the interior will issue appropriate instructions to the emigration bureau so that the processing of these families will go through quickly.

Kassa also requests a weekly progress report on families' departures. Obviously, he wants to show that there is a continual increase in the number of *olim* in order to obtain, in return, the civilian and military assistance. The fact is that even though twenty-one *olim* left today, in the whole month of October, only fifty-eight Jews have departed. This is the smallest monthly number this whole year.

OCTOBER 27, 1990 – IN MY ROOM AT HOME, ADDIS ABABA

Today is Shabbat, but today we are actually seeing the first results of the activity of Uri Lubrani's delegation. I met this morning with Colonel Mersha Ketsela, the deputy minister of the interior, and gave him the list of the twenty families who have already paid for passports but have not yet received them. I also presented him with a request to issue passports for a woman and her three surviving children. She lost her husband and three other children in the last nine months. The deputy minister, whom I met for the first time a week ago, is very short, wears eyeglasses, speaks fluent English with an Ethiopian accent, and is a former army colonel.

Even at our first meeting, he proved that, in spite of his amiable appearance, he is not going to make our labors the slightest bit easier. And yet, nevertheless, I feel that a certain chemistry has developed between us that is worth cultivating since the emigration bureau is in his direct charge.

OCTOBER 30, 1990 – ISRAEL EMBASSY, ADDIS ABABA

Tomorrow we go back to Israel, but today the things that we expected to follow the delegation's visit have taken place. The departure of the Jews is going into high gear. At half past nine, there was a working meeting in the office of Colonel Mersha. To our surprise, every suggestion that we made for facilitating the process was accepted. This meeting, in effect, has canceled the need to present a *meshenya,* as well as the notarized invitation for family reunification plus the authorization that the person requesting to leave is a Jew. Instead, there is just one form to submit with three photographs of every person age four and above. After it is handed in, one only has to wait for the payment demand for the passport.

In order to eliminate the need to bring a guarantor for the family, Colonel Mersha accepted my suggestion that I, as the Israeli consul, give a written guarantee to take responsibility for all claims on an immigrant from any government ministry, organization, bank, or even from a private individual. The embassy people warned me about signing such a document, but I see no alternative and so I'll write the letter today and present it to Colonel Mersha tomorrow, before my departure for Israel.

At twelve noon, there was another meeting, in the office of the head of the emigration bureau, Colonel Salomon. We came to an agreement concerning the person in the bureau who deals with our affairs, Kifle in room number four; two of our embassy staff will now work with him. I agreed with Avi that these two will be Zalman Perlmutter and Yaffa, my secretary, who both arrived on this morning's flight from Israel. At the same meeting, we also agreed that eighty passports that have already been paid for will be handed over to us tomorrow. In the next few days, another twenty passports will be issued so that in the course of the week, one hundred *olim* will be able to leave for Israel.

The number one hundred also appears in another document, connected with Geula Cohen, who is a deputy minister in the Israeli government. She is visiting Addis Ababa to study the situation here and had a meeting with Kassa, who agreed to accept a list of one hundred Jews from her whose exit procedures will be speeded up. We are now working on preparing the list and it will be presented tomorrow. Geula has already been here for three days, managing to visit many homes and to meet with many government officials.

Today, Geula revealed to me that before she came here, she met with representatives of the Beta Israel community in Israel and they persuaded her that the cause of the adverse aliyah situation in the last four months is none other than…me! And, therefore, I ought to be brought back to Israel immediately. Someone even told her that he saw a letter signed by me in the office of the Ethiopian president requesting a halt to the aliyah. I could have been upset about this apparent change of attitude, but then I reminded myself that there are always individuals, especially among the political activists of the community, who feel threatened by someone who is appreciated by the majority and therefore try to discredit him. Now that she has been here for three days, she realizes how very much I love the Ethiopian community and how very much they return my love. It is also obvious to her that without my work here, there would have been no progress at all. So she intends to make sure that I remain here, on the spot, in the future, as well.

I am happy that Geula sees the situation this way. She has turned out to be a most sensitive person who, in spite of her elite status, cares for people as individuals. When she met the schoolchildren this morning, she taught them to say "This year – all of us in Jerusalem" and all the children repeated in chorus after her, with shining eyes, "This year – all of us in Jerusalem."

On Geula Cohen's list, there is one family of five people that is headed by a Christian woman who is not officially eligible to make aliyah – Alemanchi Gelaye – even though her two children and two grandchildren are legally eligible since their father/grandfather is Jewish. We are all aware that the grandmother/mother will make aliyah with them since it is she who has always taken care of the children. Geula was totally enchanted by Alemanchi's eight-year-old granddaughter, whose enormous eyes captured her heart. She gave her a necklace and told her to be sure to wear it when she arrives in Israel.

But meanwhile, who knows how long we'll have to go on caring for the twenty thousand people now assembled in Addis before they all arrive in Israel? Even if they leave at the rate of a thousand a month, the last will only depart in June 1992. I only wish I could say, like Geula, "This year – all of us in Jerusalem."

After the two meetings today, I was brimming with confidence when I entered the schoolroom where we hold meetings every Tuesday with the community's representatives, the *kessoch* and the teachers. Ever since Avi initiated these meetings, we have been forced to listen to their blaming us, as though aliyah is not the main item on our agenda. We know that most of the distorted information they get comes from Israel. But today we can present them with a more optimistic forecast.

When Avi and I went into the round straw structure, those present stood up as a mark of respect. After greeting them, I started off by saying in Amharic, "Perhaps you know that recently a high-level delegation visited here, that conducted negotiations with the Ethiopian government and even met with President Mengistu Haile Mariam. Today we are seeing the first fruits of that visit and soon hundreds of *olim* will leave every month."

Applause resounded on all sides. I was careful not to state an exact number, in order not to raise false hopes among those present.

After I told them of the agreements we had made with respect to the emigration applications and the issuing of passports, I asked the community representatives to play their part by setting firm criteria regarding who has priority to leave first. For a second, there was total silence among the group. Not one of them had expected us to ask them to be partners in deciding the order of departure. After recovering from their surprise, the first to stand up was one of those longest in Addis, and he said, "The order of departure must be according to how long people have been in Addis Ababa."

Logical.

After him, one of those who had been expelled from Sudan rose and said, "Those who expected to make aliyah from Sudan, who suffered there until being expelled and are now waiting here, deserve priority in making aliyah."

Logical.

And then one of the elders rose and said, "In Addis Ababa there are elderly and sick people, and if they do not make aliyah soon, they are likely to die here and never have the privilege of seeing Jerusalem. They should have priority."

Logical.

And then another. "Many families have lost one of their dear ones and there are those who have lost more than one child. Such families should have priority."

Logical.

But then one of the most respected *kessoch* rose and said, "We, the *kessoch*, are suffering since we cannot lead the community here and at the same time it is difficult for us to keep the religious precepts here. So the *kessoch* must be sent first."

This claim did not sound particularly logical to me.

I was very disappointed, especially by the *kessoch*, who are supposed to be leaders of the community. Each one of the speakers only considered himself and so spoke on behalf of the order of priorities that would benefit him.

After a short consultation with Avi, we made the gathering an offer they simply couldn't refuse: of the forms that we present to the Ethiopian government in the future, 50 percent will be for families waiting in Addis according to seniority of stay, 30 percent will be for those who arrived from Sudan, 10 percent will be for the sick and elderly, and the remaining 10 percent will be those who have lost a family member in Addis Ababa. In addition, every month two *kessoch* will leave.

OCTOBER 31, 1990 – IN AN ETHIOPIAN AIRLINES PLANE EN ROUTE TO ROME

This morning Zalman Perlmutter and Yaffa started working in the emigration bureau and eighty Jews now have their passports in their hands. We've been promised that in another two days there will be another twenty passports.

I had to set off for the airport but I couldn't leave the embassy compound before visiting the school. It is a jewel. The children are so happy. It's difficult to detect in their faces any trace of the exhaustion and starvation that placed them at death's door only two months ago. I'm so glad that we all shared in the building of the school, even though in Israel they criticize us for it.

This is the first time in eight months that there are no *olim* with me on the flight to Israel via Rome. I didn't want to wait for the next immigrants' flight as in my bag there are eighty-eight forms that provide for about seven hundred *olim*. The particulars have to be filled in by their relatives in Israel and then the forms have to be returned to Ethiopia in another two weeks. Perhaps I'll be able to fly back with the forms and, so, celebrate the Segd festival with the community in Addis.

NOVEMBER 6, 1990 – THE JEWISH AGENCY OFFICE, TEL AVIV

According to a cabled report from Avi in Addis, there is progress. He says there was a meeting with Colonel Mersha and although the latter expressed disappointment that Israeli promises are not being kept, the emigration procedures are being satisfactorily implemented. Further shortcuts in the procedures were agreed between them, including how the forms are to be filled in, the processing of exceptional cases, and family reunifications. At the meeting, the issue was also raised of "Geula's Hundred Souls," at which Colonel Mersha expressed uneasiness at the possibility "that every politician is going to, as it were, take hostages from here." Nevertheless, it was agreed – according to Avi – that a solution to this problem would be found. At the same time, Avi stressed in his cable his own unequivocal opposition to requests from political personalities seeking instant accomplishments and media attention. He feels that these may have a negative effect in the long run.

Today, 103 *olim* left Ethiopia – the first fruits of the latest round of negotiations.

NOVEMBER 13, 1990 – ISRAEL EMBASSY, ADDIS ABABA

Zalman is getting on very well with Kifle (the man in room number four) and everyone there has gotten to know him. It's very important to have such a person manning a junction that is so sensitive.

When I arrived back at the embassy this morning, I found a large group of people, all of whom know English, sitting at the tables in the synagogue, filling in the forms for the emigration bureau and attaching photographs, all under Zalman's supervision. It's organized like an industry. Good for him!

This afternoon, Avi, Zalman, and I went to Kifle's office and suddenly I had an idea: we'd offer to computerize all the forms that have piled up in his office. The reasoning that convinced Kifle was how much time would be saved if all the forms were computerized.

Uri Lubrani is here right now with Haim Divon to take part in a trilateral meeting – American, Ethiopian, and Israeli. The US government is represented by Herman Cohen, who heads the State Department's Africa Division. The Americans are playing an important role in the diplomatic contacts and I think that it will be thanks to them that we will succeed in extracting thousands of Jews in the coming months.

Today, Uri is running from meeting to meeting. The most crucial one has been set for 12:30 p.m. in Kassa Kebede's office at

Communist Party headquarters. The Americans are represented by Herman Cohen together with the person in charge of Ethiopian affairs, Bob Hodek, and his deputy. We are represented by Uri Lubrani, Asher Naim, our new ambassador, and Haim Divon. On the Ethiopian side, there are Kassa Kebede, Colonel Mersha, and two others from Kassa's bureau.

Herman Cohen is extremely decisive and presents the conditions for improving relations between the USA and Ethiopia. He requests that the port of Massawa be opened immediately for the unloading of relief supplies for villages in the north, that peace talks be held immediately between the government and the rebels and that there be free emigration, stressing that this refers to emigration of the Falashas to Israel.

NOVEMBER 25, 1990 – ISRAEL EMBASSY, ADDIS ABABA

It is the day of the Segd and we have been waiting all morning for the Beta Israel community members to arrive at the embassy compound. They only start to arrive at around eleven o'clock, hundreds of them, all dressed in festive clothing. And then the umbrellas of the *kessoch* are seen coming up the road. The *kessoch* dance with the Books of the Law carried before them, just as King David danced when he entered Jerusalem with the Ark of the Covenant before him.

I am swept along with the people, sharing their exhilaration, as thousands flock around the synagogue. This time we are celebrating not just the renewal of the Covenant between the people of Israel and God but also the chance of actually realizing the second element of the Segd: the return to Zion.

I address the congregation in Amharic: "We are gathered here in Addis Ababa to celebrate the last festival of the Segd on Ethiopian soil and I pray to the Creator of the World is that next year we shall all celebrate this festival in Jerusalem."

Applause was heard from every corner of the embassy and then the groups started to get organized for dancing, group after group of dancers, with the youngsters leaping at the center, each one jumping higher than the next, and around them dozens of people, young and old, moving to the rhythm of the song.

In response to my question whether dancing does not contradict the solemnity of fasting on the Segd, one of the *kessoch* said that even on Yom Kippur, the Day of Atonement, it is customary to break into dance, in accordance with the injunction "You will afflict your souls."

At one o'clock, when the *kessoch* read from the Book of Nehemiah and gave a sermon on the significance of the Ten Commandments, Avi and I left the ceremony in order to meet with Colonel Mersha. The meeting started with my presenting the first fifty-two forms in the new format to the deputy minister. I am sure that Avi feels, as I do, the symbolism of presenting these forms today of all days, the day of the Segd festival.

The meeting was conducted in a very pleasant atmosphere. We thanked the deputy minister for his cooperation and expressed our satisfaction at the efforts that have been invested in issuing the passports. On the other hand, we stressed that the departure rate – 100 to 120 people a week – is not satisfactory and we are looking forward to its being doubled. Mersha promised to check into the possibilities and to reinforce the staff of the emigration bureau in order to help us. Meanwhile, the data from five hundred files in the emigration bureau have already been entered into the computer in what was previously room number four.

The Jews of Ethiopia always celebrate the evening after the Segd ends with eating and drinking. I did not join the festivities, but I celebrated the acceleration in aliyah and the decrease in incidences of death in my heart.

The acceleration in aliyah makes it necessary to step up the pace at which we prepare the forms. The forms that we have processed so far only cover about one-sixth of the Jews who are now here. I will therefore ask Israel for eight extra staffers in order to cover all the Jews in Addis Ababa within two months.

NOVEMBER 28, 1990 – IN AN ETHIOPIAN AIRLINES PLANE EN ROUTE TO ROME

After sixteen days in Addis, I'm on my way home again and 107 *olim* are with me. This month, 428 have made aliyah, slightly fewer than expected.

On this flight there are several people whose presence is especially exciting for me. There is the family of Belete Direb, "my patient," the boy for whom I totally lost my temper at the airport when he was so ill and the airline refused to allow him to fly. He has completely recovered and is now studying very seriously in a special school for educationally-deprived youngsters from Ethiopia. Also are on the plane with me Kes Samuel Negussie and his family. A few months ago, on another trip back home, I smuggled in the *kes*'s Book of the Orit, the Ethiopian Jews' Book of the Law in Ge'ez, and it is waiting for him in JDC's safe. This particular Orit is outstandingly beautiful and Ami Bergman has had it professionally photographed so that, in the course of time, it may be widely distributed.

NOVEMBER 29, 1990, 5:30 A.M. – BEN-GURION INTERNATIONAL AIRPORT

A battery of photographers and journalists are waiting for us on the runway at the foot of the aircraft steps, and in the center are Rina Engeda and Geula Cohen. Five of Geula's special cases were with us on the flight: Rina's two children, two step-brothers, and her mother. I watch as Rina and her daughter, Chana, embrace each other. Chana is the girl to whom Geula presented that lovely necklace during her visit in Addis Ababa. Chana does not forget to show Geula that she is wearing it, as promised, on her arrival in Israel. I am moved even though I know that tomorrow they are going to start a difficult new life. The parents will have to cope with bringing up two children who have not lived with them since they were babies, while the children will have to get used to the fact that it is not their grandmother who is raising them now, but their parents. The grandmother, Rina's mother, was on the flight, but now the parents will be responsible for their children's upbringing.

NOVEMBER 29, 1990, 9:30 P.M. – AT HOME

On television right now, they are showing pictures of the encounter this morning at the airport. After the *Mabat* evening news broadcast is over, Dr. Eli Schwartz calls me. He also has just returned from Addis Ababa after spending five weeks there. Eli is worried but optimistic. He singles out for special praise the work carried out by JDC with its home visits and its clinic and he recommends improvements to ensure that the number of deaths continues to decrease quickly. Many more sick people can now be saved because the Ethiopian government has agreed to evacuate serious cases to Israel for medical treatment, over and above the quota for *olim*. We will probably reach the number of fifteen hundred *olim* a month so that by the end of next year all the Ethiopian Jews will be in Israel.

DECEMBER 10, 1990 – THE JEWISH AGENCY OFFICE, TEL AVIV

The whole staff has been mobilized to prepare the forms and to correct those that have been rejected by the Ethiopians. It's hard to understand why they insist on the most minute particulars and corrections of corrections, unless it is a deliberate policy to control the numbers of *olim* and slow down aliyah. Avi also agrees with this diagnosis and wrote a cable today to that effect.

Obviously, the exit of the Jews will not be decided by the forms. It is conditional on the Israelis' assistance, at least the civilian assistance, and by American pressure on the Ethiopian government. The only one who still believes that everything depends on the forms is our ambassador, Asher Naim. That is how he expressed it today in a closed meeting that took place at the Foreign Ministry in Jerusalem. I tried to persuade him that there is no connection between the forms and the number of *olim*, but he is firm in his opinion: he says that the ball is now in our court and we must meet each requirement that filling in the forms entails in order not to give the Ethiopian government any excuse to delay the departure of the Jews.

At the same meeting, I also gave a survey of the situation concerning the Christian converts in Addis Ababa. I emphasized that the Felesmura include the grandchildren of Jews who are eligible according to the Law of Return, that they are being cared for by us and that, for them too, forms will soon be prepared, but they are the last in line. In addition to them, there are about two thousand converts in Addis today who are not cared for by the Jewish Agency, JDC, or the embassy, but are being maintained by the American organizations. These are Christian coverts who are not eligible according to the Law of Return, and, if we deal with them, it might cause a massive influx of yet more converts to the capital.

DECEMBER 17, 1990, SIXTH DAY OF CHANUKAH, EARLY A.M. – BEN-GURION AIRPORT

Just now, 194 *olim* have landed – the largest number to arrive legally in one day. A historic event. The rate now is two hundred immigrants a week, but it has to be doubled. Before leaving Addis, these *olim* and their children managed to celebrate Chanukah in the largest Jewish school in the world – serving thirty-five hundred pupils. Soon the wall will be completed around this extraordinary school that consists of straw huts in each of which fifty pupils sit, some of them barefoot. It's a pleasure to watch the children devouring their teachers' words. It's true we set up the school mainly in order to save the children from diseases, death, and the streets, but they are also learning basic Hebrew and that helps with simple communication. I really enjoyed strolling among the classes and listening to the ragged singing of the well-known children's song, *Yadayim le'ma'alah, al harosh, al haketafayim, ahat, shtayim, shalosh* (Hands up, on the head, on the shoulders, one, two, three).

Yesterday, the thirty-five hundred pupils, together with five hundred visitors, celebrated Chanukah – a festival previously unknown in Ethiopia as its Jews were cut off from the rest of the people of Israel and from the Land of Israel before the period of the Maccabees. Avi reports that the Chanukah celebration in our school's amphitheater was the most moving one he has ever experienced in his life, with the kids and the guests enjoying over four thousand *sufganiyot*, the traditional doughnuts of the holiday, made in the school's kitchen, and all the children singing Chanukah songs – somewhat off-key.

Meanwhile, here in the airport there is a reunion between Aynesagn Yimharen and his paratrooper son. The father has difficulty recognizing his son at first, but ends up clinging to his neck, unable to stop the stream of tears flowing from his eyes.

In the afternoon, I was in the office dealing with the preparation and correction of the forms and couldn't make myself available for the public. Unexpectedly, a young Ethiopian man entered wearing an army uniform and the red beret of a paratrooper. "I know that today is not a day you receive the public and that you don't remember me, but I wanted to remind you of something. We arrived in Israel six years ago with Operation Moses. You were on the bus with us and on the way we saw paratroopers. And then you said, 'In a few years, maybe you, too, will be paratroopers.' I have never forgotten that, and that was also during Chanukah. So here I am now, a paratrooper and it is Chanukah, and I came to remind you of what you said six years ago."

Perhaps the skinny kids who made aliyah today with their parents, looking with wide-eyed curiosity at all the new sights, will also be paratroopers in another few years.

DECEMBER 27, 1990 – THE JEWISH AGENCY OFFICE, TEL AVIV

Today, the last group of 1990 arrived, with 120 *olim*. Eight months ago, this was considered a large number, but now it does not satisfy us. If it were only possible, I'd bring all twenty thousand Jews from Ethiopia in daily flights over three months and there would then be no need for forms or clinics or a school in the embassy courtyard. The situation is complicated and I suspect that we are going to have to remain in Ethiopia for another year or two.

Nevertheless, in 1990, there were 4,153 *olim* from Ethiopia – of whom 769 came from Sudan and the rest direct from Addis.

JANUARY 4, 1991 – BEN-GURION INTERNATIONAL AIRPORT

Among the 195 *olim* today is Rubel Tayachew, who was a lieutenant in the Ethiopian army. He deserted after being wounded and hid for four months before at long last managing to make aliyah. I sat with him at the airport and he told me his story.

RUBEL'S STORY

I was born in the village of Aba Antonis near Gondar. I studied at the school and helped my father with the work in the fields, but when I was about twenty-four years old, I decided to leave the village and enlist in the army. My parents were not really in agreement with this decision as they wanted me to stay in the village and help support the family. But I insisted and so I joined the army.

After a few months of basic training in the region of Addis Ababa, I was sent to Ogaden. It was far away from my family and I really missed the village. Eventually, I was sent to Gondar. I was so happy because it meant that I could visit my family from time to time. It's true I'd enlisted against my parents' wishes but I missed them so much and every visit to the village was like a holiday both for them and for me.

A year ago, the rebels started to rack up victories. We fought as hard as we could but they started pushing us back on all fronts. Eight months ago, I was wounded in my hip during a battle near Adis Zemen and was taken prisoner. About eighty of my comrades were captured with me and we were kept in awful conditions. It wasn't enough that we'd been captured and some of us were wounded, but we were also on the verge of starvation – our captors didn't have enough food even for themselves.

One day, when evening fell, I went to one of the officers and asked permission to go to the nearby village to ask for food. To my surprise, he authorized this. Maybe because he hoped that I might also bring food for him and his soldiers or maybe because he thought it was unlikely that a wounded soldier would run away. Not far from the place where we captives were being held, I saw a merchant returning from the market leading a donkey. I went to him and asked him to lead me to our lines. I took out ten birrs from my pocket and gave them to him. The merchant agreed, perhaps because he wanted the money or perhaps because he wanted to help a soldier from the government side. It was dark when we arrived in the area where the government forces were deployed. I was given a great welcome and felt that my return lifted the other soldiers' morale.

We didn't waste any time and the next morning, very early, I led the soldiers to where the prisoners were assembled. That same day, we returned to our base with all eighty captives. As a reward for my help in locating the captives, and since I was wounded, I was sent to the military hospital in Addis Ababa. When I reached there, I saw many soldiers with arms and legs amputated. It was a ghastly sight that I'll never forget. All through my treatment in the hospital, I pondered how I could escape. I remembered that I had a woman relative in Addis Ababa. I wrote her a letter describing my situation.

I received a reply two weeks later. Her letter stunned me. She told me that in Addis Ababa there's an Israeli embassy that sends many Jews on aliyah to Israel. She also wrote that there were several thousand Jews now in Addis, including other relatives of mine. So, together with other soldiers who didn't want to return to the front, I planned to escape. One evening, we came to an agreement with the guard that he would allow us to escape that night. Naturally, we paid him very well for this. At two o'clock in the morning, we were outside the hospital and we walked from there to the center of Addis. At six o'clock we'd already checked into a little hotel, and then we went out to buy clothes. We got back, changed our clothes, and hid our khaki uniforms. So that my friends wouldn't be suspicious, I told them that I still had a few things to see to. I left my belongings there and found my way to my relative's address. I've not seen my friends since.

After I'd rested and eaten, my relative took me to another relative's home and he took me to you at the embassy. I remember that you kissed me when you heard my name. You told me you'd visited my village and that you'd met there – and later, of course, in Israel, as well – with my parents. I was so happy to meet a white man who knew my family and I asked you to help me to get out of Ethiopia. You promised to help.

Meanwhile, time went by and the relative in whose house I was hiding made aliyah. I moved to another relative's, but he was also on the point of making aliyah. I was worried I might be discovered and hardly ever left the house. A few days ago, I washed my clothes and went out to take them to be ironed and there, right in front of me, I suddenly saw my unit commander. He whispered that they were searching for me and if I was found, I'd be put to death. He even suggested that I return to the army of my own accord so that then I would only get imprisonment. I was shaking all over and didn't even take my laundry to be pressed, but instead rushed over to Addisu Wodaj and he took me to Zimna.

I explained my situation to Zimna and told him that unless I could leave immediately for Israel, I would be returned to the front. Zimna calmed me down and, indeed, within a few days I was told to come to the embassy with all my belongings. Yesterday, I took a taxi to the embassy. Zimna was already waiting for me, handed me a passport with my photo inside, and then went with me to the airport. When we arrived there, I got a shock – I've never in my life seen so many policemen in one place. However, I passed through the checks with no problem. But it was only when we landed in Rome that I really relaxed.

After a few hours in the airport, our escorts showed us a blue and white plane with the Star of David on it. We were so happy to fly to Israel in an Israeli plane.

Rubel's brother and sisters were already waiting for him and soon he will also be reunited with his parents. Another clandestine operation has been successfully pulled off.

JANUARY 8, 1991 – ISRAEL EMBASSY, ADDIS ABABA

I'm back in Addis. The school has changed a lot during the weeks I was away. The classrooms are a hive of activity and the decorations that remain from Chanukah add a special charm to the schoolyard. The children seem happy and very eager to learn.

On the flight, I brought Yair Feuer and his sister Navah with me. When several friends suggested I take Yair to Addis Ababa, it seemed like a crazy idea. But afterwards, Haim Halachmi, Ami Bergman, and I decided to do it. Yair worked with us from 1982 until he came down with severe diabetes and had to retire. He had devoted himself to studying the Ethiopian community and has been of invaluable assistance throughout the years in solving problems. He always knew the right thing to say and whether to use gentleness or toughness. It's so hard to see him moving slowly along with a cane, supported by his sister, but his spirit hasn't changed despite the fact that he is now so dependent. Now he is here, as excited as a young child, and his excitement grips us also. It was a good deed to bring him here. These two weeks in Ethiopia are going to add a few extra years to his life.

In the afternoon, the weekly meeting with the community representatives was held and once again complaints were heard that the proper order of priorities for aliyah is not being maintained. Once again I explained that the government continues returning forms to us for corrections and this disrupts the order in which passports are issued. At the meeting's conclusion, several *kessoch* came over to me and asked me to speed up the aliyah of the eldest *kes*, Yaakov Yitzhak. I agreed, naturally, to check into it with the authorities, but meanwhile, we have just been informed that the *kes* has passed away. We were too late.

JANUARY 11, 1991 – ISRAEL EMBASSY, ADDIS ABABA

The rate of aliyah is now 200–250 people a week. If this pace is kept up, the last Ethiopian Jews will depart toward the end of 1992. The question is whether the agreement with the Ethiopian government will hold till then. The sands of time are running fast and two years is too long a time to wait. The Eritreans and Tigreans are fighting in the north and are chalking up more and more victories while the government forces are retreating. The situation is deteriorating by the day. Apparently, the guerrilla fighters, who are equipped only with light weapons but with strong motivation, are pulverizing Black Africa's best army.

Tension is rife among us Israelis. In another four days, the US ultimatum to Iraq will expire and, although we are kept so busy, from time to time our thoughts cannot help turning to our families in Israel.

JANUARY 19, 1991 – ISRAEL EMBASSY, ADDIS ABABA

It is the fourth day of the Gulf War. It's difficult to carry on working when you know that your family is sitting in a sealed room, fearful that at any moment an Iraqi missile may strike, and no one can know where. I am angry with myself for not being there now. I am glued to the radio, following everything that is happening at home. The situation has brought the staff here closer to each other. Indeed, the whole Jewish community here is worried about events in Israel and I update those who gather here every morning. They eagerly hang on every word that I utter and I think that what I say calms them.

Next week, another three hundred *olim* will leave – a record for one week. I feel in no small degree responsible for this achievement. Who knows, perhaps it will be recorded to my credit at some stage. All the staff here shares my feeling about our work – the feeling that we are saving lives gives us the strength to carry on working, even at this stressful time.

JANUARY 23, 1991, MIDNIGHT – LEONARDO DA VINCI-FIUMICINO AIRPORT, ROME

We are with a group of 109 *olim*. In another few hours, the El Al plane will land here and we will board it and fly to Israel. Yesterday 196 people made aliyah and this month, January, we have reached a record number – 831 immigrants.

This flight has a large number of people who are being evacuated for medical reasons. Dr. David Raveh – who has the very suitable nickname "Mad Angel" – saved one woman's life when he persuaded the doctors, at the hospital where she was being treated, to give her large doses of steroids. We also have with us a boy whom Dr. Raveh nicknamed "Tiny Skeleton" because he is nothing but skin and bones.

What happened with Tiny Skeleton was even more serious. At the Addis airport, we discovered that his mother had come with an additional child for whom we did not have a passport. What were we to do? I remembered that in the office there was still the passport of a child whose Jewish father had been planning to take him on aliyah, but in the end the child went back to his Christian mother. Within ten minutes, I had that passport in my hand and, even though the photograph was not a good match for this "unauthorized" child, he flew out with that passport, so now the entire family is sitting and waiting together here at Rome's airport.

But salvation did not come in time for a three-year-old girl who was born with a heart defect. She died only one night before her family's aliyah. Michal Catvan, an Amharic-speaking social worker from Migdal Ha'emek, who took care of getting the permits, has been with the family throughout. This morning at six o'clock they hastily buried the child, threw away her clothing en route, and then rushed to the airport. It's difficult to come to terms with the destiny that decrees a small child's death a moment before redemption.

After all the *olim* had taken their seats in the plane, while it was still on the ground at Addis Ababa airport, the captain's voice was suddenly heard announcing that due to technical problems we would have to return to the terminal. I quickly went over to the chief flight attendant to clarify the cause of the delay. After some hesitation, he whispered to me, "It seems there's a man with a gun on the flight." I was relieved when I heard this. Avi Mizrahi had helped Yair Feuer board the plane and apparently his gun must have bulged out of his suit. I rushed down and explained to the security men what had happened. I said that Avi has a license to carry a gun – which is not actually true – and promised that he would never again board a plane carrying a weapon on his person.

Nerves were calmed and the plane took off. But our problems were still not over. About an hour after takeoff, Asnakew Sendeke, who is escorting the *olim* on this flight, said that one of the passengers is an impostor. In fact, the passenger was a Christian youngster who was the son of the head of the farmers' committee in Asnakew's very own village. One of the Ethiopian-born Israeli women now in Addis Ababa got him on the list by pretending that he was her sister's son. I was absolutely furious, and, what's more, I feel cheated. After all, I had put my full trust in this young woman and had even given her a job at the embassy – and this is how she repays me. Why do a few of the Ethiopian immigrants in Israel do such things? How can one explain such behavior?

I only cooled down when my thoughts turned to Dr. Raveh, the Israeli doctor on duty. He deserves a medal. He is the embodiment of a humane doctor, a doctor who always cares whether the patient is a one-day-old baby or an old man whose end is near.

FEBRUARY 14, 1991 – THE JEWISH AGENCY OFFICE, TEL AVIV

It has been four weeks now that the residents of Israel have been living in fear of another siren wail – sending them into the sealed rooms that have been created in every home. But in Ethiopia, a full-blown war is being waged. For years, the Eritrean and Tigrean rebels have been conducting a guerrilla war against Mengistu's government, but in recent weeks they have won one victory after another and now, the government forces are retreating on all fronts. On the news, it was just announced that the rebels are in control of Gondar and Gojam, two of the most important regions on the way to Addis Ababa. However, most experts rule out the possibility that the rebels intend to aim for the capital.

Because of the situation, we are talking a great deal about evacuation – evacuation of the staff's families from Addis and maybe also of all the Jews. We certainly cannot forsake them when it is clear to all of us that in between the fall of the existing government and a new government's taking charge, the Jews will be a target for attacks from their neighbors who see them as outsiders who are also rich. Although we know the abject poverty of the Jews, in the eyes of their Christian neighbors, every Jew who receives money and food from the JDC is rich. So they will be vulnerable to attacks when flour, sugar, oil, and salt are no longer available in the markets.

Kobi, of JDC, has already started getting organized for these eventualities and has turned the Housing Committee – which until now dealt with relocating families from unwholesome lodgings to other accommodations – into the Emergency Committee. At this stage, it is carrying out an exact listing of all Jewish addresses in Addis Ababa. Kobi is also organizing a store of fuel, nearly all of it purchased on the black market. In case of need, this fuel will be used for the trucks and buses to move the staff, and maybe the general Jewish population, to the airport or out of Addis.

Meanwhile, we in Israel continue with our normal routine, making corrections on the forms that were returned by the Ethiopian authorities and preparing the latest forms received. By the end of this month, we will have covered the 16,500 candidates for aliyah who are now crowded into Addis Ababa. While all this is going on, twice a week another group of about two hundred *olim* arrives here. And with all the joy that gives us, there are cases where we are conned by those very same *olim* to whom we devoted the greatest attention.

In today's group, a family of seven arrived who had pressured us constantly, practically daily, to bring them on aliyah as quickly as possible. And at long last, they arrived here, but even at the airport we realized that they were not two parents with their five children as they claimed. In fact, only one of those listed on the form is the real son of the two parents. The other children are either relatives or are not even related to the family at all. One of the daughters – apparently – is a girl of fifteen whose father had agreed to give her in marriage to the *oleh*'s adult son. Her father had been persuaded to send her from Addis and in exchange she will be the slave of a man over thirty years older who is cared for by his eleven-year-old daughter – only a little younger than her stepmother.

When this whole story became clear to me, a few minutes before the families were to get into the taxis taking them to the absorption center in Nazareth, I asked my secretary, Yaffa, to tell the girl she should go with them as far as the absorption center, but not to let the man touch her. I will make sure that within two days she is placed in a boarding school. Yaffa came back immediately and said that the girl refuses to join her "husband" because if she does not comply with his wishes, he will beat her. I should have thought of that from the first and not suggested that she go with him at all. One telephone call was enough and the girl was already on her way to a boarding school. I felt that I had rescued her.

But the peak of *chutzpah* was that one of the "daughters" of this same *oleh* is not Jewish at all, but is a native of Addis Ababa and it is not clear at all why she has been brought to Israel. It may well be that the man was bribed in some way to bring her.

Tomorrow, I'll make arrangements for returning her to Ethiopia.

MARCH 8, 1991 – ISRAEL EMBASSY, ADDIS ABABA

I returned this morning to an Addis Ababa that is different from the one I left. On the surface nothing has changed, but in fact a whirlwind is blowing through the length and breadth of Ethiopia and that includes the capital city. First of all, the people we meet actually dare to express their true feelings about Mengistu's regime, even their hope for his downfall. And indeed, the rebels are increasingly successful and it looks like they will soon conquer Gondar, Ethiopia's historic capital and the symbol, more than any other place, of ancient, independent Ethiopia. Gondar is a source of pride to any Ethiopian and above all to members of the Amhara tribe. Its fall will, without a doubt, lead to a decline in the morale of Mengistu's supporters.

The economic situation is deteriorating as a result of the military losses. Food prices have doubled in the last two months and the poverty is even more widespread. As a result, we hear of more and more cases of robbery and every night shooting is heard, even in our neighborhood, which is considered to be upper-class and comparatively safe.

In the embassy, an evacuation plan has been prepared, but one cannot compare our situation with that in other embassies. We have our additional concern for over sixteen thousand Jews who place their trust in us. We cannot just get up and walk away, abandoning them. The horrific pictures that were shown on all the world's television screens showing residents of Mogadishu, the capital of Somalia, being murdered by robber gangs for a few pounds of flour, are engraved deeply in our minds. When the situation reaches crisis point and the rebels threaten the Ethiopian capital, those scenes from Mogadishu may well be repeated here, but this time the victims will be Jews.

During my last visit to Israel, we were called – the people from the JDC, the Jewish Agency and the Foreign Ministry – to the army's General Staff Headquarters located at the Israel Air Force headquarters. A woman soldier was waiting to conduct us several stories below ground to where a large number of officers and a few civilians were crowded into a spacious room. There, the general outlines of an evacuation plan were presented to us. At this stage, only one thing is clear: the day is near when we will have to evacuate the Jews from Addis, but it is still not clear whether it will be by a direct airlift or other means.

The operation has already been given a name: Torrential Rain.

The division of labor between the IDF – in effect, the IAF – and the civilian side – in other words, the embassy, the JDC, and the Jewish Agency – was clear. We are responsible for assembling the Jews, identifying them, organizing them into groups, and transporting them to the point where the IDF takes over responsibility for their safety during the journey to the airfield and their flight to Israel. I will now utilize the time to prepare, together with Kobi and Ami from the JDC, and with Avi and Zimna and the other Jewish Agency staff, a plan that will resolve the three main problems we face: gathering the Jews at the embassy without missing even one family; identifying those who are eligible for aliyah while preventing the infiltration of any others; and transporting the people to the assembly point for the flight to Israel.

But meanwhile, the Ethiopian government has stopped all aliyah and for the last two weeks no passports have been issued. The Ethiopians' formal pretext for the cessation of the emigration is that we bribed emigration bureau staff and tried to transfer people without passports. Above all, they claim that we mock them by continually submitting forms that are faulty, in spite of their comments. The truth of the matter is that they are shaken by the many defeats suffered by the Ethiopian army in recent weeks and Ethiopia's rulers are trying to put pressure on the Israeli government to supply them with heavy armaments to bring about a turnaround in the fighting. We are not willing to do this and the Americans give us full backing. At the same time that they encourage us not to respond to the Ethiopian demands, they also check to make sure that we do not deviate from our agreement with them.

Because of the situation, we are evacuating the embassy staff's families to Israel and in another week there will only be eight of us left.

MARCH 12, 1991 – A CLASSROOM IN ADDIS ABABA

At the weekly meeting with the community representatives, their worry is obvious. We try to calm them down while also trying to encourage them to be extremely cautious. Especially at night. The rebels are advancing and it is now clear that they are heading for Addis Ababa. At the meeting, the representatives raise the problem of the halt of aliyah and I promise them – without any clear basis for doing so – that it will soon be resumed. We end the meeting at half past five so that everyone can get home before dark.

MARCH 14, 1991 – ISRAEL EMBASSY, ADDIS ABABA

This morning, agreed the ambassador and Kassa that aliyah will start again, and we have already reserved a plane on Wednesday for two hundred *olim*. The ambassador even speaks of increasing the number of those leaving to twelve or thirteen hundred per month. It's hard to believe that the Ethiopian government will agree in light of our refusal to supply them with arms.

MARCH 20, 1991 – THE AIRPORT, ADDIS ABABA

Two days ago, a military delegation arrived from Israel, dressed, of course, in civilian clothes, to examine the options for evacuating the Jews. It is headed by a brigadier-general. Since one of the options is an airlift, I took the delegation to the airport so that they could get their own impressions and, primarily, so that they could film it on video. I convinced the airport authorities that they were an Israeli film crew wanting to document the aliyah of the Falashas and, indeed, just then 202 were leaving for Israel.

In order not to arouse any suspicion, I told the *olim*, who were sitting in their best finery in the departure hall, that these Israelis wanted to film them boarding the aircraft and that each one should wave good-bye from the door of the plane. And that is just what they did, while the brigadier-general used the opportunity to film the whole airfield.

When we got back to the embassy, we met again with the brigadier-general and his people and, for greater security, we held the meeting in one of the school's classrooms and not inside the embassy building. We all had the feeling that we were making history, even though these historical deeds involved a great deal of detailed work and the solving of many tiny problems. Fortunately, Ami and Kobi from the JDC are both here now. And, to our great relief, they have solved two of our three problems.

It was Ami's idea to turn the Housing Committee into the Silent Signal Network, such as we have in Israel to call up the reserves in an emergency. Reservists are alerted either by radio or by sending people from house to house. We will do the same here. Addisu Ambaw is in charge of it. This young Jew, who was born in one of the villages in northern Ethiopia, studied engineering in Addis Ababa and reached a senior position in the Ethiopian Ministry of Housing. He was recruited a few weeks ago by Kobi and is now in charge of a signals network that encompasses almost four thousand households. Of these, the addresses of 98 percent are registered in our computer. Addisu directs five neighborhood heads who, in turn, direct 120 heads of units. Each unit head knows the addresses of the twenty-five to thirty-five families for whom he is responsible. We call this setup Addisu's Pyramid.

Fortunately, the problem of identification has also been solved. Recently, all those eligible for aliyah were issued with family ID documents. One side of the document has a photograph of the head of the family, with his particulars as they are registered in the embassy's computer. The other side has a list of the dependents of that family head. Each family now possesses such a document and on the day of evacuation it will entitle that family to make aliyah.

The problem of transportation is the one that remains to be solved. Meanwhile, we are storing gasoline and diesel oil. In the embassy's courtyard and in the courtyard of Kobi's house, dozens of drums of fuel will be ready when the crisis erupts.

MARCH 26, 1991 – THE AIRPORT, ADDIS ABABA

I am back at the airport and another 205 *olim* are leaving for Israel. But sixteen thousand Jews are still waiting to make aliyah while the situation here deteriorates by the day.

Shoshana Zinger is also leaving on the flight today, the last woman in our embassy in Addis. In preparation for an emergency, we are starting to dispense food and medicines so that these necessities will be as close as possible to the Jews' homes. Eventually, every neighborhood will have a depot of food and medications. Today, we also moved about a quarter of the medications into the embassy and started a stockpile of emergency food rations in the school's kitchen. Ami Bergman is orchestrating all this in his usual quiet way, using his discretion in assigning the most important tasks. It's the first time that I've seen Ami displaying any excitement. Until now, he has always managed to conceal his emotions. But, indeed, we are all being swept away by this endeavor because Jewish lives are in our hands. We have to be prepared for the possibility that the Jews will be forced to rely on us for everything that they need during the period when there is no one in control in Addis.

Amid all the commotion, we hear the news that the students have interrupted their studies at the university because they apparently want to join the government's fighting forces. Our sources later amend this information, clarifying that the government stopped studies and the students are being forced to enlist. Tomorrow, apparently all the high schools will be shut down and we are worried that they will also recruit pupils from the older grades of our school.

MARCH 27, 1991 – ISRAEL EMBASSY, ADDIS ABABA

Today 108 *olim* are supposed to leave, and the total number for this month is over five hundred. I was convinced that today there would not be any mishaps and so I stayed in my office at the embassy, but suddenly Benny called me from the airport and said I ought to get over there.

It turned out that everything had gone smoothly and all the *olim* were already sitting in the plane, including the children. But one fourteen-year-old girl, named Fenta, decided at the very last minute that she did not want to make aliyah. When I reached the airport, I saw Fenta throwing herself to the ground beside the departure gate. There were about thirty security people standing around her, some unknown to me. I went up to the girl and said to her very forcefully that she had to join her parents and her brothers and sisters who had already boarded the plane. My words only made her more agitated. I decided to play my last card and took her parents off the plane with their other six children.

The father made a heartrending appeal to the girl but to no avail. On the contrary, the girl attacked her father, shouting at him in a way that I have never heard even in Israel, where children treat their parents with far less courtesy than in Ethiopian families. In the end, the whole family remained behind and the flight left without them.

I decided to deal with this matter immediately, so I took the family back to the embassy with me. It turns out that the girl had fallen in love with a non-Jewish boy and wanted her parents to say that he was the mother's brother so that he could also go on aliyah. This situation has arisen because her parents refused to do so. There is nothing left to do but to hope that the whole family will leave on next week's flight.

APRIL 2, 1991 – ISRAEL EMBASSY, ADDIS ABABA

My hope was in vain. The family left today for Israel without the daughter, who prefers to stay here with her boyfriend. Yesterday, the parents signed their consent to making aliyah without their daughter. One can see from their faces how hard this is for them and I also felt that what I am asking of them, I perhaps would not ask of myself. The mother was crying constantly so I have promised her that I will not forget the daughter and will send her on aliyah as soon as possible. But what will I do if she refuses? All the way back from the airport to the embassy compound I remembered the mother's weeping. I am very unhappy that I almost forced her to go without her daughter. They could have stayed, but that, too, would been a poor decision for the rest of the family. It was a no-win situation. What else could I do?

The ambassador has just received a cable from Uri Lubrani:

> We all share the feeling that the time of crisis is clearly upon us and we have to put our heads together to search for the most practical and effective methods of ensuring our basic interests.
>
> In light of the circumstances, we must manage our concerns and our struggle vis-à-vis Ethiopia on two parallel tracks. Each track has its own elements, limitations, and risks.
>
> On one track, routine obliges us to carry on doing everything as before to advance the process of family reunification – filling in forms properly and maintaining essential contact with all the Ethiopian agencies that deal with the issue. All this has to be done in an effort to obtain the maximum possible number of departure visas in the routine way, with all the annoyances and the mistakes and the returning of forms involved. All this has to proceed as though Ethiopia were not in crisis and the process of family reunification were progressing according to the rate that can normally be achieved. And, indeed, this track is productive, at least for the present, and we are all happy about each additional immigrant who arrives in Israel this way.

> The second track is based on the conviction that there is an emergency, based on the information received on the military situation which also accords with every evaluation that has reached us – from you, from the USA, and from European countries with whom we are in contact. In our opinion, in recent weeks, the capability of Mengistu's troops seems to be irreversibly eroded and the question is no longer whether this government will hold on with the troops at its disposal, but rather when it will collapse. We are informed that it is a matter of between two weeks and two months. So far, we have not heard of any change or improvement in this estimate. On the contrary, there are signs, even today, that the rebels are advancing in spite of the logistical difficulties that are apparently holding them up. But even though their advance is slow, they continue to achieve successes and their aim is to tighten the noose around Addis Ababa. As things stand, it is impossible for us to ignore a scenario in which the time will probably come when chaos and lawlessness reign in Addis Ababa. There will then be a situation in which the Jews waiting to make aliyah may well be the first to be exposed to acts of robbery, plunder, and perhaps even worse than that, and it will not be possible to help them in their distress. All this is based on the assumption – a realistic assumption in our opinion – that this period will force you all to effect your own flight from the embassy, and you yourselves will, therefore, be largely neutralized.

I agree with Uri Lubrani's assessment. Let's hope that if chaos reigns here, there will no longer be any Jews left in Addis Ababa.

APRIL 4, 1991 – ISRAEL EMBASSY, ADDIS ABABA

It is clear that the Ethiopian army is going to be defeated soon and no one believes that there will be an immediate change of government without bloodshed in the city. We live in a state of tension, but meanwhile we are also witnessing joyous events because of the military developments. Today two prisoners arrived from Gondar: they were released a few days ago when the rebels entered the city.

The family of the older one left for Israel some time ago, but the wife of the younger one – his name is Alene Azezew – has been waiting for him here and already has his passport, as well as the passport of his sister's daughter, Dembernesh Yirga. I watched them. This slender girl, Dembernesh, is deeply devoted to her uncle, even feeling a sense of responsibility for him. In spite of her young age, it looks like the uncle depends on her and not the other way around. In fact, this girl stayed behind when her family left Gondar for Addis Ababa. She remained in Gondar in order to take care of the uncle and brought him meals in prison every day. Now that he has been released, she, too, can savor redemption. Soon, she will be reunited with her mother and siblings in Israel.

APRIL 6, 1991, SHABBAT – IN THE MEN'S APARTMENT, ADDIS ABABA

From the window of our apartment, the chirping of the birds can be heard and the city can be seen, drenched in green with tints of gold from the sun. Everything is so quiet one could be mistaken into thinking that this is one of the most peaceful cities on the globe, but beneath the surface it is all seething, like a volcano about to erupt.

Rumors are widespread throughout the city that about one hundred thousand Tigreans are just waiting to go into action on orders from the underground movements that are fighting the government. The populace is on edge and hoarding anything it can lay its hands on, from flour and coal to car tires and household utensils. Naturally, prices are going up and up. Every day, we get updates from various sources and a picture of the situation is becoming clear. The rebels are gradually closing in on Addis Ababa and within a few weeks the city will be under total siege.

But it is not only in Ethiopia that things are happening. The military plan, Operation Torrential Rain – for the evacuation of the Jews from Addis Ababa – is ready. Now all that is left to do is to negotiate the level of compensation that the Ethiopians will receive for their agreement to release the Jews in a mass airlift.

Meanwhile, we carry on with our regular business, running to the emigration bureau, receiving passports, ordering flights, arguing for another family, another Jew that we want to bring out of the filth. And, naturally, we carry on smuggling out Jewish defectors – "Greenies," as we call them, because of the green ink we once used to mark their names.

My thoughts wander to my family in Israel. I close my eyes and see Ruthie and the children, as though they are with me. In another five days, I'll no longer have to close my eyes to see them, but then I'll be missing my Jews here.

APRIL 10, 1991 – ISRAEL EMBASSY, ADDIS ABABA

Yesterday, Colonel Mersha contacted me, asking that we transfer his wife and two sons to Israel. In fact, all the country's leaders are doing the same, utilizing their connections in various embassies in order to save their families from the terrible fate that awaits them after the rebels enter the city. This is perhaps the most conclusive proof that Mengistu's regime is nearing its end. I already asked the ambassador yesterday to look into the matter with our Foreign Ministry in Israel and I think that the response will be positive.

Now, I am sitting with the deputy minister and asking him to release Atanaw Biruk, the uncle of my secretary, Yaffa. Today, his turn arrived to make aliyah and he turned up with all his family at the airport. But a police officer with the rank of major stopped him and gave instructions that he be transferred to the police headquarters in Addis Ababa. Atanaw was in the Treasury Police and did not bother to get a release from them before his departure, so he was arrested. The deputy minister has already been fully informed by the minister and his answer is that he cannot help in this matter since it is a serious crime.

I cannot do anything and I go to Kobi Friedman's home, where Avi is expecting me together with Kobi, Amir Maimon (the administrative officer of the embassy), and Moshe Edri, who was once our security officer and has now returned here as a guard.

We sit in Kobi's spacious living room and drink Ethiopian coffee. It is time for us to plan the last details of the rescue operation. I shut my eyes for a moment in order to imagine how sixteen thousand Jews would look en masse. A picture flashes across my mind of a football stadium full of faceless figures.

We discuss the problem of those who are hospitalized. In a group as large as this, there are always some people in the hospital. To make sure that none of them is left behind when the operation takes place, we decide to write a list of hospitalized patients on the notice board in our room at the embassy and to update it every single day. When the operation takes place, we will send the embassy car to the hospitals with letters requesting that the patients be transferred to Israel for treatment. Let's hope that no problems arise with this and that the sick will also reach Israel with their families.

So now, only the transportation hurdle remains and Kobi has promised to investigate the possibility of organizing trucks and possibly buses.

In another few minutes it will be midnight and the curfew will begin, but tomorrow I am going home and will be able to report that preparations are proceeding smoothly.

APRIL 11, 1991 – ON AN ETHIOPIAN AIRLINES FLIGHT EN ROUTE TO ROME

Among the 192 *olim* on the plane are Alene Azezew, his wife, and his niece, Dembernesh Yirga. Once again I am impressed by the fourteen-year-old girl's devotion to her uncle, who spent three years in prison. Alene did not want to fly today, claiming that he has pains in his heart. When I responded that in Israel we have good doctors to treat him, he said that he can't make aliyah because he is still wearing the same shirt and trousers that he wore when he went into prison. How can he go through the gates of Jerusalem wearing prison clothes? I refused to heed his words and would not yield, so he is here in the plane but his face does not express joy. Why?

At the airport in Rome, I buy him a shirt, but when I present it to him, no sign of happiness appears on his face.

APRIL 16, 1991 – THE JEWISH AGENCY OFFICE, TEL AVIV

We plan, plan, and plan some more, one meeting hard on the heels of another. The day before yesterday, the concluding meeting was held at General Staff Headquarters. Both yesterday and today, meetings were held in our Jewish Agency offices attended by Foreign Ministry representatives, headed by Haim Divon, Ami Bergman of the JDC, Haim Halachmi, and all those in the Jewish Agency who are involved, headed by our department's director-general, Arnon Mantver.

Ami and I report on the Silent Signal Network that has been put in place and computerized. We are cautious, taking into account that mishaps are likely to happen when we gather all the Jews and within thirty-six hours transfer them in trucks from the embassy to an assembly point that is to be decided upon – at the rate of one thousand per hour!

Today we received the operational order for Operation Torrential Rain. On the first page its goals are defined: "The rescue operation of Ethiopian Jews (hereinafter 'the operation') aims to rescue, within the shortest time possible, the Ethiopian Jewish community, about eighteen thousand in number, who are today concentrated in the capital, Addis Ababa. An essential condition for the operation is authorization and agreement from the head of the Ethiopian government according to conditions that will be determined in advance by both parties."

I actually have my doubts regarding the number that is stated. In Addis there was a disagreement between Kobi Friedman and myself regarding the number of Jews still in Addis. Kobi always stated a higher number and his thinking was accepted by the army in preparing its operational order, even though the number is actually lower than sixteeen thousand. In any case, there is no harm in preparing to rescue a slightly higher number than is, in fact, expected.

Personally, I find it difficult to believe that the Ethiopian government will agree to the actual Israeli military operation. But I do think that they'll let us take out one thousand Jews a day – not in the context of the Operation Torrential Rain – which, in any case, means that we'll be able to rescue all the Jews from Addis within a period of about two weeks.

APRIL 17, 1991, 3 A.M. – MY ROOM IN THE MEN'S APARTMENT, ADDIS ABABA

I'm back in Ethiopia in order to prepare a drill to test the Silent Signal Network. Arnon Mantver and his deputy, Brachyahu Mantzuri, are also here to observe the drill.

An urgent telephone call from the ambassador wakes me up. Senator Rudy Boschwitz has just arrived as the envoy of the US President, George Bush, and late this morning he is supposed to tour the neighborhoods where the Jews are living. The ambassador asks me to take the senator to visit one of the families, preferably one living in harsh conditions. I decide to shock the senator.

APRIL 27, 1991, LATE AT NIGHT

This has been a tumultuous day. To start with, we took the senator and his entourage to a courtyard where three Jewish families are living – eighteen souls in three rooms, which are in fact three holes, each one measuring two by two meters. But what shocked the senator most was the fact that the three families are living right next to three cows, who reside in the fourth room of the same structure.

During the day, we also deployed for our "mobilization drill." We put Addisu Ambaw in charge of summoning about a thousand people to the embassy. These are all people for whom aliyah forms have not yet been prepared. Addisu activated the network but in the course of the day only 850 of those who received the signal actually turned up at the embassy. We sent them along a prepared route that all the *olim* will pass through if the operation takes place.

In light of the exercise, it was made clear that improvements have to be made in the route. We will, indeed, be able to carry out the identification and grouping processes and be able to give out the boarding cards for the trucks and planes to each family at a rate of one thousand per hour, as required by the operational order. However, I am worried by the fact that 150 of those summoned – about forty families – did not arrive. This means that on the actual day of the operation, there could be over two thousand people who do not show up. This is unacceptable.

APRIL 28, 1991, MORNING – IN MY ROOM

I have calmed down.

After a sleepless night I realized why the forty families did not arrive. They quite simply saw no need to do so, since they already possess a duplicate of the identity documents and their aliyah forms had already been filled in for them using other ID documents.

Why is a duplicate ID necessary for the Jews in Addis Ababa? The answer is obvius to anyone who lives and works here. These documents are used by each family here to receive financial assistance and food every month.

MAY 1, 1991 – ISRAEL EMBASSY, ADDIS ABABA

The situation grows continually worse and the army is constantly suffering defeats. It can now be said that Addis Ababa is almost under siege.

Over the past few days, the option of an evacuation of one thousand per day has been discussed. The day before yesterday, Colonel Mersha mentioned this as a possibility and today the ambassador called us to an urgent meeting at which he laid out a plan to start evacuating the Jews at the end of next week, at the rate of one thousand per day.

Tomorrow, I'll be on my way home with a group of 208 *olim*. We carry on taking out as many Jews as possible by the normal channels, but it is obvious to all of us that there has to be a faster evacuation method.

Uri Lubrani is already on his way to Addis Ababa to negotiate with the Ethiopians to let us evacuate all the Jews quickly, perhaps all of them within hours. But even at a rate of one thousand per day, we can still save them.

MAY 8, 1991 – THE JEWISH AGENCY OFFICE, TEL AVIV

Uri has sent a cable to Israel saying that the days of Mengistu's government are numbered. At his meeting with Kassa, the Ethiopian government agreed to a speedy evacuation that would be carried out with absolute secrecy and – of course – large financial compensation.

MAY 12, 1991 – THE JEWISH AGENCY OFFICE, TEL AVIV

Addis is under siege. The rebels are in control of all the routes leading into the city except for the Addis-Debre Zeit road. Uri continues his meetings. He has now been in Addis almost two weeks and the reports from there indicate that the evacuation operation will take place soon.

Meanwhile, in Israel it is Jerusalem Day and the Ethiopian Jews assemble in Ethiopia Forest, next to Kibbutz Ramat Rachel, to commemorate the thousands of Jews who perished in Sudan before Operation Moses. What a pity that we cannot announce to the gathering that soon no Jews will remain in Ethiopia because soon those who are now suffering in Addis will be flown out "on eagles' wings," as the Yemenites said about their own airlift in the early fifties.

MAY 20, 1991 – THE JEWISH AGENCY OFFICE, TEL AVIV

Uri returned two days ago and is now giving his report to the prime minister, Yitzhak Shamir. The rebels, who are now on the outskirts of Addis, are unstoppable. The Americans inform us that they prefer that the Jews leave now, before the present government falls, but they promise that if that does not work out, the new government will continue with the process of family reunification.

The prime minister is absolutely unwavering in his determination that all the Jews leave immediately. He has given Uri full responsibility to finish the negotiations and stick to the current plan for getting the Jews out without delay. The meeting ended with the prime minister deciding that the entire operation will be called, so appropriately, Operation Solomon. Now it's really going to happen!

MAY 21, 1991 – THE JEWISH AGENCY OFFICE, TEL AVIV

This afternoon, it was announced that Mengistu Haile Mariam, the president of Ethiopia, has fled to Kenya in a small aircraft and will apparently proceed to Zimbabwe, where his wife and children are waiting for him.

Meanwhile, Uri has agreed with Kassa on a payment of $35 million in exchange for the right to evacuate the Jews in our planes and on condition that the evacuation operation end before May 25, the date of the start of the conference in London between the Ethiopian government and the rebels' representatives.

Uri is trying to drag out the time and to pay only part of the sum right away, but Kassa is sharp enough to demand all the money in advance. We will have to deposit the money in the Ethiopian government's bank account in New York. Simcha Dinitz, chairman of the executive of the Jewish Agency, is already on his way from the West Coast to New York to prepare for the payment.

At the embassy in Addis Ababa, they are deploying for the operation, but the problem of transportation from the embassy to the airport had still not been resolved until this task was given to Ami Bergman, who managed to make contact with a wealthy dealer who has a fleet of available buses. And so that has also been dealt with.

Yesterday evening, Uri Lubrani, Eli Eliezri, and Kobi Friedman flew with El Al to Nairobi, and this morning they landed in Addis.

I'm angry that I was not informed of their trip and quickly contact the director-general of my department, Arnon Mantver, who is now in the USA. I ask him to authorize that I fly tomorrow on the special El Al flight to Rome. The plane is scheduled to return to Israel with the eighty-eight *olim* who will leave Addis tomorrow morning. Arnon does not agree and tells me to wait for the staff plane that will be the first to land in the rescue operation. His reasons appear to make sense, among them the worry that I may end up stuck in Rome because of possible flight delays.

Part Six

That's It, We're Done

MAY 22, 1991 – LEONARDO DA VINCI-FIUMICINO AIRPORT, ROME

The reasons made sense, but I've flown here anyway on the special El Al plane to Rome – Benny Harel and I were the only two passengers on board.

In Rome, we meet the group of *olim* who will fly back on the plane. They are escorted by Haim Baynesagn, another of the Kfar Batya graduates from the fifties. He gives us a report on the bad situation in Addis and says that the rebels are likely to enter the city within hours. He is amazed that now, of all times, we are going to Addis, but in order to prevent any break in operational secrecy, I explain that we decided we want to be with the Jews right now, precisely when things are so hard.

MAY 23, 1991, 7 A.M. – IN AN ETHIOPIAN AIRLINES PLANE TO ADDIS ABABA

Benny and I are on the plane. It may well be that our journey is destined to help put an end, forever, to the Ethiopian exile and that in another forty-eight hours the last Jew there will board a plane for Israel. The countdown to Operation Solomon has already started and in another twenty-seven hours the first planes are supposed to land at the Addis Ababa airport.

In another two days, there is certainly going to be tremendous rejoicing in Israel. It's really happening! The families' suffering is almost over.

MAY 23, 1991 – HILTON HOTEL, ADDIS ABABA

We have all gathered in the room of the ambassador, Asher Naim. Uri Lubrani is here, as well as staff from the embassy, the JDC, and the Jewish Agency. The final go-ahead for the operation was given five hours ago and now we are reviewing the final preparations, checking every single stage of the operation. The meeting is continually interrupted by telephone calls from Israel and the USA.

Amnon Lipkin-Shahak, the deputy chief of staff, is scheduled to arrive with the rescue force tomorrow at ten o'clock in the morning and he wants to check with Uri that everything is proceeding according to plan. Amnon will command the operation here and the chief of staff will command it in Israel.

A few minutes ago, Uri finished a telephone conversation with Bob Hodek, who is in charge of the US embassy in Addis Ababa, informing him of the deployment of the forces in the evacuation operation. This information is intended for the rebel leaders, who are delaying their entry into Addis Ababa until we take out the last Jew. Uri told him that eighteen Hercules planes, painted gray and without the identifying insignia of the Israel Air Force, will be taking part in the operation. Additionally, there will be three El Al jumbo jets without the Magen David, and other Boeing 707 and 767 aircraft – some belonging to El Al and some from the IAF. The rebels will no doubt be observing these planes when they land and take off at the airport.

All of us in the room are tense and apprehensive about the operation's success.

But even before we started with the preparations, a group of us embassy staffers went to the city center. Opposite the African Unity Center, thousands of the town's citizens had gathered and, with the aid of a tall crane, were attempting to knock the statue of Lenin, the symbol of Communism and repression, off its pedestal. We didn't have time to wait until the statue actually toppled, but we saw the happiness on the people's faces and heard the joy in their voices. The end of tyranny.

We hurried back to the embassy. The buses that Ami and Kobi mobilized from the managing director of Addis Ababa's bus company, Mr. Eyob, were already waiting. Yesterday, these two succeeded – with the help of a bottle of whiskey and a few 100 birr notes – in persuading him that it was worth his while to make twenty buses available for the embassy's use, to take the school children for a visit to the zoo.

Driving up the hill, we saw the bus drivers practicing reversing their buses on the slope in the embassy courtyard. We realized that the buses could not turn around inside the embassy courtyard as the road is too narrow and there are deep drainage ditches on both sides. So the only remaining possibility is for the buses to back in. Since some of the drivers could not manage this, and some of the buses almost fell into the ditches, we are now holding training sessions for the drivers.

While this is going on, we announce to the school pupils that tomorrow there will be no classes and that we are taking those who study in the afternoon shift on a trip to the zoo – that is our cover story.

Meanwhile, we take our own trip – along the route that the Jews will take tomorrow and the day after. It has several stops along the way. The first is the school gate, which is iron, about two meters wide and set into a wall that was built by the *olim* themselves. At this point, each family will have to present its family ID and our people will make sure that the number of arrivals is the same as that registered on the document. When the two numbers match, the family will enter and wait to be summoned to the next station. Whenever there is a smaller number than that registered, the family will wait at a special assembly point until the family head returns, bringing the rest of the family. A family arriving with a larger number than that registered will quite simply not be allowed to enter the embassy.

We also deliberated on what to do with families who arrive without documentation because it had been lost or stolen. In such a case, the family will have to go through an eligibility check, for which purpose we have set up an additional station where there is a linkup to our computer. Once again, whoever is found eligible will wait his turn at the second station and whoever is found to be ineligible for aliyah will be sent away from the embassy.

At the second station, the family's identity will be checked once more and if, indeed, the family is as it appears on its ID, a family boarding card for the plane will be issued. This simple card, in three copies, provides basic information on the family, such as the number of their file in the computer, the name of the family head, and the number of people in the family. According to the plan, only two copies will be handed over to the family, while the original will be torn off and passed to Shoshana Zinger, who will check off on the computer that the family has gone through the procedure. The two other copies will be used by the family to board the bus and the plane.

Also, at that same station, stickers containing numbers will be placed on the upper folds of the immigrants' clothing. These numbers will be used to form them into clusters, each cluster consisting of 190 people. The air force is planning to load 190 *olim* into each 92-seater Hercules aircraft, after removing the seats and spreading mattresses on the floor. In the 707 aircraft, intended for 180 seated passengers, the IAF will carry 570 people – three clusters of 190 each. The jumbo will have enough room for five or six clusters.

On his last visit to Israel, Ami Bergman brought the boarding cards and the numbered stickers with him. When the secretaries at the JDC in Jerusalem, who were preparing them, asked him what they were for, he said that they were for a gathering of the mentally disabled so that they could play Bingo!

From the second station, the people will go to the area of the embassy's main exit gate, which we call "the assembly triangle." At its end, we have created two "holding areas," each of which has space for 190 people, so that it will always be possible to contain the groups as they wait to board the buses.

From the exercise with the buses this morning, we saw that each "holding area" will suffice to fill three buses, so six buses must always be ready inside the embassy compound.

Just as we finished our tour of inspection, the buses returned from the zoo. The children who got off the buses were told that tomorrow there would be no classes and they ran off home. In my imagination, I see them, in another two days, running through the corridors of an absorption center in Israel. But they still do not yet know anything about the dramatic changes in store for them.

After we sent the children off, some of the teachers came over to us and apologetically said, "We don't understand why you did this. The children are not used to traveling by bus and some of them threw up. And what is there to see there at all? Five lions from the time of Haile Selassie."

It's true that the Addis Ababa zoo is no great attraction. But at that minute I couldn't come up with a better excuse to explain to the teachers why we had carried out this exercise. So I just made do with a slight hint about the operation: "We Israelis have all sorts of crazy ideas. Soon you'll be living with us, so you should try to get used to us." The teachers didn't exactly understand me and were whispering to each other as they left. Most of them went home, but a few stayed in the embassy because they were part of our Silent Signal Network. Kobi instructed the network members that they should wait with us until about half an hour before dark.

At half past five, the network members ought to have left the embassy compound in order to get home before dark. But the final go-ahead for the operation had not yet been received from Israel. Then, at six o'clock – exactly when we were about to send the network members home – the authorization came. From the ambassador's hotel room, we got a call that at 4:30 a.m. the rescue planes would be taking off from Israel for Addis Ababa. It was now up to us to start assembling the people immediately.

We gathered the Silent Signal Network people in the waiting area near the embassy building and I said to them in Amharic,

"The great day has arrived. Out of concern for the situation of the Jews here in Addis Ababa, the State of Israel has decided to evacuate all the Jews to Jerusalem, and tomorrow the evacuation will commence. Within forty-eight hours, not even one Jew will be left in Addis Ababa and you in the network are the people responsible for bringing the whole community here, without leaving a single person behind."

Their surprise showed clearly on their faces and it took them a few minutes to digest the full implications. Then their joy and happiness were obvious.

Kobi took over from me, telling the network members that first they had to bring their own families – that is, their spouses, children and parents – to the embassy between six and seven o'clock in the morning. They must come with no baggage except for religious books and family photographs. Since we would not have time to carry out a security check of luggage, they would have to leave their possessions behind. They all nodded their heads in agreement.

Kobi went on to explain the identification and grouping route, at the end of which the families would board the buses, travel to the airport, and from there be flown to Israel in Israeli planes.

That was when they really took in the full significance of the tremendous endeavor that was about to take place. Their exhilaration spilled over. They all hugged each other over and over and their whisperings turned into shouts of jubilation.

Kobi then continued his explanations, describing the next stages of the operation. After separating from their own families, it would be their responsibility to bring about one thousand people to the embassy every hour, according to the prearranged plan. The network members were asked not to mention one word to anyone about the operation and at this stage only to prepare their own families. Tomorrow also, when they signaled the families in their charge, they should tell them that they must not divulge one word of the operation to anyone else, so that the embassy would not be mobbed outsiders.

While Kobi was finishing up the last details with the network people, I saw Tiruwork Mekete by the embassy door. She is the coordinator of mathematics studies at the teacher training college of Addis Ababa and works with Andy Goldman from NACOEJ. I've known her for a long time, and I also know that her husband serves as deputy commissioner of the Ethiopian police in a small town about 170 kilometers from Addis Ababa. I couldn't do otherwise than hint to her about tomorrow's operation. I did a forbidden thing, saying in one sentence, "Make sure that tomorrow your husband is here and don't ask me why."

I saw from her face that she understood.

To allow us to control the large number of people arriving at the embassy before the evacuation force lands from Israel, it was agreed to bring representatives of the American organizations into the picture and incorporate them into the various processing stations: at the gate, in the waiting area, the identification and grouping area, and the "holding area" prior to getting on the buses. I am worried about what may happen in the first hours. We only have a total of sixteen staffers, of whom six are from the American organizations. Rescue operation staffers are scheduled to land in the first plane around ten o'clock tomorrow morning. Three hundred people will be arriving; the plan is to bring thirty-three of them to work with us in the embassy. We have chosen these people very carefully, trying to bring in people who have worked with us in the past at the embassy.

At twelve noon, an Ethiopian Airlines plane is supposed to take off, escorting two of the IAF 707s containing the first thousand people. We are then supposed to transport one thousand people to the airport every hour, which is the rate at which the *olim* will fly out of Ethiopia in El Al and IAF planes. If everything proceeds as planned, it will be possible to conclude the airlift of fifteen thousand people by two o'clock in the morning and then we can all go home.

But meanwhile, I am worried about things going wrong. Will all the Jews be contacted and not one be left behind? Will we manage to keep out the ones who try to sneak in at the embassy or the airport? And what will happen if in the middle of the operation one of the rebel commanders decides to break the agreement and occupy the airport? We will then have to take control of the airport by force in order to continue the operation, but at what cost?

Uri suggests that we now disperse and grab a few hours' sleep. We are not sleeping in our homes tonight but here in the hotel.

Before bidding us goodnight, Uri says that in Israel the preparations are finished as well. At an IAF airbase near Ben-Gurion airport, three hundred buses will be waiting tomorrow morning to carry the *olim* to a rest stop and from there to absorption centers, mobile home sites, and hotels. Over the past two days, the Jewish Agency's Department for Immigration and Absorption has mobilized hundreds of workers while preserving the strictest secrecy. Indeed, each one of us is keeping the secret of the operation. I didn't even tell my wife why I was leaving for Ethiopia so suddenly yesterday.

Tomorrow, the last coordination meeting will be held in Colonel Mersha's office.

MAY 24, 1991, 5 A.M. – HILTON HOTEL, ADDIS ABABA

I couldn't fall asleep. I kept on imagining all the things that might go wrong during Operation Solomon.

Even though the Americans promised us that the rebels would not enter Addis Ababa while the operation was taking place, over and over I envisioned pictures of soldiers armed with Kalashnikovs, their belts hung with hand grenades, taking over the airport. And our Jews being returned to their homes, devastated.

I don't bother shaving and leave immediately for the embassy. Who knows whether I'll be back in this hotel? Inwardly I bid farewell to this place where we have spent so many evenings in heart-to-heart talks and secret planning.

The JDC people arrive at 5:40 a.m. and I ask Kobi to see about putting up a fence between the upper waiting area and the identification point where every family will be checked, given its boarding card for the plane, and its cluster number stickers.

MAY 24, 1991, 8:40 A.M. – THE ETHIOPIAN MINISTRY OF THE INTERIOR

The meeting that should have started at 7:45 a.m. is only starting now. We arrived here in time and gathered in the meeting room, but proceedings have been delayed because some of the Ethiopian participants were not summoned on time. It turns out that the rebels have managed to cut some of the city's telephone lines.

The meeting opens after a fifty-five-minute delay. After each side introduces its representatives, we announce that within an hour four Israel Air Force aircraft will arrive at the Addis Ababa airport – two Hercules with equipment for setting up the command post and two Boeing 707 planes with the three hundred people required to handle the departures. In prior conversations, we had definitely informed the Ethiopians of our intention to deploy this large number of people, but Colonel Mersha puts on an amazed expression and asks whether these people have visas to enter Ethiopia. I respond immediately, "Not only do they not have visas, they also don't have passports with them. They will be identified by the name tags on their lapels. But if you are worried that one of them will want to remain in Ethiopia illegally at the end of the operation, I, as the Israeli consul, am ready to give my official word that such a thing will not occur."

The meeting drags on. It is already 9:45 a.m. and we have to wind it up soon, as our planes are already over Addis Ababa. They must land in the next few minutes as they cannot refuel here because of the fuel shortage. And now, of all times, when we are waiting for permission to land, Colonel Mersha raises another problem. He wants to receive a passenger list before each takeoff. I respond immediately, asking him why he wants this. His answer astounds me: "It simply cannot be allowed that Ethiopian citizens should leave the country without being registered."

I answer impatiently, "It's an impossible request. We're talking about fifteen thousand people."

My answer does not satisfy the deputy minister of interior and he hardens his stance: "Yesterday the ambassador promised that we would receive these lists." There is no time to waste, so

I answer immediately, "If the ambassador promised it, you will receive the lists." I know that I'll never be able to provide him with genuine lists, but perhaps we will provide him with fictitious lists from our computer.

The meeting is over and permission is received for our planes to land. I hurry to announce this to Avi at the embassy and he sends a bus to the airport immediately.

I run down the steps and drive like a maniac to the airport. The planes have already landed and are drawn up by the parking area at the western edge of the airfield. Among the arrivals, I greet Dr. David Raveh, whom I have recruited to be the physician on duty at the embassy, and Moshe Edri, the former security officer, whose job will be to ensure the *olim*'s orderly entry through the school gate, as well as to photograph the operation as much as possible. Among those alighting from the plane, I am particularly pleased to see Haim Halachmi, who has been dealing with aliyah from Ethiopia since 1977 and for whom this unconventional visit is the first time he has been here in fourteen years. We agree that Haim will help Avi Mizrahi at the airfield and I leave for the embassy with thirty-three people.

En route, I explain to them how we expect events to unfold. Most of them have served here in some capacity or other in the course of the last sixteen months – that is, in the period since the embassy was opened – and they understand the directions without my having to go into detail, while the others will get an additional explanation when we reach the embassy compound.

The journey from the airport passes without mishap and then we are on the last stretch before the embassy. I look to the left in the direction of the Shola neighborhood and see family after family making their way in the direction of the embassy. I recognize some of the people, and others I identify by their festive clothing, which they have been carefully keeping for the day of their aliyah to Israel.

It is eleven o'clock and I should see about two thousand people waiting outside the embassy and approximately the same number inside. The spectacle that greets our eyes stuns and shocks us. The road and its edges simply cannot be seen at all. The entire area is a mass of people, all dressed in white. Our bus even has difficulty carving a path through the people in order to reach the embassy gate.

When we approach the main gate, we come upon a scene of total tumult – a giant human wave pressing up to the school gate. Zimna is trying to control this wave, without success. I realize that this is our weakest point and send a large number of our people to the main gate, headed by Moshe. Now I hope it will be possible to contain the pressure.

Within the embassy compound, eight buses are already waiting, containing three clusters, almost six hundred people, mostly members of the families of the unit heads. When I pass by the buses, children's heads peep through with numbers stuck on their foreheads – 1, 2, 3. There is also movement throughout the other areas of the embassy. Two of the "holding areas" are full of people with the number 4 on the heads of those in the first area, and the number 5 on the heads of all those in the second.

In the upper grouping point, Benny Harel and Yehoshua are dealing with those waiting to receive their boarding cards for the plane and the stickers with the cluster number. At the moment, there are about five hundred people and there is not too much pressure. We are all on edge. There are two main problems to address: the first is the gate, which apparently will now be solved with the addition of the extra staff there. The second is the airport, where there is no permission yet for takeoff. That is why the buses full of people are waiting on the steep road and not yet moving off toward the airport.

Uri was with Kassa Kebede at nine o'clock. It was decided that the sum agreed on beforehand, $35 million, would be deposited in the Ethiopian government's bank account in a New York bank. The chairman of the executive of the Jewish Agency, Simcha Dinitz, has been in New York since yesterday and the required amount was there, donated by American Jewry. We receive an announcement by telephone from New York that the money has been deposited as requested but we have still not received permission for the planes to take off.

Why?

The ambassador explains that the Ethiopian government's representatives in the USA have not located the money in their account and it is only after they are informed a second time of the number of the account where the money has been deposited that they realize that they checked an account in another bank. But eventually the money is located, so let's hope that we can start transporting the people to the airport and commence the airlift. It is already 12:50 p.m. and we are running well over an hour late. But our problems are not yet over. I am called to the telephone. Colonel Mersha is on the other end of the line. He is waiting for the passenger lists that were promised. I calm him down and ask that he authorize departure of the first planes. "The lists are already on their way over to you," I tell to him.

At long last, permission is given for takeoff. The first eight buses set out.

Out of the mass of people, two people approach me. They are Kfar Batya graduates who rose to important positions in the Ethiopian government. Zimna took the trouble of informing them by telephone about the operation and they rushed to the embassy in their official limousines. Now they want to give me the car keys, telling me that the cars are parked opposite the embassy. Official limousines such as these have a special number plate in Ethiopia and I understand how dangerous it is to leave them here. I hand the keys to one of our drivers, ask him to take two other drivers with him, and dump the cars as quickly as possible. He returns half an hour later and hands me back the keys. Impatient, I shout at him, "I don't need the keys. Throw them in the river!"

Among those who arrive, I see Tiruwork Mekete and her husband. He managed to get here in time and now the whole family is in the embassy compound.

I explain to these people who have top-level jobs that they have to merge into the crowd and not stand out in any way. They must get rid of their neckties and change their clothes, because if they don't, they could be recognized at the airport, putting the whole operation at risk.

At the gate, the situation is growing worse and some families are being divided. The number of families in the waiting area inside is growing, while outside the number of people is increasing instead of decreasing. In the ambassador's room, which is being used as the embassy's command post, we receive an announcement that the planes that had taken off for Ethiopia and are now over Eilat are now being called back to the base, because we are not keeping to the timetable and are not sending one thousand people an hour to the airport.

Suddenly Zimna rushes over to me and shouts, "It's a disaster. Babies are being crushed to death on their mother's back because of the pressure from the others outside." I go out to the gate. Fortunately, Zimna's fears prove false. Nevertheless, we still have not solved the entrance problem. We open and close the gate, but the pressure does not let up. We threaten the people that they will not fly out, but the pressure is unceasing. We promise them that they will all fly, but the pressure continues. In the end, I make a really cruel decision. There is no alternative but to push them back by force. We are careful not to injure anyone, but at last, some of them draw back from the gate and it is now possible to let those waiting enter in a more regulated fashion.

I am still not sure whether we are going to bring off this mission since outside there are still at least twenty thousand people – not all Jews, not all eligible for aliyah. The Felesmura are there, and some of the crowd who watched the fall of Lenin's statue yesterday are now watching the spectacle at the Israel embassy.

It is now 6:45 p.m. and night is falling over Addis. The curfew will start at 9 p.m. I take up a portable loudspeaker and announce to those who are not eligible for aliyah that there has been a change in orders and that the curfew will now start in another quarter of an hour, at seven o'clock. Not a single person believes this announcement and not one of them moves away.

In another two hours, the curfew will really start and then it will be easier.

I am called to the telephone. The call is from the prime minister's bureau in Jerusalem. Someone there is asking if the converts can be identified for certain, in case it is decided to bring them on aliyah as part of this operation. I go to look for Andy Goldman from NACOEJ. I know that Andy has issued all the Felesmura in his care with family ID cards, similar to those we issued to those eligible for aliyah. Andy says that it is indeed possible to identify the families using the IDs he issued and I give a positive answer to Israel.

The question makes it clear to me that an argument is taking place in Israel as to whether or not to bring the two thousand converts in Addis on aliyah. I don't have time to delve into this matter at the present moment but obviously, we here will obey all the instructions that come from the Israeli government.

Since I am now inside the building and near the telephone, I keep my promise to Geula Cohen. Geula made me swear before I left for Ethiopia that I would inform her when the operation began. I promised I would contact her as soon as I could and that, to preserve secrecy, my manner of greeting her on the telephone would be inappropriate to the time. When I manage to get through, I say, "Good morning" instead of "Good evening." At the other end of the line, Geula responds with a surprised, "Good morning?" And then she happily bursts out, "Good morning. Good morning!"

At nine o'clock in the evening, the curfew begins. The spectators leave the area of the embassy, while about five thousand Jews remain outside.

From Israel there is an announcement that it has been decided not to include the Felesmura in the operation. But then Avi announces that the deputy chief of staff has received a cable instructing him to include the converts; however, since he did not understand exactly what it meant, he asked Avi. Avi drew the deputy chief of staff's attention to the fact that it is not clear who sent the cable and suggested that he contact Israel. Indeed, after clarification, the deputy chief of staff was also told that the

Felesmura were not to be included in the operation. It would be interesting to know who sent the cable.

MAY 24, 1991, 11 P.M. – THE AIRPORT, ADDIS ABABA

Throughout the whole day I have been worried that we were not going to bring off this mission, but now that the eight thousandth *oleh* has left the embassy for the airport, I can afford to join the convoy of buses in order to see from up close what is happening there. The sight that meets my eyes is so different from the events at the embassy. Here there is no turmoil. The *olim* sit on the green grass on the edge of the parking area. They are arranged in clusters according to the numbers on their foreheads. So that not one of them can go astray in the darkness, a thin cord is tied around each cluster and Israeli soldiers of Ethiopian origin, wearing jeans and colorful parkas, lead the people to the planes by cluster number.

The Exodus from Ethiopia is happening here, right before my eyes. The aliyah that I have dreamed of for so long is becoming a reality.

Everything is done quietly. It is only when people arrive at the foot of the aircraft that there is some slight tension. Those are the moments when Haim Halachmi's presence is so important. He calms the people and directs them to the plane. I marvel. Where does this sixty-five-year-old man get such strength and energy?

An Ethiopian Airlines cargo plane is now landing. I watch the man on the tarmac directing it and to my surprise he is an officer of the Israel Air Force. The Ethiopians are not interfering at all with events. Avi tells me that they are so stunned that they are not even trying to sneak onto the aircraft.

There is only one government clerk on duty at the airport. This is the representative of the emigration bureau who receives the boarding cards for each flight before takeoff. This arrangement is in response to the deputy interior minister's requirement for passenger lists before each takeoff.

Then this young clerk, who knows me from my visits to the emigration bureau, comes up to me and says, "Mika."

"Yes."

"I'm cold."

"So what can I do about it?"

"Please, get me one of those jackets," he says, and points to one of our soldiers.

I try to get him a parka, but not one of the soldiers is willing to give up his own protection against the cold.

"You'll get one tomorrow morning at six o'clock," I tell the young Ethiopian, thinking this will satisfy him.

Five minutes later he is there again.

"Mika."

"Yes."

"I'm cold."

"So, what do you want now?"

"I want to go home."

"So go home."

And that is how the last of the Ethiopian clerks leaves the airport.

MAY 25, 1991, 1 A.M. – ISRAEL EMBASSY, ADDIS ABABA

It's as though a magic wand has released the pressure at the entrance gate and the people can now be brought through in an orderly fashion. Our warriors are tired and many come inside the embassy to grab a nap. Now I feel hungry. It turns out that we quite simply forgot the whole matter of food. It was also overlooked in the army's operational order. But we have to carry on; we have to impose order on the line that stretches in front of the synagogue, which is now the center for identification and grouping. Our success is already evident. Everything is running as planned. But the staff is starting to wilt from fatigue and only Dr. Raveh, Moshe, Zimna, Zeev, and Zalman are bearing up. My task now is to awaken those who are sleeping and encourage those who are awake not to slacken their efforts.

MAY 25, 1991, 5 A.M. – ISRAEL EMBASSY, ADDIS ABABA

Dawn has already broken. Apparently, I also fell asleep for a short time. I go to Shoshana and Dalit in the computer room and they tell me that we are near the end. Also outside, the network people report that no Jews remain in their homes and the last are now waiting in the embassy courtyard. Avi Mizrahi and Haim Halachmi say that many flights left during the night and there were no problems whatsoever.

We feel that the operation is drawing to a close.

MAY 25, 1991 – ISRAEL EMBASSY, ADDIS ABABA

The last bus is waiting beside the gate for latecomers. A last look at the school. The fences that were constructed to separate the various areas in the embassy courtyard have fallen to bits. Only the straw huts that served as the classrooms of the largest Jewish school in the world – and now, it turns out, also the shortest-lived in the world – remain sturdy.

I make a last tour of inspection in the school's courtyard. The whole area is covered with papers, orange peels, and remnants of food. The sight of this garbage exhilarates me. It is the tangible sign that we are done.

I am suddenly called to the area of the synagogue. In the waiting area beside the synagogue, about sixty of the Felesmura are standing. Somehow, they managed to infiltrate the embassy courtyard. When I approach the group, the members of one family all run toward me. The head of the family begs me to allow them to make aliyah. His wife nods her head while tears pour from her eyes, and the children are squealing and pulling their hair out.

It is a difficult sight to bear.

Wubie Gedamu is standing beside me. He is one of the longest-settled Ethiopians in Israel and these are his relatives. He came yesterday with the rescue force in order to work with us. Wubie wants to help me explain to his weeping aunt that according to the law, she is not entitled to make aliyah since the family has not kept the faith of our fathers.

However ghastly I feel about this, Wubie feels a hundred times worse. After all, these people are his own kin. I see the deep disappointment on the woman's face, not disappointed by me but rather by her own nephew. He should be assisting her, not abandoning her.

While the argument carries on, the last Jews arrive. They include many citizens of Addis Ababa who only came now because they wanted to make use of the time for shopping and there are also some who have managed to sell some possessions. The last bus leaves. The converts remain behind, weeping and wailing. The last of the staff depart in the embassy car to go to their flats, collect their personal belongings and proceed to the airport. I lift my hand in a last salute to the guards at the gate.

Will I ever see them again? Will I ever return to this embassy that became like a second home to me?

I have to hurry to the airport. The streets of Addis Ababa are crowded today, too. Again it looks as though no one is going to any particular destination. No one hurries. On the street corners men stand, women stand, leisurely chatting as though the ground were not burning beneath their feet, as though there were no siege around the city, as though the rebels were not going to flood into it within hours.

Now, in the final minutes of the operation, an additional operation takes place – the operation to evacuate the president's adviser, Kassa Kebede, and Deputy Minister of the Interior Mersha Ketsela. It was agreed yesterday evening that they would be taken out by us in one of the last planes. This morning at eight o'clock, they were told to come immediately to the Hilton Hotel. In one of the hotel rooms, the orders to evacuate them were received.

MAY 25, 1991, 10 A.M. – HILTON HOTEL, ADDIS ABABA

In the parking lot opposite the side entrance of the hotel, Colonel Mersha is waiting in his car for Kassa Kebede. Kassa is supposed to travel in Mersha's car. Ami Bergman is watching events from a distance. He is to lead them to a nearby meeting point.

Kassa enters the parking lot in his car and gets out. He carries an executive briefcase and, as usual, is wearing an expensive suit and the most elegant leather shoes. Crouched over, he runs to a parked car that looks like Mersha's. In fact, behind the wheel sits a lady who is on the point of leaving. Kassa hastily opens the door, but then a shout is heard from inside the car. Kassa quickly slams the door shut, looks around, identifies Mersha waiting in his car, and runs over to him. Now that they are both in the one car, Ami signals Mersha to follow him.

Within two minutes, the cars arrive at the area of the filling station that is only a few meters away from the police station. Ami stops his car beside a Toyota that belongs to the JDC. Beside this car, the JDC's Eli Eliezri and Doron Tashtit are already waiting. They hasten to open the rear doors of the large car. Kassa propels himself inside, as though jumping into a swimming pool. Mersha leaves the keys in his car and gets out, but then he spots Kassa's briefcase, which he has left behind because he is so flustered. Mersha takes the briefcase and also jumps hurriedly into the waiting car. The two are then covered from top to toe with sheets.

Doron takes the wheel and Eli sits beside him. Now it's Ami's turn to take his own private revenge on both of them. There have been so many times when we were all furious at Kassa for the problems he caused us and the obstacles he raised to keep the Jews from leaving. Mersha was also a pain in the neck with his nitpicking insistence that we make corrections in the forms, thereby slowing down the departure of the emigrants. So Ami decides to drive via every single pothole on the roads of Addis Ababa – and potholes there are in abundance. Doron and Eli understand what is happening and don't hesitate at any point in this Via Dolorosa. Over and over again, Kassa and Mersha are thrown about, jerked up, tumbled down, jerked up into the air again and then onto their backs, throughout the whole drive.

When the car reaches the airport gate, Ami brakes, points to the car behind and tells the guards at the gate that he has brought two more sick people. Yesterday, Ami conducted carloads of patients from the hospitals and from the JDC's clinic. The guards do not suspect him, and both cars drive though the gate and up to one of the two Hercules aircraft. It is being loaded at that moment with the equipment that was used in our command post at the airport. Doron backs the car to the plane's opening so that when Kassa and Mersha enter the aircraft, no one outside can identify them.

While I am observing events on the tarmac, a thought suddenly crosses my mind: less than twenty-four hours have passed and we have already finished the operation! Then one of the air force officers comes to me and says worriedly, "One of my men is missing. I can't find him anywhere."

Since the officer chose to come straight to me, I realize that the soldier is of Ethiopian origin. And after the officer tells me the soldier's name, I calm him down, saying, "Don't worry. He met up with his parents who were here in Addis and it made him completely forget that he's here as a soldier. He's already in Israel with them." I hope I'm not mistaken.

Then another mishap. After we have already announced that all the buses are present at the airport and only two Hercules planes remain on the runway, jam-packed with people, plus a Boeing 707 holding some of our staff, a bus suddenly draws up with about sixty *olim*. It's true that on the runway there is another Hercules without passengers, but one of its engines has failed and it has been forbidden to carry any load. We will be forced to wait another six hours until another plane arrives, and when we were thinking that we'd be home in another four hours.

Then I have an idea. Maybe we can add thirty passengers to each of the two planes that are already filled to the brim. I go to the first plane and ask the people to get up. In spite of their fatigue, the people do as they are asked. Then I ask them to move forward toward the nose of the plane and, amazingly enough, a two-meter-wide strip is revealed. I transfer half of the bus into the strip that has opened up and repeat this exercise with the second plane.

That's it, we're done.

The two planes, filled with passengers, take off from the runway. As they turn their noses northward, a large limousine enters the area under our control. From this vehicle, the senior official of the US embassy, Bob Hodek, emerges. Saturday is not a working day in the American embassy and so Bob is casually dressed. His bearded face has a satisfied smile. I find myself hugging him and thanking him and his government for assisting in the operation's success.

I thought we were done. I was wrong.

Two taxis appear at the end of the runway. Inside are eight women from four different generations: a great-grandmother, her daughter – the grandmother and her unmarried daughter, a second daughter with a baby and a third daughter with twin girls. I run toward them, amazed that their taxis managed to enter the airport without permission. Perhaps the soldiers responsible for guarding the gate have already given up in despair, knowing that the rebels are watching the airport from the hills around us and are waiting only because their leaders have promised the Americans that they would not enter Addis Ababa as long the operation was taking place.

I ask the new arrivals to show me their identity cards. They do not all have the correct ID cards and when I point this out, they react with outrage. Hearing the tumult, General Amnon Lipkin-Shahak comes over and asks what's happening. I explain to him that they don't have the proper plastic ID cards. The deputy chief of staff says angrily, "Plastic-shmastic – put them on the plane." I quickly obey.

Since most of the people are already on the plane, I also board. In the front row of seats, the deputy chief of staff is sitting with Uri Lubrani beside him. Amnon halts his conversation with Uri for a moment, winks at me and says, "Believe me, if they knew how uncomfortable it was in a Hercules, even if they'd had the plastic IDs, they wouldn't have shown them to you." In my heart of hearts, I'm pleased that he ordered me to put the women on the plane.

I find an empty seat in the last rows. Behind me two of the Silent Signal Network people are sitting and the eight women from the taxis. Most of the passengers have fallen asleep. A few take the prepared meals from the forward part of the plane. I distribute several trays to the immigrants and take one for myself. Now I feel my hunger; after all, we haven't eaten a thing for almost thirty hours.

I want to share with someone what I am feeling right now, but everyone around me has fallen asleep, so I can only confide in my diary, which I've kept faithfully all these years. I write this, overwhelmed by what we have done – that in the course of twenty-two hours from the first plane's takeoff to the last plane's takeoff, we have brought fifteen thousand *olim* home to Israel.

MAY 25, 1991 – BEN-GURION INTERNATIONAL AIRPORT

I awoke a few minutes ago, when the plane lowered its flaps for the landing. We descend from the plane – Zimna and Avi and Mamush and Asnakew and Shoshi and Dalit and Zeev and Zalman and Benny and Yehoshua, as well as Barbara, Andy, and Salomon from NACOEJ and also Ladena and Susan and Glen from AAEJ. We are all tired and dirty, we are all thinking of a shower and bed, but something draws me to what is apparently the wrong bus, a bus that takes a few of us to the airbase where the *olim* have been landing nonstop during the last twenty-four hours.

When we reach the assembly area, we discover that the whole "Who's Who" of Israel is there. I am happy to see Uri Gordon, my department head, and Arnon Mantver. Geula Cohen is also there. They all welcome us with kisses, as though we had returned from a battlefield.

And then the two Hercules approach carrying the last busload of passengers that we loaded six hours ago. We rush over to where they land and wait for the *olim* to descend.

One Hercules opens its rear door and the *olim* pour out of it. They look tired after their sleepless night and their faces are numb. But when they see me, they smile and their eyes sparkle. The elders take the initiative and come over to me and kiss me. One of them whispers in my ear, "Thank you very much, Abba Mika."

The last of the 14,310 *olim* who arrived in Operation Solomon boards the last bus. I go home by taxi to my family, to a shower and my bed. The television at home is on and the whole time they are showing pictures of the operation. The people of Israel are all celebrating with us.

I am totally exhausted, overtired, but have no trouble falling asleep.

Epilogue

MAY 26, 1991, 5 P.M. – THE PRIME MINISTER'S OFFICE, JERUSALEM

The telephone hasn't stopped ringing, especially with all the journalists who want to interview me, perhaps because they saw me on television last night. The term "heroes" is being used to describe those who took part in the operation. In the afternoon, they interviewed me for the TV program *A New Evening*, and from there I hurried to a meeting of the Interministerial Coordinating Committee for Immigrant Absorption, chaired by Minister Ariel Sharon.

Outside the prime minister's office, four Ethiopian immigrants were standing. They were all known to me: Yefet Alemu and his wife Edna, Wolelaw Abera, and Takele Mekonen. I said hello, but instead of returning my greeting, one of them, Yefet Alemu, scowled, his face twisted with emotion, and said, "At long last you've managed to carry out the 'selection' you wanted."

Yefet was referring to the converts whom we left behind in Addis Ababa. I was horrified by his words. In effect, he was calling me a Nazi. Grieved as I was by his lack of understanding, this was neither the time nor the place to tell him my own story: how many of my family went through Nazi selections in the death camps in Poland. The time will come to discuss with Yefet and his friends the complicated question of the aliyah of the Felesmura. I have no doubt that this issue is going to engage the attention of the Israeli public for many years to come.

JUNE 21, 1991 – DACHAU

I arrived at ten o'clock this morning at the Munich airport. I'm here for Keren Hayesod, to speak to the Jews of Germany about the operation and its human and financial costs. At twelve o'clock, Colonel Nechemia, the commander of one of the Hercules squadrons that participated in the operation, landed with Mamuye in a plane from Vienna. It was a very emotional reunion. We decided to drop off our things at the hotel and go by train to Dachau, which is very close to Munich. We arrived an hour ago. On our way to the camp, we passed through a residential neighborhood that is right next to the camp fence. We know that during the Holocaust, people were living beside the fence and did nothing. Colonel Nechemia – like me, the son of Holocaust survivors – also does not understand how people could carry on living their normal lives, as they did, beside those walls and that electric fence. Mamuye shared our feelings when we toured the museum and the barracks that still stands. And then, actually right opposite the crematoria, images of the operation crossed my mind. As a human being and particularly as a citizen of Israel, I feel such pride in having taken part in it. Because the State of Israel exists, there will be never another Dachau or another selection of Jews – a selection of who shall live and who shall die.

SEPTEMBER 15, 1992 – ON A DIRT PATH BETWEEN GONDAR AND TEDA

This is my last trip to Ethiopia. Since Operation Solomon, another 4,402 Jews from Ethiopia have also made aliyah, including nearly the whole Jewish community from Quara. I had met some of them in the past, and had even gone with Avi, Ami, and Zimna to the foot of the Quara Mountains, but it was quite impossible to reach their villages.

Later, we sent out emissaries on the ten-day walk to Quara to tell the Jews there that we would wait for them and send them on aliyah to Israel. Together with the JDC, we set up two transition camps in Teda and, at the rate of five hundred per month, the Jews of Quara were transferred to Addis Ababa and from there, without much delay, they made aliyah to Israel.

Now, we really can say that nearly all the Jews of Ethiopia are in Israel. There are very few left. Some do not make aliyah because they do not want to do so right now and some because they cannot yet do so. The issue of the Felesmura, which renains unresolved, comes up from time to time in newspaper headlines.

I am at the wheel. Zimna is beside me and we have summed up our years of working together. I feel a special affection for him, a closeness that is closer than family.

Then, after a few moments of silence, while we both enjoy the view of the hills that are so green after the rainy season, Zimna breaks the silence by saying, "You know, Micha, sometimes I get fed up with all the pressures and the running around in Israel and I see myself settled here in the hills, in a straw hut like the one I was born in, keeping bees. I so miss the landscape here. I so miss the silence and tranquility of the mountains of Ethiopia."

I don't answer. Perhaps many of the Jews of Ethiopia feel that way about leaving behind the landscapes, scents, and culture of their childhood. Perhaps it is difficult for them to cope with the murderous pace of Western life in spite of their burning desire to live in Israel.

It is that way, for sure. We saved the lives of many Ethiopian Jews, but did we also save their souls?

We did. I'm sure of it. As I continue driving in silence, I see in my mind's eye the thousands of people waiting outside the embassy in Addis and the dead girl whom I carried in my arms during Operation Moses. I picture Zimna in Sudan and the Israeli ship, *Bat Galim*, receiving Agerie, the girl-woman who made aliyah in one of the marine operations, and I hear Galit Halili's poem:

Behold, look, I am coming to you, my land.
Sing as I laugh and let us rejoice.
Embrace me with others who once were alone,
Embrace me, kiss me, feed me fine fruits of choice.
Stretch out your hands to shelter those ground in the dust,
Stretch out your arms, ignoring distance and bounds.

***

Adisalem started a family in Israel. He lives and works in Beersheba, but is still called Eddie.

Agerie is now called Dina Cohen. After divorcing the husband she married in Sudan, she married an Israeli. She has three children and works as a nurse in the hospital in Afula.

Maeysho discovered that her husband was alive. The couple now lives in Ashkelon and two of their daughters are married.

Zena divorced her husband and returned to her studies. Today she is a social worker in a town in the center of the country.

Workitu lives with her husband and children in Migdal Ha'emek. Ajalew has finished high school with excellent grades.

Mekonen is now a major in the army, has a family, and lives in Petah Tikva.

Aba Samuel lives in a modest apartment in Ramle with his wife, surrounded by his children, grandchildren, and great-grandchildren.

Fikadu converted to Judaism, is married and has a family. He lives and works in Kiryat Yam in the Haifa Bay area.

The parents of Shimshon Kebede, the high-school student who sent me such a touching letter, made aliyah even before Operation Solomon. He is now a lieutenant in the regular army and recently married.

Shoshana, the thirteen-year old girl whose letter made such a deep impression on me, reverted to her Amharic name, Shoanesh, and is now a student at the Hebrew University of Jerusalem.

Wubnesh Mera and her children arrived in Israel just before Operation Solomon, and she and her husband now live in Kiryat Gat.

Lakech and her son also made aliyah before Operation Solomon, and she lives near her sister, Zehava, in Netanya.

Addisu Wodaj lives with his family in Kiryat Gat. He bought a minibus and makes his living as a driver.

Rubel is married with children, lives in Rishon Lezion, and is a manual laborer in the central region near Tel Aviv.

One of the most dramatic stories is that of Zewditu, her father Genetu, and the sister, Manale, who disappeared on the way to Sudan in June, 1983. About nine years after Manale disappeared, news reached Israel that in the Chilga region there was a girl of about fourteen, who had been found one rainy morning, some nine years earlier, standing outside a farmer's hut. When the man saw her there, completely naked and shaking all over, he did not know at first whether she was a human or an animal.

The man's father told him to bring the girl into the hut and he did so. He raised her together with his own children and even sent her to school, where she finished fourth grade.

On the strength of the information that we had received, we sent the father, Genetu Dessie, to Ethiopia. After a long search, he found the peasant's house, but not his daughter. In the meanwhile, she had been abducted by a thug who claimed her as his daughter. Genetu continued searching and eventually reached the kidnapper's home, but it turned out that the man's wife had fled from her abusive husband, taking the girl with her. Genetu's further searches proved fruitless. In shame and distress, he returned to Israel.

Then Zimna contacted the same man who had found Manale on that cold, rainy morning and asked him to abandon his work and devote himself entirely to searching for the girl. The man agreed and, after several months' searching, he located the kidnapper's wife, but the girl was no longer with her. She had sent her away to be a maidservant or, to be more exact, to be a slave to a foreign woman.

The man did not give up, but set out for the township of Bahir Dar where the girl had been sent. He systematically explored the streets of the town, almost house by house, until he eventually found Manale, managed to have her released from her servitude, and then brought her to Zimna at his office. Zimna paid him all his expenses, as promised, and as a bonus, gave him two bulls.

In May 1993, almost ten years after her disappearance, Manale was returned to her family. Today, she lives with them in their apartment in Bat Yam.

Her sister, Zewditu, has almost finished her degree at the University of Haifa.